PRELUDE TO PRISON

Syracuse Studies on Peace and Conflict Resolution
Robert A. Rubinstein, *Series Editor*

Other titles from Syracuse Studies
on Peace and Conflict Resolution

Back Channel Negotiation: Secrecy in the Middle East Peace Process
Anthony Wanis-St. John

A Band of Noble Women: Racial Politics in the Women's Peace Movement
Melinda Plastas

The Bernal Story: Mediating Class and Race in a Multicultural Community
Beth Roy

Democracy and Conflict Resolution: The Dilemmas of Israel's Peacemaking
Miriam Fendius Elman, Oded Haklai, and Hendrik Spruyt, eds.

Exploring the Power of Nonviolence: Peace, Politics, and Practice
Randall Amster and Elavie Ndura, eds.

Globalization, Social Movements, and Peacebuilding
Jackie Smith and Ernesto Verdeja, eds.

Jerusalem: Conflict and Cooperation in a Contested City
Madelaine Adelman and Miriam Fendius Elman, eds.

A Place We Call Home: Gender, Race, and Justice in Syracuse
K. Animashaun Ducre

PRELUDE TO PRISON

Student Perspectives on School Suspension

MARSHA WEISSMAN

Syracuse University Press

This book is dedicated my husband, Jim, and my sons, Evan and Casey, and to the memory of my parents, Al and Lillian Weissman, whose belief in education as a liberating force has guided my life.

MARSHA WEISSMAN is the founder and executive director of the Center for Community Alternatives. For more than thirty years, the Center has worked to end mass incarceration through alternative-to-incarceration programs for youths and adults, and research and policy advocacy to educate the public and policy makers regarding the need for a more effective juvenile and criminal justice system. Dr. Weissman holds a PhD from the Maxwell School of Citizenship, Syracuse University.

Contents

Illustrations and Table

Preface

THE MOST INSPIRING experience in my work life—and there have been many—came when I traveled with four young people engaged in programs operated by my organization, the Center for Community Alternatives, to Geneva, Switzerland as part of a US Human Rights Network delegation. The youths, along with other delegation members, would testify before the United Nations Commission on Ending Racism in All Forms. The kids were asked to speak about their direct experiences in the juvenile justice system, and the increasing nexus with school discipline that had come to be known as the "school-to-prison pipeline."

I spent a week in awe of these young people, observing their poise in traveling on an airplane for the first time, taking what was their first trip out of their home communities, and their openness to meeting other members of the delegation that represented virtually every dispossessed and marginalized group in the United States. I watched with delight as they relished new foods, the free transportation available in Geneva, and the French language spoken by native citizens. I sat proud as a peacock as they testified with dignity about the conditions in their lives, their entrapment in schools that offered them no hope but instead relegated them to educational settings without opportunities for real learning, and worse yet, the dungeons of this country—its jails and prisons.

This experience inspired me to write a book, this book, that elevates the voices of these young people. I have tried to do justice to their stories, neither sugarcoating them, nor ignoring the ways that so many adults in their lives have failed them. I have tried to connect their individual experiences to a set of structural conditions and policy choices that dismisses their humanity and promise.

Almost all of the youths interviewed said something to the effect that their success in school rested solely on their shoulders. At the end of the interview, I would tell them that adults in their lives—parents, guardians, teachers, faith leaders, neighborhoods—are obligated to help them negotiate their transition to adulthood and that all of us are responsible for their struggles. Absent significant social change, this will be an empty promise.

The book begins with chapters that present the "big picture," the data and research that describe the advent of mass incarceration in the United States and how social control has been extended to multiple domains, including schools. The middle chapters describe this "school-to-prison pipeline" experience through the eyes and voices of the young people who travel this path every day. The concluding chapters place these insights into a body of literature that speaks to the role of schools in the reproduction of current social patterns. Tragically, in twenty-first century America, this means inuring poor, young people of color to the carceral institutions of the United States.

Acknowledgments

THIRTY YEARS AGO, I left academia to pursue a life that involved working "on the ground" with kids pushed out of school and into prisons. Yet I always had a desire to return to research, a desire fulfilled with the publication of this book. None of this would have been possible without the leap of faith and the intellectual support of colleagues, friends, and family, and of course, the generosity of the young people who shared their stories with me. Although there are many who have encouraged this work, Robert Rubinstein quite simply stuck his neck out for me, prodded me, and shared his considerable wisdom. To be fair, Robert's neck would not have been extended so prodigiously had it not been for the inestimable Sandy Lane, Robert's partner in crime, so to speak. Sandy Lane reflects the scholar as mountain climber: there is no peak that she considers too high to scale. Don Mitchell, Diane Murphy, and Arthur Paris made time to provide thoughtful comments as I completed this study.

This work has fundamentally been inspired by the young people who agreed to be interviewed for the study. The kids gave freely of themselves, answered all my questions with detail and feeling. The stories that they told me, not only of their suspensions, but their lives, are what make this study important. We simply have to do something to stop pushing young people with such promise into the margins of community life and into prisons and ghettos. I hope that I have done justice to their narratives.

I am also fortunate to be part of a community of advocates, many of them part of the Dignity in Schools Campaign, and most especially, my colleagues at the Center for Community Alternatives, the organization I have been privileged to lead for three decades. My life and work has been enriched beyond measure by a network of friends who have, in their own ways, traveled a journey in the struggle for justice with me. These range from the "hula girls" who take me on an annual bacchanal that keeps my spirits going, to Susan who has been just about everything to me including my labor coach. My comrade in heart, Alan, has shaped my thinking and has been a model of principle and dedication to social justice from our first day of college to this day.

At the end of the day, however, it does come down to family. In some respects, I have a family like the kids I interviewed—serpentine connections that defy easy definition. My parents, Al and Lillian, long deceased, privileged education above all else, and thus allowed for whatever path it took me on, as long as it was grounded in learning. Lolly and Ted Levy offered their generosity of spirit and material support that has seen me through a lifetime. Debby Weissman and Louis Perez have shared wonderful, magical summers of work, debate, discussion, and the goofiest moments of my life.

My husband Jim Vermeulen has been quite simply my rock. He reminds me that life can be joyous, calm, reasoned, and stable. His parenting has made it possible for me to take on my crazy work and know that our kids would be fine. I end with a very special thank you to the children of my family who are now taking up their responsibilities in the struggle for justice as community organizers, agitators, "people's" lawyers, teachers, artists, and doctors. My sons, Evan and Casey, their partners, Erin and Sarah, the cousins, Lisa, Josh Alann Rima, Keith and Greg cement my hope for the future. The building of the movement now passes to them and their children, Rowan, Èamon, Desmond, and Lorna and those yet to be born. I have no doubt they will live to see the kind of just society that I have dreamed of.

Prelude to Prison

Introduction

Learning from Jayda

JAYDA[1] **WAS** sixteen years old when she accompanied me and three other young people as part of the 2008 US Human Rights Network delegation to review the United States' compliance with the United Nations International Convention on the Elimination of All Forms of Racial Discrimination.[2] The review was held in Geneva, Switzerland, a place that Jayda never heard of a mere three months before. It was Jayda's first trip on an airplane . . . her first trip anywhere beyond her hometown. She was off to testify about her experiences being suspended from school. This is an excerpt from her testimony:

> I would like to tell you what it is like to be sent to an alternative school. You always feel judged; teachers don't give you the benefit of the doubt. Out of the seventy students [who] actually attended school every day, I remember seeing only one white boy. At my regular school about 60 percent of the population is white.

1. In order to protect the privacy of students and others mentioned in this study, the names of individuals (who are not widely known public figures) have been changed to pseudonyms, as have the names of specific schools.

2. The International Convention on the Elimination of All Forms of Racial Discrimination is a United Nations (UN) treaty adopted in 1965 by the United Nations' General Assembly. Its signatories, of which the United States is one, commit to eliminating racial discrimination. See International Convention on the Elimination of All Forms of Racial Discrimination, available at: http://www.ohchr.org/EN/ProfessionalInterest /Pages/CERD.aspx.

Mid-year I was put in a program, called "three to five," which means I went to school for two hours a day. I fell behind in my schoolwork and was only taught math once a week. The teacher who was there every day didn't really teach, either; she only gave me worksheets. I am in the tenth grade but I have to take ninth grade classes.

I felt like I was in jail when I was in the alternative school. Sometimes I had to be checked three times a day and checked before I went into certain classrooms. It is very uncomfortable being searched because I really don't like being touched by other people, especially people I don't know very well. It is more uncomfortable for girls because sometimes they check you around your most private areas, and it's just uncomfortable.

I feel like the alternative school system has set up kids like me to fail. You go back to school so far behind that you just want to drop out of school or sometimes you get sent back to a regular school where you get targeted, and you just get fed up and drop out. I would like to end by saying that we need to look at why kids like me are suspended and if at all possible get rid of alternative schools.

Jayda, whose testimony introduces this study, is one of the twenty-five students I interviewed who spoke to me about their experiences and perceptions of being suspended from school. The students interviewed all attended school in the Syracuse City School District, a poor urban district in a mid-sized city in the northeastern United States. The students were in the seventh, eighth, or ninth grade at the time of their suspension and were sent to an alternative school (named Brig) for students in grades K–8, or an alternative school (named Steel) for youths in grades 9–12. Almost all were children of color—predominantly African American. Thirteen of the youths were girls and twelve were boys. Jayda's story was repeated to me many times by teenagers who were also suspended from school for behaviors that ranged from acting the class clown to more serious incidents and fights.

Her story is likely typical of children across urban America. The City of Syracuse faces myriad challenges typical to northeastern, "rust belt" cities, including a deteriorating economic base, declining population, and concentrated poverty. The 2011 Syracuse population is estimated to be just over 145,151, representing approximately a 6 percent decline since 2000, and almost a 60 percent decline since 1950. The city's minority population is 30 percent (compared to the county's minority population of 11 percent). Nineteen census tracts—roughly one-third of all Syracuse communities—are characterized as census tracts of extreme poverty, defined as neighborhoods with more than 40 percent of their residents residing below the poverty line (Kneebone, Nadeau, and Berube 2011). The Syracuse metropolitan area ranks as the ninth most segregated housing area in the country (Frey 2010). Correspondingly, for blacks, the Syracuse metropolitan area ranks the seventh in the country for segregated public primary schools (Osypuk et al. 2009). Forty-five percent of all children in the city are below the poverty line (New York State Community Action Association 2009). The majority of the youths sent to alternative schools come from three inner city neighborhoods that form the urban core of these census tracts, which are 70 percent African American, 10 percent Latino, 2 percent Native American, and 20 percent Caucasian.

Forty-three percent of the population in these neighborhoods is under the age of twenty-one, with 44 percent of families living below the poverty line, compared to a citywide average of 20 percent. Syracuse City Police data show that 60 percent of juvenile arrests are made in these neighborhoods; in contrast, these neighborhoods only comprise roughly 30 percent of the total population of the city.

The high poverty rates among Syracuse minority communities are due to the loss of employment opportunities, notably the loss of the industrial base that once made Syracuse known as a city with a diverse economic base. One by one, industries have moved out of Syracuse—Carrier Corporation (absorbed into United Technologies), Solvay Process (absorbed by Honeywell), General Electric, and even the city's Syracuse China—taking with them good-paying blue collar jobs, some of which were even available to the black population.

Even as the metropolitan area as a whole declined, Syracuse was particularly hard hit as the remaining industry and white middle class moved to the suburbs. The city, which is home to 30 percent of the Onondaga County population, has only 18 percent of its taxable property (American Institute of Architects 2006). The limited tax base supports 60 percent of the low income population in the county, who are disproportionately minority and are concentrated in neighborhoods characterized by abandoned and substandard housing, high crime rates, and a lack of neighborhood amenities such as grocery stores. Socioeconomic and health risks are prevalent in these inner city neighborhoods, as well. The neighborhoods exhibit high rates of unemployment, the lowest [adult] educational levels, the greatest indices of health problems (HIV and AIDS, teen pregnancy, infant mortality, low birth rates, STDs, cocaine, and opiate hospital discharges), and other measures of social disorganization (New York State Department of Health 2000; Lane et al. 2004).

The War on Drugs has taken a particularly hard toll on Syracuse's black population. More than two-thirds of people arrested for drug crimes are black and most arrests are made in the poor, black, inner city neighborhoods (New York Civil Liberties Union 2009). The prison admissions in some of these neighborhoods are as high as twenty to forty residents per 1,000 people. The profound racial disparities in incarceration rates are demonstrated by data that show that in Syracuse, ninety-nine blacks are incarcerated for every one white when the crime involves illegal drugs (Beatty et al. 2007).

The high rates of incarceration in Syracuse, as in most if not all inner city neighborhoods, has come to be known as "mass incarceration." This phenomenon affects virtually all aspects of ghetto life—the absence of fathers and husbands, the language and fashion of urban youth—reflecting what Wacquant (2001) refers to as the "deadly symbiosis" between ghetto and prison. Increasingly, this deadly symbiosis extends to urban school systems, which become institutions focused on social control. This book explores how social control through school suspension and exile to alternative school becomes a prelude to prison for young people like Jayda.

A Troubling Symbiosis: Schools and Prisons in the Age of Mass Incarceration

There are likely no more distinct institutions in a society than schools and prisons. One, the school, is considered an institution that builds capacity, a ticket out of poverty, and the gate that opens to a better future. The other, the prison, is used to contain those whom we consider a drain on and threat to social well-being, a barrier that closes off a segment of the population from the rest of us. For most of the history of the United States, schools were celebrated as an institution with open access to all, while prisons were relegated to a despised and marginal role (Coleman 1966; Rothman 1971).

By the close of the twentieth century, however, these two institutions had dramatically reversed their place in the social order. Public schools are now under attack for their failure to educate children, and are disparaged as bureaucratic, violent, and amoral, if not immoral. Charter schools, school vouchers, eroding property tax bases, and general taxpayer revolt undermine funding for public schools. In contrast, the US prison system is robust, taking up increasing portions of state and federal budgets. By 2009, the United States had imprisoned 1.94 million people—making the United States the global leader in terms of total numbers and per-capita incarceration rates (Glaze and Parks 2012). The widespread use of incarceration or mass incarceration is characterized by a rate of imprisonment that is both historically and comparatively high and concentrated in specific segments of the population (Garland 2001a).

For poor children in the United States, particularly children of color, the view of school as a ticket to the future has always been fraught with contradiction. There is no doubt of the correlation between academic achievements (graduation, college, and post-baccalaureate degrees) and improved life chances on a range of outcomes from economic well-being to health (Stoops 2004; Ross and Wu 1996). Yet poor children of color are less likely to succeed in school, as evidenced by various traditional measures of school success—graduation rates, academic diplomas, test scores, attendance rates (Rouse and Barrow 2006; Kozol 1991; Orfield et al. 2004). Conversely, they are more likely to be suspended and then drop out of school without graduating (Orfield et al. 2004; Wald and Losen 2003).

Starting in the latter part of the twentieth century, for children of color, the absence of a high school diploma has done more than relegate someone to the economic margins of society. For youths of color, dropping out of school not only diminishes one's employment prospects, it increases the likelihood of winding up in jail or prison. By the time they reach their early thirties, 52 percent of young, male, African American high school dropouts have spent some time in jail or prison (Western, Pettit, and Guetzkow 2002).

The junctures throughout the educational experience that move a child away from education and graduation to incarceration have come to be known as "the school-to-prison pipeline." The connecting links in this pipeline are policies such as high stakes testing and zero tolerance disciplinary codes that push youths out of mainstream school and into alternative schools. Suspension to alternative schools is often the last step before youths drop out of school completely, thereby increasing the likelihood that they will get arrested and incarcerated.

The role of school in pushing young people into the prison system contradicts the view of public education as a transformative institution in American culture. Education in American mythology is enshrined for its ability to introduce young people to new worldviews, which in turn help to shape their future goals and aspirations. The Supreme Court's decision in Brown v. Board of Education aptly captures the American belief in education as our chief means of providing equal opportunity, deeming it "perhaps the most important function of state and local governments," and essential to both individual opportunity and democratic society.

Yet a body of conceptual literature and empirical research calls into question whether schools facilitate upward mobility or instead preserve the existing social structure. Social reproduction theory asserts that the methods and processes embedded in schooling perpetuate social inequality across generations. Subsets of this literature—correspondence theory, cultural reproduction theory and critical resistance theory—address the interaction between the school environment, its culture, curricula, rules, policies, and the student and how these aspects of the school experience slot youths into predefined economic and social roles.

Althusser (1971) and Bowles and Gintis (1976) argue that schools play a major role in reproducing the class structure necessary to sustain a capitalist economy and specifically socializing young people into workplace hierarchy. However, Bowles and Gintis's articulation of correspondence theory, which looks at the relationship between education and labor status, may seem to have little utility in explaining the school-to-prison pipeline, as they considered how schools help sort students into their future places in the workplace. The school-to-prison pipeline metaphor does not foresee youth entry into the workforce. Rather it is concerned with the pathway from school suspension, to dropping out, to the criminal justice system. Instead of joining the workforce, the young people pulsing through the pipeline will become part of a permanent underclass whose future lies behind prison walls. However, the tremendous expansion of incarceration and the particularly high rate of incarceration of people of color that has taken place since Bowles and Gintis authored their 1976 study make it important to examine the role of schools in reproducing prisoners.

There is no question that school suspensions have increased, particularly since the introduction of "zero tolerance" laws enacted as part of the federal Safe and Gun-Free Schools Act of 1994. Despite the rhetoric suggesting that suspensions are used to respond to the most egregious behaviors, such as the possession of dangerous weapons, students are suspended for a hodgepodge of behaviors that reflect subjective, sometimes racially biased, decision making by teachers (Skiba et al. 2003). Bowditch's study of a northeastern urban high school found that most suspensions were a response to behaviors that require subjective interpretation on the part of teachers and administrators. She concluded that schools "punish behavior that threatens the school's authority rather than its safety" (Bowditch 1993, 499). The application of disciplinary sanctions can also vary by school characteristics (Brantlinger 1991; Kaeser 1979; Wu et al. 1982).

Bowles and Gintis's thesis has been enriched by consideration of the role of resistance and human agency, and of the ways that race, gender, ethnicity, and culture shape the interactions between schools and students (Walker 2003; MacLeod 1995; Giroux 2003; Bourdieu and Passeron 1979; Willis 1977; Rikowski 1996, 1997). The dominant school culture rewards the "cultural capital" of the middle and upper classes with its emphasis on preparation for learning and a belief in education as the means to social and economic success (Bourdieu and Passeron 1979). As the ethnographies of Willis (1977) and MacLeod (1995) show, students who come to school with behaviors and attitudes that match the "achievement ideology" of schools are rewarded for their conformity, while those who do not fail and are "pushed out" or "jump out" of schools because they do not fit in. Family and life circumstances that impede success in school are often treated as indicators of troublesome behavior rather than risk factors (Bowditch 1993). Students who miss school because of other family responsibilities are classified as truants comparable to students who willfully miss school. Parents who do not show up for teacher conferences because of a lack of "family-friendly" work policies are viewed as dysfunctional (Bowditch 1993; Fine 1991). These assumptions constitute a form of profiling that inflicts particular harm on youths of color much in the same way that police profile youths of color on the streets (Bowditch 1993; Solomon and Palmer 2004). Fine's (1991) study of students in a New York City high school describes how disrespectful or dismissive treatment of parents, discouraging comments from teachers predicting students' life outcomes, unintentional but nonetheless disparaging comments about neighborhoods and communities, and Eurocentric curriculum produce school dropouts. These experiences make it difficult for poor, largely minority, students to believe that formal education has relevance to their lives.

Resistance theory helps to explain how the behaviors of young people contribute to their journey through the pipeline. Giroux (1982) asserts that student resistance is a logical response of young people to an educational system that has little meaning or value to their lives. By responding to the ways that schools push them out through behaviors that are likely to result in suspension, young people in a sense become complicit in their own marginalization. These dual forces, the conditions of school and the behaviors of youths, in combination produce dropouts.

The role of agency—deliberate actions on the part of youths that contribute to their suspensions—is intertwined with the school environment and culture. Youths come to believe that schools dismiss them because of their cultural, racial, and class differences. Their misbehavior is a form of resistance to messages that they should become something or someone they are not. The working class youths, "the lads" in Willis's (1977) *Learning to Labour*, rejected the dominant middle and upper class aspirations projected in schools because these did not reflect their own experience, culture, and identity. In the world of these "lads," academic success was considered unmanly. Fordham and Ogbu (1986), Fordham (1996), and Howard (2003) document how black students are forced to choose between "acting white" to achieve academic success or maintaining the integrity of their racial and ethnic identities as African Americans, identities that are not rewarded by schools, which have been made in the image of the white middle class. Students who feel misplaced in and dismissed by schools also experience a forceful assault on their self-esteem. They in turn repudiate their educational environments through behaviors that reject and are antagonistic toward school.

This book extends the inquiry about youths' perceptions of why and how they are pushed from or jump out of schools to explicit questions about whether or not young people in this predicament see that the school environment may be putting them on the prison or jail track. Existing research informs us about the various forces that contribute to youth suspensions and expulsions, such as zero tolerance policies. However, we know less about how young people themselves evaluate processes associated with zero tolerance and the impact on their future lives (Giroux 1982; Willis 1977; Smith 2000; Stevick and Levinson 2003; Fine 1991). Dunbar provides one of the few studies that explicitly look at young people who travel the school-to-prison pipeline, from alternative school to detention and prison. These young people clearly articulate a lack of hope and a sense that they will wind up in prison or dead: *"By da time I'm 21, I don't know where I'll be. I don't even know. Da way I'm going now, I'll probably be in jail or dead. I be gangbanging, carrying guns, and all that"* (Dunbar 2001, 162). This young man (Peter) was prescient as Dunbar tells us that he was subsequently incarcerated.

With few exceptions, the research has not explored the school-to-prison pipeline experience through the voices of youths despite the growing quantitative evidence of the connections between school suspensions, dropouts and incarceration, that is, the school-to-prison pipeline. We know almost nothing about the extent to which youths perceive themselves to be driven not only out of school, but into the justice system and prison. Are youths aware of the similarities between school and prison, or is this a meaningless analogy for them? Do they expect that in light of their lack of success in school, they too will become a prisoner like many of their relatives and neighbors?

The "Deadly Symbioses" of School Suspension
and Criminal Justice: Observations on Parallel Processes

I have spent time in courtrooms, jails, and prisons for almost twenty-five years as part of my work, first as a sentencing advocate, working with defense attorneys to provide information to judges and prosecutors to reduce the use of incarceration, and eventually as the director of an advocacy organization, the Center for Community Alternatives (CCA). I have spent almost as much work time with young people, also in courtrooms, jails for children, and alternative schools. Over these many years, I have seen the two systems converge. Messages conveyed to youths about why they are in an alternative school, the organization and structure of the school, and the role of the police in the school often mirror the rhetoric and practices of prisons and the criminal justice system.

The Syracuse Police Department makes no secret that they view their roles and responsibilities in the schools and the streets as one and the same. During the writing of this book, a widely publicized altercation between a school-based police officer and a female student took place in one of the district's high schools (Kollali 2008). The girl suffered a broken nose when she was punched in the face by the police officer. The incident resulted in an outcry from parents and the district convened a public meeting, which I attended. The meeting was led by the superintendent of the district: the police chief was given an opportunity to describe the incident to the audience, which was largely made up of the parents of the students who attended the high school. In his presentation, the chief referred to the student as "the female suspect" and painstakingly explained the growing problem of "aggressive violent females" who were inflicting injuries on school police officers and police officers working the streets. The chief used typical police terminology to describe the incident in the school, interspersing his account with reminders that "female defendants can hurt or kill, same as men." He carefully set a stage that depicted the district schools as dangerous places, noting that in 2007 there were 2,037 "conflicts" involving "physical fights, or almost physical fights," 370 arrests, and 235 weapons seized (knives or "knife-like" weapons). As the audience recoiled from these descriptions, the chief ended this part of his presentation with the statement that "schools are no longer havens."

After presenting schools as dangerous places, the chief then went on to justify the behavior of the officer in the specific incident and placed this incident in a history of heroic duty to the city and the district. According to the chief, Officer Selton, the officer in question, had been in the school for many years and had suffered injuries (including two injuries that required surgery) in his efforts to break up fights in schools. The chief further reported that his information showed that the "female suspect" had a "history of disobedience" and that the [male] police officer was justified in entering the girls' bathroom (where the incident began), as "bathrooms are hideouts." The chief stated that Officer Selton's punch to the girl took place after she refused to follow him to the principal's office and instead proceeded up the stairs. The chief described a chain of events that began with the officer following the girl up the stairs and physically blocking her from continuing further. The girl then allegedly pushed the officer and they proceeded to scuffle down the steps, each throwing punches at the other. The incident ended when the officer punched the girl three times in her shoulder and chest and once in her face, subdued her, cuffed her, and arrested her.

The chief concluded his version[3] of the incident with a careful explanation that the job description, roles, and responsibilities of police officers in school are exactly the same as their responsibilities on the street. Police job responsibilities, as defined in the New York State Penal Law, include the use of physical, even deadly force, handcuffing, and arresting, which

---

3. The police chief's version of the incident was challenged in part by the district superintendent who asked that the officer in question be reassigned. The chief reluctantly complied with the request, and relations between the district and the police became strained. The chief's version was more fully challenged by a community activist who had obtained a transcript of the meeting that took place in the principal's office immediately after the student was subdued and arrested. In the activist's version, she pointed out that Officer Selton was more than forty years old and 6'2" while the teenage girl (aka "female suspect") was fifteen years old and 5'1".

are applicable to any setting to which they are assigned. He pointed out that the police do not have to be present in the school, but cautioned that, "[i]f you [parents, teachers, and administrators] decided that you want police in schools, we have the very legal right to do what Officer Selton did in this incident."

Beyond the way that police view school-based incidents as actions committed by "suspects" rather than teenage students, there are other ways that school suspension has come to resemble the criminal justice system. Both defendants and students go through judicial or quasi-judicial processes to determine guilt, which involve witnesses and the presentation and refutation of evidence to an authoritative figure who determines culpability and renders a decision. If found "guilty," both a defendant and a student may receive a sentence that removes them from the normal social environment and places them in a setting designated for others who have been found to violate social or institutional norms. In prisons and alternative schools alike, those sentenced to prison or sent to alternative school are disproportionately people of color (Harrison and Beck 2006; Kleiner, Porch, and Farris 2002). In contrast, the authority figures (wardens and guards in the case of prisons, and principals and teachers in the case of alternative schools) are predominantly white (US Census Bureau 2000).

My interviews with students who have gone through the suspension process lend credence to the analogy of the "deadly symbiosis" of school suspension and the criminal justice system. While listening to these young people, I continually recalled my experiences representing defendants in the criminal justice system. Youths often complained of having their behavior misinterpreted—which I likened to the overcharging that is prevalent in the criminal justice system (Miller 1996). The boys in particular were more likely to speak of being under surveillance by school authorities—administrators, teachers, and school police—whom they believed expected them to misbehave. The fatalistic attitudes about school surveillance were similar to opinions that I have heard from young people in the system regarding racial profiling by police. Even when the young people acknowledge their wrongdoing (which was the rule, rather than the exception), they were distressed by the lack of interest on the part of principals and hearing officers about the circumstances surrounding the incident. This, too, is a characteristic of the criminal justice system, where the context of offense behavior and mitigating circumstances are rarely considered. Zero tolerance policies in both systems tie the hands of decision makers who might otherwise be inclined to look behind the behavior to understand reasons, as well as to consider a more total portrait of the human being.

The suspension hearing itself was described in ways that were eerily familiar to what I observed in my work in the court system. The youth, much like many defendants I have encountered, were not really clear about the procedures governing these processes. Young people were often not aware they could have formal representation, but did know that they could and should bring someone with them to the hearing. That "someone" was typically a relative, most often a parent or grandparent. From their descriptions, the parents were ill prepared to serve as an effective advocate for the child. Rather, the young people described parents or guardians sitting passively just trying to keep up with what was happening or being frustrated that they could not get their point across. The youths themselves felt that they were not listened to: in some instances the experience of being ignored reinforced preexisting cynicism, but to others it was a shock, dismantling their belief in fairness. This, too, is a common experience among defendants who often complained that their attorneys did not effectively represent them and that they were not given an opportunity to tell their side of the story.

Finally, students suspended to alternative schools and people sentenced to jail or prison describe common reactions to their first entry into these institutions. Much like young people who enter prison for the first time, they are fearful, uncertain, and filled with a sense of loss of family, friends, community, and "freedom" (Harvey 2007). The kids I interviewed had many of the same trepidations that Jayda describes:

When I first walked into Steel [an alternative school], I wasn't nervous, but I was nervous at the same time. . . . This school, it looks different. It looks weird. Then when you first get there, they gonna label you as a bad child. That was always in my mind . . . they gonna probably label. Some of them will say, "Oh this one, she's a bad child." So yeah, sometimes

I felt nervous, ashamed, different. I had different emotions, but when I was there I felt embarrassed, nervous, and ashamed when I first started going to Steel.

Jayda and other young people become demoralized knowing they are being sent to a place for "bad kids" or "bad people." While security and surveillance measures at prisons and jails are far more extensive than at alternative schools, virtually all of the youths I interviewed were struck by the extent of searches they had to undergo simply to enter the school, as well as the special restrictions on their clothing and possessions, which Celia described to me:

You're not allowed to wear nothing with no zippers like a hoodie. You can't wear a hoodie; you can't wear nothing with no hood on it. And your coat, you can't wear no coat.

Many of the youths likened their alternative school to a jail or prison and one student actually likened the jail to the alternative school. She refused to visit a family member in prison as she said it brought back memories of her unhappy time in alternative school. Her comment struck me as one of the clearest examples of what Wacquant describes as the symbiosis between ghetto communities and prisons.

Organization of the Book

This is a qualitative study in which I represent authentically and give voice to young people who seem to be trapped in the school-to-prison pipeline. I give a glimpse into their lives, the challenges they face, and their efforts to overcome those challenges. In particular, I illuminate what happens to them when the educational system excludes them from regular school. I elevate their voices so that adults—researchers, schoolteachers, administrators, policy makers, and the general public—can hear what these kids go through when they are suspended. I hope, however naively, that through this work, adults in policy-making positions take heed of how policies like zero tolerance damage children.

It is easy to ignore, understate, or dismiss the cruelty of suspension if we learn about this only through newspaper reports or even data documenting the extent of the problem. There is much to cause us to disregard the fact that these young people are still children, just entering their teens with many developmental hurdles to jump over. It is easy to forget that they are children and instead think of them as dangerous, disruptive, or "super predators" and deserving of isolation and exclusion. However, talking to the kids, hearing the catch in their voices as they ponder why so many adults think they are "bad" puts a human face on destructive zero tolerance policies. A qualitative, interview-based method is an excellent way to learn more directly and profoundly what these suspension policies are doing to so many young people in our country.

The book is structured to follow how young people are run through the pipeline. In the first three chapters, I look at factors contributing to the school-to-prison pipeline, including the broad social policies as well as specific criminal justice practices that have fostered the phenomenon of mass incarceration. Chapter 3 looks specifically at relatively recent changes in education including the transformation of alternative schools—institutions once intended to enrich learning—into warehouses for misbehaving students, and how zero tolerance policies contributed to such changes. Alternative schools have a history rooted in the struggle for educational equality that was a core value of the civil rights movement (e.g., "Freedom Schools"), as well as experimental schools reflecting the 1960s counter-culture movement (e.g., "free schools"). Yet by the end of the twentieth century, reference to alternative schools brings to mind the prisonization of American education and a betrayal of the fundamental principle of an equal educational opportunity.

The methods used to collect information and the setting where the research was conducted are summarized in chapter 4.

The remainder of the book is devoted to understanding the suspension process as experienced by young people who find themselves pushed out of school. I describe the lives of young people outside of school: because so much of the rhetoric around the lives of poor minority children focuses on dysfunction, I was particularly interested in hearing how they described their family relations, despite obvious hardships. The dissection of school suspension is based upon the students' descriptions of the suspension incident itself, what behaviors prompted their suspension, and how school authorities, including school police, reacted to these behaviors. The student accounts include details about youth experience with surveillance and security, as well as student perception of education in an alternative school and the stigma that lingers even after their return to mainstream school. Chapter 10 offers a glimpse into what is lost by the dismissal of these children, by their placement onto the prison track. I recount the kids' assessments of what they need to learn, the value they place on education, and how caring adults can make a real difference in helping them cope with the emotions that often drive misbehavior.

The book concludes with a review of the theories, literature, and research that place youth perspectives in context. The concluding chapter contains recommendations for policy, practice, and political changes that could decouple schools from the carceral state.

2

The American Gulag

Entwining Schools into the Carceral State

THE TERM "GULAG," which originally referred to the Soviet system of penal labor camps (Solzhenitsyn 1973), has come to symbolize prisons generally. Ruth Wilson Gilmore (2007) refers to the "Golden Gulag" in describing the expansion of prisons in California, now the largest state prison system in the United States, which itself maintains the largest prison system in the world. With more than two million people in prison, the US criminal justice system is widely viewed as a system of mass incarceration driven by a confluence of governmental and economic forces now known as the "prison-industrial complex" (Mauer 2001; Simon 2001).

The circumstances and factors that have created the American Gulag have become an increasingly important link in the carceral state. By carceral state, I mean the way that law enforcement techniques, methods, and tools are ubiquitous throughout all facets of American society. A synthesis of ideas from Foucault (1979), Garland (1990, 2001b), Wacquant (2001, 2006), and Simon (2007) suggests that the carceral state consists of spatial ordering of control both within and external to prisons through gated communities, mall security, metal detectors in schools, security cameras, and the physical presence of public and private police, as well as the prisons and detention centers that dot the American landscape. The carceral state also consists of zero tolerance policies that criminalize an increasing range of human behavior including homelessness, mental illness, addiction, and noise on the street, and increasingly, student insubordination and normative adolescent behavior in the schools. Those who transgress are considered different and dangerous and can be incapacitated even

17

outside the prison wall through house arrest and electronic monitoring. They are labeled ex-con and ex-offender, labels that exclude them from participation in most aspects of civil society, for even without incarceration, a criminal conviction of even a minor sort can result in bars to employment, college, housing, licenses, voting, and volunteering.

Mass Imprisonment

In 1971, US prisons captured the attention of the American public with the Attica rebellion that took place in a maximum security prison in Batavia, New York, a small town outside of Buffalo.[1] I was one of those caught up in the unveiling of twentieth-century American punishment. My discovery of these institutions was serendipitous—a product of time and place—as experienced through the eyes of a then young graduate student who in the early 1970s became involved in efforts to defend prisoners charged in the aftermath of the Attica prison uprising of 1971.

In 1971, there were no prisoner's rights projects and only a handful of people were at all concerned about prison conditions. Prisons were a relatively insignificant institution in American life in 1971, with the rate of incarceration (96 per 100,000) relatively constant all through the 1900s to that point in time. In fact, by 1971, there had even been a small decline in the incarceration rate.

There were a few lawyers who did prison work, and they took on the defense of the sixty-one prisoners charged in the uprising and recruited law and graduate students to help with the various aspects of the work. I first became involved in efforts to survey community attitudes toward prisoners as part of the legal strategy to obtain a change of venue to move the trials from the virtually all-white prison town of Batavia to Buffalo, New York, a city with a more diverse population that would be more representative of the largely black and Latino prison population. I also became

1. The prison uprising took place at the Attica prison in upstate New York from September 9 through September 13, 1971. Wicker (1975) provides an observer's view of the takeover of the prison by the inmates and the state's retaking of the prison.

involved in the community organizing strategy to build support for the "Brothers," as the prisoners charged in the Attica case came to be called. As time passed (the first case went to trial in 1974), more and more of the prisoners were able to post bail and become active in their own legal and community organizing strategies. I came to know many of them, not just as "clients" but as friends. I came to learn firsthand the connections, direct and indirect, between community conditions and pathways into crime, and to think more critically about how the United States constructs its punishment system.

The cumulative experiences stemming from the Attica insurrection—the substantive work, the community organizing, and personal connections—were transformative for me. I spent the last thirty years working in community organizations in an effort to reduce the use of incarceration. Forty years after the rebellion at Attica, the incarceration rate had increased six-fold: in 1980, there were fewer than 140 people per 100,000 in state and federal prisons but by 2011 that rate had risen to just over 716 per 100,000 or more than 1 out of every 130 US residents (Sentencing Project 2011). The incarceration rates for people of color are much higher—black, non-Hispanic males are imprisoned at a rate of 4,749 per 100,000, representing more than 2.3 million people confined in US jails and prisons (West and Sabol 2010). One in nine black men between the ages of twenty and thirty-four is now in prison or jail (Pew Center on the States 2008). America's "gulag" now stretches from coast to coast in institutions that contain men and increasingly women, who are isolated from families and communities.

David Garland (1990) describes mass imprisonment as a form of social control that reflects the social and economic changes of late modernity. In *The Culture of Control*, Garland (2001b) elaborates on the arrival of mass incarceration and its connection to changes in social, economic, and cultural relations ("late modernity") and the ascendance of socially conservative politics. These changes are characterized by the transformation of US capitalism from a manufacturing to a service economy, increasing globalization of capital with the associated insecurity, deterioration of public goods, and increasing income inequality and effects on social reproduction (Katz 2001). The "culture of control" is a reaction to these economic, political, and social changes. Poverty and crime become equated, and both are characterized as the individual choices of unworthy individuals (Hagan 1993). The conflation of poverty and crime has made it easier to replace social welfare programs with punitive crime control policies resulting in a reliance on incarceration (Simon 2007; Garland 2001b).

Through her case study of California, Gilmore (2007) explains the orgy of imprisonment in the United States in the latter part of the twentieth century. She traces the expansion of prisons within the context of changing economic structures and political ideology. Surpluses in capital, land, labor, and state capacity make prisons an increasingly attractive investment. Economic and political changes create a large urban underclass, a surplus humanity that in essence becomes the commodity that stokes the prison-building boom. Prisons were built on surplus land, formerly used for agricultural purposes, in an effort to shore up rural economies that were decimated by climate-induced crises and agribusiness. The prisons were financed by public borrowing that was "off-line," that is, not included in state budgets and therefore immune to right-wing organized taxpayer revolts exemplified by California's famous "Proposition 13," which starved public goods such as education. The dismantling of welfare supports for the poor and near poor was supported by the consolidation of right-wing Republican power through the administrations of Ronald Reagan, George Deukmejian, and Pete Wilson. The politically expedient "get tough on crime" mantra created harsh sentencing laws (e.g., "three strikes") that ensured a steady stream of humanity into the large number of new prisons being built in rural areas throughout the state.

California's "Golden Gulag" is perhaps the most dramatic example of the role of prisons in the political and economic landscape of the late twentieth century, but it is not the only example. New York State mirrors much of the California experience, although the prison expansion in the state occurred under the liberal administration of Mario Cuomo. Sidestepping the state's regular budget process and even its bonding process when the voters of New York rejected a prison bond referendum in 1981, the state government turned to the Urban Development Corporation (UDC) to fund the building of new prisons. UDC was originally established to fund low- and moderate-income housing, but in 1982, during the dramatic increase in homelessness throughout the state, UDC funds were redirected to pay for prison building (Schlosser 1998). There were twenty-eight prisons built in New York between 1981 and 1990, prisons that were readily filled through enforcement of New York's mandatory drug sentencing laws.

Mass incarceration has become a uniquely American institution, one that is intimately tied to structural changes in the larger society, both economic and social (Garland 2001a; Wacquant 2001). Wacquant (2001) specifically considers incarceration to be the most recent iteration of social control of African Americans. He places mass incarceration in the coterie of the American "peculiar" institutions—slavery, Jim Crow, and the ghetto—directed at controlling black people. In keeping with Garland's explanation of prison as the social control mechanism of late modernity, Wacquant asserts that prisons are particularly directed at controlling the no longer employable black population, that is, surplus labor for whom there are no jobs. Under the race-neutral rubric of crime control, "tough on crime" became a code word for containment of the largely African American "castaways" (Wacquant 2006, 5) of the US population. Disciplinary policies and practices, such as those that mandate the suspension of young people out of mainstream schools, play a critical role in rendering young people of color superfluous and unemployable.

Race and Incarceration

Incarceration rates vary dramatically for whites and minorities. In 2011, the rate of incarceration in state and federal prisons was 478 per 100,000 for white males, 3,023 per 100,000 for black males, and 1,238 per 100,000 for Hispanic males (Sentencing Project 2011). The incarceration rate of black people in the United States exceeds the rate of black incarceration in South Africa at the height of apartheid (Mauer 1994).[2]

2. The incarceration rate for people of color ("blacks" and "coloureds") in South Africa in 1993 was 851 per 100,000.

The tremendous growth in the numbers of black and Latino males in prison has been the most troubling aspect of the prison-industrial complex, but is not the only demographic characteristic to consider. The number of women incarcerated increased by 757 percent between 1977 and 2004 (Frost, Greene, and Pranis 2006). Racial disparities are even more pronounced among the female prison population: in 2011, black and Hispanic women made up more than half of the population of women incarcerated (Carson and Sabol 2012). The incarceration rate for black women, at 129 per 100,000, was about three times the incarceration rate for white women, which was 71 per 100,000. Hispanic women, with an incarceration rate of 142 per 100,000, were about two times more likely to be incarcerated than white women (Carson and Sabol 2012).

Erecting the "Peculiar Institution": Drug Laws and Mandatory Sentencing

Legislative changes and changes in the implementation of criminal justice procedures and processes have situated the criminal justice system as a critical tool in the management of marginalized populations (Wacquant 2001; Gilmore 2007). The "War on Drugs" is most often pointed to as the cause of the astonishing growth in the US prison population and the specific containment of poor people of color. Indeed, drug laws are considered the single most important legislative factor driving the expansion in imprisonment, first in New York State, and then throughout the United States.

Mandatory prison sentences for drug crimes were first introduced in 1973 in New York State. Under what became known as the Rockefeller Drug Laws, New York's prison population grew from 12,500 in 1973 to a peak of 71,500 in 1999 (Correctional Association of New York 2006a).[3] People convicted of drug offenses were 11 percent of new commitments in 1980, but by 2006, drug offenders represented 36 percent of New York's

---

3. The New York State prison population declined to about 58,000 in 2010 (New York State Department of Correctional Services 2010).

prison population (Correctional Association of New York 2006b). Drug law reform in New York was enacted beginning in 2004, and by 2012, 14 percent of the state prison population was incarcerated on drug crimes. Despite the reforms, almost 8,000 people are still incarcerated for drug crimes and racial disparities persist with 75 percent of prisoners being people of color (New York State Department of Corrections and Community Supervision 2012).

New York's draconian drug laws were replicated in states across the United States as well as by the federal government. In roughly the two decades between 1980 and 2000 the number of annual drug arrests tripled, reaching 1,579,566 by 2000 (King and Mauer 2002). Between 1980 and 1990 alone, there was a five-fold increase in the rate of imprisonment, from 19 prison commitments per 1,000 arrests to 103 per 1,000 arrests. The rest of the country followed New York's example: prison cells were increasingly taken up by drug offenders. In 1980, people convicted of drug crimes were only 6 percent of the state and federal prison populations, but by 2008, 17 percent of state and federal prison populations were drug offenders (Carson and Sabol 2012).

The enforcement of drug laws—arrest, prosecution, and sentencing—have been most felt in communities of color (Tonry 1995). While drug use is not distinguishable by race or ethnicity among African Americans, Latinos, and whites (Substance Abuse and Mental Health Services Administration (SAMHSA) 2007), drug laws have been far more aggressively enforced in poor communities of color than in white middle class neighborhoods. The result of this disparate application of drug laws is apparent in the US prison population: almost three-quarters of all people in prison for drug offenses are black or Latino (Human Rights Watch 2000; Mauer 2006; Blumstein et al. 1983).

While important, drug laws are not the only laws that have increased incarceration. Mandatory sentencing laws, i.e., laws that require imprisonment for certain crimes (crimes involving the use or possession of a weapon, robbery, and other crimes involving violence, as well as drug crimes) or criminal histories (e.g., the infamous "three strikes" laws) result in the incarceration of people who previously might have received non-custodial (typically probationary) sentences (Wolf and Weissman 1996).

By 1996, all states had implemented some form of mandatory sentencing (National Center on Crime and Delinquency 1998). Mandatory sentencing has led to higher incarceration rates (Stemen, Rengifo, and Wilson 2006) and exacerbated racial disparities in the criminal justice system (Mustard 2001; Albonetti 1997). The most egregious examples of these mandatory sentencing laws are federal drug laws that include mandatory minimum sentences for crack and cocaine offenses (US Sentencing Commission 1995; Human Rights Watch 2000; Free 1997).[4] However, state drug laws affect more people, given that law enforcement remains predominantly a state function.

Beyond driving more people into prisons, mandatory sentencing laws also have institutional effects on the administration of justice. The balance of power is shifting in court rooms as mandatory sentencing laws remove judicial discretion and increasingly make prosecutors' charging decisions the key determinants of the sentence outcome (Albonetti 1997; Bureau of Justice Assistance 1996).

Changes in parole and probation supervision have also been a part of the building of the carceral state. First, these community supervision options have been proscribed through mandatory sentencing laws that eliminate the prospect of a noncustodial probation sentence at the front end, and by the elimination of parole at the back end (Wolf and Weissman 1996; Travis and Lawrence 2002). Federal "truth in sentencing laws," notably The Violent Crime Control and Law Enforcement Act

[handwritten margin note: mandatory minimum taken power away from judge]

4. There have been recent reforms to federal sentencing guidelines and support for further reforms is gaining momentum. Effective November 1, 2007, the US Sentencing Commission amendment revised the federal guidelines for crack cocaine sentencing and reduced prison time for people convicted of crack offenses. Congressional legislation to eliminate the disparity in crack versus cocaine sentencing is under consideration and, if passed, would equalize federal sentences for offenses involving crack and powder cocaine. Attorney General Eric Holder supported sentencing reform in a June 24, 2009 speech before the Charles Hamilton Houston Institute for Race and Justice and the Congressional Black Caucus Symposium "Rethinking Federal Sentencing Policy: 25th Anniversary of the Sentencing Reform Act." Available at: http://www.usdoj.gov/ag/speeches/2009/ag-speech-0907221.html.

of 1994, as amended in 1996, played a role in eliminating or reduc[ing] the use of parole. Under this law, federal funding for prison construction was made contingent upon the state increasing the length of sentences and requiring that certain categories of offenders serve at least 85 percent of the sentence imposed (Sabol et al. 2002). Second, probation and parole supervision approaches moved away from a rehabilitative focus and became increasingly law enforcement oriented (Clear and Byrne 1992) and heavily reliant on sophisticated methods of surveillance and control (e.g., electronic monitoring, urinalysis). These methods in turn resulted in greater numbers of people being returned to prison for "technical" violations[5] of their conditions of release rather than new criminality. Travis and Lawrence (2002) report that the number of parole violators returned to prison increased seven-fold between 1980 and 2000, noting that the number of parole violators re-incarcerated in 2000, 203,000, approaches the total number of people imprisoned in state prisons in 1980. In some states, such as California, parole violators are the largest single segment of the prison population (Travis and Lawrence 2002).

The Color of Justice: Disparities in Arrest, Prosecution, and Sentencing

The socioeconomic characteristics of the US prison population show that the phenomenon of mass incarceration has not affected all segments of the population equally. A body of research and data demonstrates disparities in the criminal justice system by race and ethnicity (Golub, Johnson, and Dunlap 2007; Mauer 2006; Tonry 1995; Nelson 1995; Baldus et al. 1998). Discrimination is historical and current, deliberate and inadvertent, and occurs at every stage of the criminal justice system from arrest to sentencing. The stage-based nature of discrimination has a cumulative

---

5. A technical violation of parole or probation reflects an alleged failure to abide by conditions of release for reasons other than a new crime. Examples of technical violations include drug use, association with other people on parole, changing residence without parole or probation officer approval, failure to maintain employment, and failure to report.

effect that lends itself to the adage the "the whole is greater than the sum of its parts."

Regardless of the source, the result is the over-representation of minorities at each of the key stages of the criminal justice system. Cumulative disparity plays an insidious role in the criminal justice system. The American Bar Association's (ABA) (2004, 9) Kennedy Commission concluded: "the cumulative effect of discretionary decisions at each step of the process ultimately contributes to the racial disparity in our prisons and jails."

A number of scholars have attributed racially disparate sentencing outcomes, whether or not a person is incarcerated, to legally relevant factors such as longer criminal histories (Hagan 1974; Blumstein et al. 1983). However, legally relevant factors at sentencing cannot be separated from broader criminal justice practices along the continuum of the system, including the harsher treatment of minorities as juveniles (Pope and Feyerherm 1990; Sampson and Lauritsen 1997; Poe-Yamagata and Jones 2000), and at each stage of the [adult] criminal justice system (Nelson 1995). Moreover, the criminalization of student behavior, with its attendant racially disparate effects, positions the school as the new entryway into the criminal justice system continuum.

Studies of each distinct stage of the criminal justice system have found evidence that race influences outcomes. The deployment of police resources in inner cities and certain practices, such as police stops, have been found to result in disparate arrest rates for minorities (Blumstein 1982; Blumstein et al. 1983; Langan 1985; Hawkins and Hardy 1989; Crutchfield, Bridges, and Pitchford 1994). The National Organization of Blacks in Law Enforcement (NOBLE) (2001, 4) asserts that "[b]ias-based policing impacts all aspects of policing and should be considered the most serious problem facing law enforcement today." Blumstein (1982, 1993) found that 75–80 percent of the racial disparity in the prison population is explained by racial differences in arrests. Using different methods and levels of analysis, subsequent research essentially confirmed Blumstein's findings (Langan 1985; Hawkins and Hardy 1989; Crutchfield, Bridges, and Pitchford 1994). Disparity tends to be greater for the less serious and nonviolent crimes where there is typically more discretion in police decision making (Austin and Allen 2000). For example, racial profiling in traffic stops has been a widely acknowledged problem (New Jersey Office of the Attorney General 1999; Ramirez, McDevitt, and Farrell 2000; Harris 2000). While the problem of "driving while black" has been the most visible example of racial profiling, the pattern of police deployment in venues and neighborhoods with higher concentrations of people of color also contributes to the higher arrest rates of minority populations (Cole 1999; Tonry 1995; Sampson and Lauritsen 1997). Between 2002 and 2012, the New York City Police Department made more than four million "stop and frisk" interrogations. The overwhelming majority of people stopped—87 percent—were black and Latino (New York Civil Liberties Union 2012).[6]

Arrest is followed by the decision to detain or to release on recognizance or to set bail: defendants detained pretrial are more likely to be convicted of the charges, and if convicted, are more likely to be incarcerated (Ares, Rankin, and Sturz 1963; Taylor et al. 1972; Hermann, Single, and Boston 1977; Hart and Reaves 1999; Spohn 2000; Williams 2003; Taxman, Byrne, and Pattavina 2005; Phillips 2007). Critical bail and pretrial release decisions are influenced by the defendant's racial and ethnic characteristics, with minority defendants more likely to be detained prior to trial than whites facing similar charges and with similar criminal histories (Goldkamp 1979; Mahoney et al. 2001; Demuth and Steffensmeier 2004; Free 1997). Racial disparities are also present in the next step in the criminal justice system—prosecution and charging decisions. Minorities are less likely to have charges dismissed or reduced. An investigation of about 700,000 criminal cases from California between 1981 and 1990 revealed statistically significant racial disparities in prosecutors' willingness to dismiss charges or reduce charges to crimes that would permit diversion (Schmitt 1991). Albonetti (1997) also found differences by race in federal prosecutors' willingness to grant sentencing reductions based upon "substantial assistance." Whites who provided substantial assistance received an average 23 percent reduction in the likelihood of incarceration, while similarly situated blacks received a 13 percent reduction and

6. About 90 percent of the stops did not result in any arrest, indicating that stop and frisk practices are less about public safety and more about social control.

Hispanics received a 14 percent reduction. The actions of many different criminal justice system "actors" along a multi-stage continuum impact the basic "in/out" sentencing decision.

Economics and Social Control: The Prison-Industrial Complex

The tremendous growth in the prison population has made criminal justice big business. The economic interests that now connect industry to prisons go beyond the public sector workforce of police, court personnel, and prison guards. It extends into companies that produce and sell an array of products, both security-related and more basic supplies to these various sectors. It also includes the use of prison labor to produce goods and services at below-market price for private corporations and local government (Nagel 2002). A *New York Times* report (Santos 2008) on a possible prison closing in upstate New York captured the small town dependence on prisons:

> The reliance on Camp Gabriels extends well beyond jobs. Small businesses have staked their survival on the prison workers who patronize their stores. Local governments and charities, meanwhile, have come to depend on inmate work crews to clear snow from fire hydrants, maintain parks and hiking trails, mow the lawns at cemeteries and unload trucks at food pantries.

Mike Davis (1995) first introduced the term "prison-industrial complex," likening the burgeoning prison industry to the "military-industrial complex" exposed by President Dwight Eisenhower. Schlosser (1998, 54) defined the term as referring to "a set of bureaucratic, political, and economic interests that encourage increased spending on imprisonment, regardless of the actual need." Like the military-industrial complex, the prison-industrial complex entwines diverse public and private interests. The economic interests include unionized public sector workers, public and private corporations that bond, construct, and supply prisons (architects, construction companies, investment houses, bond counsel firms, and telephone companies), industries devoted to the technology of social

control, and the growing role of private corporations in the direct operation of prisons that are contracted out by state and federal government.
Private corporations and governments also benefit from the use of prison
labor that takes on public sector work (e.g., maintenance of state parks) or
joint ventures between states or the federal government and private companies to produce goods and services using prison labor (Sexton 1995).

Prisons are also increasingly privatized and run by large corporations
such as the Corrections Corporation of America and Wackenhut, whose
profits are dependent upon the continuation of punitive policies. A *Businessweek* article headlined "Private Prisons Have a Lock on Growth" noted
that the Corrections Corporation of America stock price rose 26 percent
in the first six months of 2006 (Ghosh 2006). The Correctional Corporation of America (the largest private prison company) manages or owns
at least sixty prisons in nineteen states and Washington, DC, with these
facilities having a "bed" capacity of 80,000 (Correctional Corporation of
America 2010). It is a publicly traded corporation and posts a web page
for investors with up-to-date share prices. As of 2009, there were 127,688
people held in private prisons under contract to the federal and various
state governments. In but one year (July 2005–June 2006), the use of private prisons increased by almost 13 percent (Sabol, Minton, and Harrison
2007). Moreover, these publicly traded companies, driven by financial
profit, have become significant and sophisticated lobbyists on criminal
justice legislation[7] that would sustain or increase the prison population
(Chang and Thompkins 2002).

Private corporations are not the only group lobbying for tougher sentencing laws and against sentencing reform. Prison guard unions also do
so (Doster 2007; Center on Juvenile and Criminal Justice 2007; Chang
and Thompkins 2002; Davis 1995). Unions have combined and spawned
victims rights groups that together form a formidable lobby for "tough

---

7. Seeing detainees as a lucrative market, private prisons are also involved in craft-
ing harsh immigration laws. An investigation by National Public Radio (Sullivan 2010)
revealed that the Correctional Corporation for example was involved in the drafting of
the 2010 Arizona Immigration Law (S.B. 1070).

on crime laws." Davis (1995) points to more than one thousand new laws enacted in California between 1984 and 1992 with the strong support of the guards union and victims groups. Rural communities without another source of jobs join in the clamor for prison expansion and prison construction (Gilmore 2007). A *New York Times* article (Confessore 2007), quoting Kent Gardner, president of the Center for Government Research, captures rural support for prisons in New York State: "Up in the north country, you used to just think of hanging out a sign that says 'PrisonsRUs' . . . ; pretty much every rural town in the state was angling for these facilities." Prisons have become the largest local employer in many rural communities, which over the last twenty years have become home to about 60 percent of new prisons (Beale 1993, 1997; Wagner 2003).

There are no comprehensive measures of the overall economic power of the prison-industrial complex. However, the Bureau of Justice Statistics tracks employment and spending in various government functions that form the criminal justice system—police, prosecutors, courts, and corrections. Overall, expenditures in the multiple sectors that make up the criminal justice system have increased dramatically between 1980 and 2010. In 1982, criminal justice prison spending was calculated at just under $36 billion dollars. Within ten years, spending grew by 125 percent to $79 billion and by the end of the 1990s, spending exceeded $146 billion, another 85 percent increase in less than ten years and an astounding 300 percent increase between 1980 and 2000 (US Department of Justice 2002).

The increase in spending on corrections has outpaced spending on education. Between 1977 and 2003, corrections spending alone increased by 1,173 percent, while spending on education increased 505 percent. Criminal justice functions became a larger share of state and local spending, while spending on education decreased as a proportion of state and local budgets (US Department of Justice 2002). Employment in criminal justice functions increased by 77 percent between 1982 and 2003 (US Department of Justice, Bureau of Justice Statistics 2002). By 2006, the federal and state criminal justice systems employed more than 2.4 million people, accounting for 10 percent of federal government employees, 31 percent of state employees, and 58 percent of local government employees (Perry 2008).

Mass Incarceration and the Social Control
of Superfluous Populations

While crime control defines the public view of the purpose of prisons, mass incarceration is driven by other agendas, including economics and politics (Garland 2001a; Wacquant 2006; Gilmore 2007). Incarceration rates increase independently of changes in crime rates, growing even when crime rates go down, such as occurred during the 1990s, and outpacing crime rates when these rates are high, such as during the 1980s (King, Mauer, and Young 2005).[8] Moreover, only between 10 and 25 percent of the decrease in crime has been attributed to the increase in incarceration (Levitt 2004; Spelman 2000; Western 2006). Incarceration rates continue to climb even in the face of evidence that it is itself a destabilizing force, particularly when meted out in concentrated forms on specific communities (Rose and Clear 1998).

Mass imprisonment is a tool to address the growing unemployment of young, unskilled men and is most readily imposed upon African Americans. As explained by Western (2006, 53):

> Underlying these political and economic explanations of mass imprisonment is a broader account of political reaction to the upheaval in American race relations through the 1960s and the collapse in urban labor markets for low-skill men. The social turbulence of the 1960s—a volatile mixture of rising crime, social protest, and the erosion of white privilege—sharpened the punitive sentiments of white voters. The economic demoralization of low-skill urban blacks in the 1970s presented a vulnerable target for the punitive turn in criminal justice. These were the basic preconditions for mass imprisonment.

The work of Wacquant (2001, 2006), Gilmore (2007), Garland (2001a), Western and Beckett (1999), Western and Pettit (2005), Western (2006), and Davis (1995) all offer perspectives on the prison as a mechanism for

8. For example, during the 1990s, the crime rate declined by 17 percent, yet the rate of incarceration increased by 65 percent (King, Mauer, and Young 2005).

absorbing surplus labor. Western and Beckett (1999, 1031) discuss how prison acts as a regulator of the US labor market, serving the role that social welfare institutions do in European democracies: "Incarceration generated a sizeable, nonmarket reallocation of labor, overshadowing state intervention through social policy."

Incarceration hides joblessness by taking labor out of the market. Western (2006) demonstrates that the economic boom of the 1990s and its ameliorative effect on unemployment and the poverty rate, particularly for African American males, disappears once prisoners are included in calculations of economic well-being.[9]

Wacquant (2001) attributes the rise in incarceration in the late twentieth-century United States to signify the declining ability of the ghetto to contain poor African Americans due to economic restructuring, which included mechanization and globalization that made African American labor even more expendable. Like slavery and Jim Crow laws, prisons are the latest means for keeping (unskilled) African Americans in a subordinate and confined position—physically, socially, and symbolically (Wacquant 2001, 97). Wacquant defines the extreme containment of the prison as the "hyperghetto." The carceral culture has become the dominant culture in poor, urban, African American communities, revealing not only the profound lack of jobs, but also other indices of the abandonment of inner cities: "As the ghetto became more like a prison (what I call the 'hyperghetto') and the prison became more like a ghetto, the two institutions increasingly fused to form the fast-expanding carceral system that constitutes America's fourth 'peculiar institution'" (Wacquant 2001, 103).

Prisons become more like ghettos in their racial divide, increased violence, and chaotic street culture that meshes with convict culture. This should come as no surprise as poor communities of color are populated by people who cycle in and out of prison, doing life on the installment plan. Ghettos take on the culture of prisons, most profoundly, in

9. Western and Pettit (2005) show that by 1999, the exclusion of prisoners in earnings calculations inflated the relative earnings of blacks by between 7 and 20 percent among all working age men, and by as much as 58 percent among young men.

Wacquant's words, by "official solidification of the centuries-old association of blackness with criminality and devious violence" (2001, 117). The material manifestations of the merging of prison and the street is evident in street gangs in prison and prison gangs in the street, prison slang, such as "homeboy" or "homie," and even fashion trends such as sagging pants, a style with roots in the prohibition against belts in prison. Shabazz Sanders (2008) explored the meshing of the ghetto and prison in the culture and consciousness of black men. He points to the hyper-masculinity of black men, including their body sculpture, tattooing, and physicality as moving from the prison to the community. The ghetto also prepared young black men for prison through the spatial contours of geographical isolation, policing, and surveillance, physical overcrowding, poor nutrition, and compromised health. Shabazz Sanders joins many public health scholars in pointing out the interaction between prison and the ghetto in the spread of HIV (Lane et al. 2004; Freudenberg 2008; Adimora and Schoenbach 2005).

The merging of race and criminality also depoliticizes issues of racism. Under the guise of a race-neutral criminal justice system, social and economic problems of the ghetto that result in alienation and its attendant behavioral manifestations are redefined. For example, the condition of urban schools is transformed from an issue of resource distribution to a problem of violent, delinquent children and their dysfunctional families. Moreover, community level disenfranchisement effects associated with the large number of people barred from voting because of a criminal record undermine the possibility of effecting change in educational practice and policy through the political process (Uggen, Manza, and Thompson 2006).

Prisonizing Schools: Police, Security, and Surveillance

As a core institution, public schools in poor urban communities of color are not immune from the symbiotic relationship between prison and community. "Public schools in the hyperghetto have similarly deteriorated to the point where they operate in the manner of *institutions of confinement* whose primary mission is not to educate but to ensure 'custody and control'—to borrow the motto of many departments of corrections" (Wacquant 2001, 108; emphasis in original).

School as the initiation to mass incarceration is a recent consideration. The ghetto school reflects the carceral culture in many ways, from zero tolerance policies requiring suspension, which can be analogized to mandatory sentencing, to pervasive police presence, pro-arrest policies, and expanded surveillance and security. As Shabazz Sanders (2008) points out, the carceral culture is also seen in the appearance and behaviors of youth. This melding of prison culture and school operation collapses the pipeline: schools become a place that readies some youths for prison.

While there is a rich literature on the role of the school in reproducing cultural and class relationships, until the late 1990s, schools were not thought of as training grounds for prison. The first national level conference to examine the school-to-prison pipeline was held at Harvard University in May 2003. That conference, the research that preceded it, as well as much of the subsequent research has focused on documenting and analyzing the problem, showing how the punitive policies of the criminal justice system have come to permeate the US school system, particularly inner city urban schools. The "school-to-prison pipeline" has become a phrase used to describe the connections among school policies and practices that result in a more punitive approach to student misbehavior.

The links between school disciplinary policies and practices and criminal justice system involvement are both direct and indirect. The direct link is the increased presence of police in schools such that student misconduct and noncompliance that were previously addressed by teachers or school administrators now become the purview of school-based police. Police presence and criminalization of misdeeds have resulted in an increase in the number of in-school arrests (Advancement Project 2005).

Regular police presence in schools is a relatively recent phenomenon. In the late 1970s, there were only 100 school police officers nationwide (Brady, Balmer, and Phenix 2007). Between 1999 and 2003, the number of schools reporting the regular presence of safety and police officers increased by 30 percent, according to the US Department of Education (DeVoe and Kaffenberger 2005). The number of school resource officers peaked at just over 14,300 in 2003 and, due to federal funding cuts, declined to about 13,000 in 2007 (Justice Policy Institute 2012).

By the mid 1990s, the number of police deployed in New York City schools exceeded the size of the entire Boston police force (Beger 2002) and now at 4,600, exceeds the number of officers in most US cities (New York Civil Liberties Union (NYCLU) 2007). As might be expected, police presence results in the treatment of student misbehavior as criminal justice matters. While New York City has refused to disclose the number of arrests made in schools, the NYCLU study shows that increased law enforcement and school security measures are concentrated in schools where the student body is disproportionately students of color: 82 percent of children attending schools with metal detectors were black and Latino, surpassing their representation in the citywide school population by 11 percent.

While national data are not available, information from individual cities show an increasing number of arrests of children while in school. For example, in the 2010–2011 school year, 16,377 students in Florida were sent directly to the juvenile justice system, an average of forty-five students per day. Black students make up only 21 percent of the Florida youth population but made up 46 percent of all 2011 school-related referrals to law enforcement (Florida Department of Juvenile Justice 2011). In 2003 in Chicago, Illinois, 8,539 students were arrested in public schools (Advancement Project 2005). Almost 10 percent were children age twelve or younger. Black students made up 77 percent of the arrests, but were only 50 percent of the school population. Half of the students arrested in Chicago schools are sent to juvenile or criminal court. In Palm Beach County, Florida in 2003, black students make up only 29 percent of the student population but were 64 percent of arrests in school (Advancement Project 2006). The racial disparity in school arrests is not limited to large urban centers: in 2003, according to the *Des Moines Register*, black students constituting 15 percent of Des Moines's high school student population were 33 percent of the 556 arrests in that city's high schools (Deering, Alex, and Blake 2003).

Data on school arrests for school districts with more than fifty thousand were made public by the US Department of Education in 2012. The data showed that over 70 percent of school-based arrests or referrals to law enforcement involved minority students. Males were more likely than females to be arrested in school (US Department of Education 2012).

Especially disturbing is the fact that many of the school arrests are for non-criminal activity and are carried out without regard for the age of the student or the context of the child's misbehavior. Media accounts of these sorts of arrests abound and have been chronicled by the Advancement Project (2006) and the Advancement Project in collaboration with Alliance for Educational Justice, Dignity in Schools Campaign, NAACP, and Legal Defense Fund (2013). Examples include the arrest in St. Petersburg, Florida, in 2005 of a five-year-old African American girl by police for throwing a tantrum and hitting an assistant principal. Also in that year, in New York City, a sixteen-year-old girl was arrested for shouting an obscenity in the hallway. When the school principal attempted to stop the police from detaining the girl, the principal and a school aide were also arrested. In May 2012, an honors student in Houston, Texas spent a night in jail when she missed class to go to work to support her family. In April 2012, a kindergarten student in Milledgeville, Georgia was handcuffed and arrested for throwing a tantrum. In Palm Beach, Florida, 22 percent of the in-school arrests were for miscellaneous non-criminal behaviors such as "disruptive behavior" (Advancement Project 2005, 2006).

The prisonization of schools through ubiquitous presence of the police undermines the authority of principals and other school administrators (Devine 1996). There are formal and informal policies that now require incidents to be turned over to the police for action. Several years back, I attended a meeting of a New York State board with planning responsibility for the state's juvenile justice system. A school administrator was chastised for requesting funding to establish an anti-graffiti program that would retain school authority over such behavior. The administrator was sharply reminded that graffiti was a crime and therefore school police, and not the school principal, were to be the arbiters of whether or not a student could be admitted into the diversion program or arrested and prosecuted under the penal code.

The widespread introduction of police in schools has been accompanied by enhanced security technology. In schools throughout the country, including Syracuse City schools, entryways to schools are often limited to one door. On entering the school, students are subject to metal detectors, wands, electronic identification systems, and biometric technology such as eye-scanning cameras and fingerprinting that allows admission to preapproved students (Atlas 2002; Cohn 2006). Halls are equipped with alarm systems and cameras and some districts have installed panic buttons in classrooms. In addition to hard technology, schools now employ security guards to monitor entry and egress. In some cases of school searches, the police use dogs to sniff out drugs. Data from the US departments of education and justice that track the types of security measures used by schools show that between 1998 and 2000, 75 percent of public schools limited access to schools during school hours, 7 percent used random metal detector checks, 21 percent used dogs for random drug checks, and 19 percent monitored students' whereabouts with security cameras (DeVoe and Kaffenberger 2005). Private security firms have identified schools as a lucrative market, with business magazines sprouting up that focus on the selling of security systems to schools. There are a large number of vendors who set up booths at school-related conferences as well as security industry-organized conferences on the topic of school safety (Casella 2003). The industry magazine *Security Management*, for example, posts a web page[10] listing its collection of articles on school security. There is an overlap between companies that design prisons and jails and sell security equipment to correctional facilities and those that are now involved in designing and equipping K–12 schools.[11]

School Disciplinary Policies: Bringing Zero Tolerance to Schools

Arresting young people in school is the overt connection between school and the criminal justice system. Increasingly punitive disciplinary policies

10. See http://www.securitymanagement.com/library/000760.html.
11. Randall Atlas, for example, whose essay is cited above, is vice president of Atlas Safety and Security Design, Inc. His resume describes him as an architect specializing in "criminal justice architecture" and cites his experience as a consultant to the Florida Department of Corrections and the National Institute of Corrections, among others.

are less obvious, but play a more significant role in disconnecting youths from education by pushing them out of the school by expulsion or suspension.

Zero tolerance grew out of federal drug enforcement policies of the 1980s and was adapted to aggressive quality-of-life policing in urban centers, notably in New York City during the Giuliani administration (Bowling 1999). The 1994 Gun-Free Schools Act brought the zero tolerance policies of the criminal justice system into the school setting. The act made federal funding to schools contingent upon the local adoption of school disciplinary policies that mandated expulsion for weapons possession.

Much as zero tolerance policing increased the number of people brought into the criminal justice system, zero tolerance disciplinary policies have played a major role in the increase in school suspensions. While the federal law requires a one-year expulsion for possession of a weapon, over time many jurisdictions came to apply mandatory expulsion policies to other behaviors, including drug possession and fighting, and even lesser "offenses" such as swearing (Skiba and Knesting 2001). The interpretation of zero tolerance and expulsion varies by state. In some states, expulsion means virtual exclusion from all educational settings; in others, such as New York, school suspensions can result in assignment to "alternative" educational settings.

By the close of the twentieth century, school suspensions became the indirect link between American education and the US prison system, as suspended students became more likely to drop out of school, and dropouts acquired a high risk of being incarcerated at some point in their lives. Western's (2006) empirical work found education to have the most profound impact on the likelihood of incarceration, with high school dropouts five times more likely to go to prison than high school graduates regardless of race. The combination of race, gender, and education level is devastating. By the late 1990s, one in six black male dropouts annually went to prison. For young black men in particular, dropping out of school foreshadows incarceration. Western, Pettit, and Guetzkow (2002) estimate that one in ten young (age 22–30) white high school dropouts and 52 percent of African American male high school dropouts have been incarcerated by their early thirties.

Educational level demarcates the prison population from the general population. Among whites for example, those with only a high school education get imprisoned at a rate twenty times greater than those with college degrees. Sixty-eight percent of state prisoners in the United States do not have a high school diploma and 41 percent have neither a high school diploma nor a GED[12] compared to 18 percent of the general population (Harlow 2003). While the prison population as a whole is characterized by extraordinary levels of high school dropouts, prisoners of color are more likely to be dropouts than are white prisoners. Forty-four percent of black prisoners and 53 percent of Hispanic prisoners in state prison did not graduate or earn a GED, compared to 27 percent of white inmates (Harlow 2003).

School suspensions, which play a critical role in producing dropouts, have significantly increased over the period of time that also saw the growth in incarceration. US Department of Education, Office of Civil Rights data on school suspensions and expulsions show that between 1974 and 2000, the rate at which America's students were suspended and expelled from schools almost doubled from 3.7 percent of students in 1974 (1.7 million students suspended) to 6.6 percent of students in 2000 (3 million students suspended) (Wald and Losen 2003). By 2012, the number of students suspended at least once reached over three million students, more than seventeen thousand students per day (Orfield and Losen 2012). Much like arrest and incarceration, suspensions fall disproportionately on youths of color. African American students are 3.5 times more likely to be suspended or expelled as white students (US Department of Education 2012). Also, the use of punitive school discipline can be decoupled from school violence in the same way that incarceration rates are not related to crime rates. Out-of-school suspensions increased despite a documented decline in school violence, student victimization, and student fear of violence during the 1990s (Donahue, Schiraldi, and Ziedenberg 1998; Kaufman et al. 2000).

---

12. The majority of prisoners who earned a GED did so while incarcerated (Harlow 2003).

School suspensions are predictors of dropping out of school. The National Center for Educational Statistics shows that 31 percent of students who had been suspended three or more times before the spring of their sophomore year dropped out of school compared to only 6 percent of students who had never been suspended dropping out (Livingston 2006, table 27-2). The dropout rate for suspended high school sophomores is three times greater than for students who were not suspended (Skiba and Peterson 1999). While not all dropouts wind up in prison, dropping out does increase one's prospects for becoming a prisoner and most people in prison are high school dropouts.

We have then a perfect storm: young black men who drop out of school are very likely to wind up in prison; the likelihood of dropping out of school is increased by suspension; and black male students are the most vulnerable to being suspended from school.

3

Alternative Schools and Zero Tolerance

From Liberation Learning to Social Control

> They really don't do nothing in Brig. So like we all used to just walk
> out of the class, go play through the hallways, run up and down the
> stairs and we never used to get in trouble. So nobody really cared. In
> Brig, they was passing you anyways. So like nobody really cared but
> you wasn't really learning nothing.
> —Celia

CELIA OFFERED these comments to me when I asked her what it is
like to attend an alternative school. She was enrolled in Brig, the alternative school for kids in eighth grade or below. The essence of her statement,
as well as other comments that I heard from young people, depicted alternative schools as little more than warehouses. Learning and education
were secondary to just having a place to hold kids who were put out of
mainstream school, but too young to drop out.

Alternative schools predate zero tolerance policies, with some established to offer curriculum and pedagogy that could engage and educate
youth who, for a variety of reasons, did not thrive in mainstream settings.
However, zero tolerance policies have largely transformed alternative
schools into a key juncture in the school-to-prison pipeline.

The push for zero tolerance policies, the increase in police presence,
and the growing use of surveillance technologies have been supported
by politicians, school administrators, parents, and teachers as a necessary
evil to counter what is alleged to be increasingly violent student behavior. Schools, once thought of as safe havens, are increasingly viewed as
dangerous places. How accurate is this description? Were the schools of

41

yesteryear trouble-free venues and are the schools of today violent, out-of-control environments?

School discipline runs the gamut from teacher admonitions in classrooms and teacher contact with parents to more formal school procedures including suspensions and expulsions. Suspensions can be in-school (ISS) or out-of-school (OSS). ISS suspensions typically involve placement in a specialized, segregated setting within the mainstream school for a specified and relatively short period of time that may range from a school day to several school days. OSS suspensions can be also short-term, e.g., three to five days, after which the student returns to his or her school. However, OSS suspensions may be long-term, typically involving placement in an alternative school or other educational setting. Long-term OSS and expulsions are often considered one and the same, although there are differences in how states implement these actions. New York State, for example, does not permanently exclude students; the state's response to the zero tolerance mandates in federal law was to set up alternative education settings that were called "programs" rather than schools. In Pennsylvania, students are expelled and their parents are given thirty days to enroll them in another school district. If they are unable to do so, the expelling district is obligated to establish some form of education service for the student, and the type of program is at the discretion of the district.

This chapter looks at development of the alternative school as the means for meting out school discipline. I first consider the question of what has prompted the increase in out-of-school suspensions. I ask, what is the extent to which suspensions and zero tolerance rules are a response to increasing violence in the schools? I then look at how alternative schools have evolved and their varying uses in the history of American education. I conclude with a discussion of how the current iteration of alternative schools resemble prisons in how they punish and whom they punish.

The School House Hype: Creating Support for Punitive School Discipline

In a May 1996 speech delivered at a high school near St. Louis, Missouri, during his reelection campaign, President Clinton took credit for the passage of the Safe and Drug-Free Schools and Communities Act. He reminded the crowd that the bill

> gives money to schools all across the country to do what they think they need to do. Here [Webster Groves High School], our program has helped station a plain-clothes police officer at the school. People should be safe in schools; if there's any place on earth young people should be safe all day, every day, it is when they are in school. Every young person should be safe. . . . I want us to be safe and secure. . . . I know, too, that unless we can purge ourselves of crime and violence and drugs and gangs, your future will never be what it ought to be. So I ask you to stand up as you have here for the concept of zero tolerance in school; stand out for the concept that gangs and drugs are wrong; stand up for the idea that you have to participate in a partnership with police if you want a safe neighborhood, a safe street, and a safe school. (Clinton 1996)

Clinton's statement implied that crime was rampant in the nation's schools and that introducing law enforcement personnel and practices was needed to restore safety to schools beset by gangs and violence. Political rhetoric and tragic, albeit aberrational school shootings, such as those at Columbine High School in Colorado, fanned by media "hype" (Donahue, Schiraldi, and Ziedenberg 1998), made schools a receptive venue for carceral control.

Yet, contrary to public perception about school violence, data and research show that there has never been a plethora of school-based violence in the United States, and that school crime was on the decline even prior to the enactment of the 1994 Safe and Gun-Free Schools Act (Small and Tetrick 2001; Donahue, Schiraldi, and Ziedenberg 1998; DeVoe and Kaffenberger 2005); and finally, positive behavioral supports and broader changes in school environment may contribute more to school safety than punitive disciplinary policies (Chen 2008).

A focus on student perpetrated school violence emerged in the 1960s based upon the perception that the climate in schools had changed dramatically from the 1950s (Rubel 1978). Establishing the level of concern about school crime in general and violence in particular that existed before 1968 is challenging, since school districts did not compile such information prior to that date. Growing attention to student violence took place within the context of the entry of baby boomers into schools and increasing school desegregation. Rubel (1978) notes that by the late 1960s, media reports on school crime and violence shifted from contextualizing school disruption as political (sit-ins and protest riots) to ordinary crime. Moreover, media accounts of school crime defined the problem as specific to inner city schools, ignoring that reports of school crime were increasing in suburban schools, as well (ibid.).

The first national study on school violence undertaken by the National Institute of Education at the request of Congress (Asner and Broschart 1978) found an increase in school violence and vandalism during the 1960s. School crime began to level off in the early 1970s and generally continued to decline through the present day. The decline in reported school crime began prior to 1995 when the implementation of the Safe and Crime Free Schools Act began and continued even as the rhetoric about violent schools escalated (Kaufman et al. 2000). The rate of reported crimes per 1,000 students in 1992 was 144 for all crime, with violent crime lower than other types of crime, e.g., 95 per 1,000 students for theft, 44 for violent, and 10 for "serious violent" crime.[1] By 2004, the comparable rates per 1,000 students were 55 for all crime, 33 for theft, 22 for violent, and 4 per 1,000 for "serious violent" crime. By 2010, the total rate of self-reported school-based offenses per 1,000 students fell approximately 79 percent from 1992 (Robers et al. 2012).

Empirical studies of factors that contribute to the decrease in school crime point to school climate, teacher training, positive behavioral interventions such as character education, and social skills training as more significant than punitive disciplinary policies (Chen 2008). Smaller schools that provide environments conducive to greater individual attention and bonding between students and school staff are also associated

1. The survey at times uses broad definitions. While serious violent crimes is rather precisely defined as rape, sexual assault, robbery, and aggravated assault, the category violent crime includes both serious violent crimes as well as simple assault, which can include pushing and other forms of uninvited touching. Total crimes include violent crimes and theft.

with lower school crime rates (Chen 2008). In contrast, punitive disciplinary policies may result in higher rates of crime (Mayer and Leone 1999) or have a small, but insignificant association with school crime reduction (Chen 2008).

Not only was school crime on the wane at the time that zero tolerance was being introduced into the school setting, but the behaviors targeted were largely nonviolent in nature. In 2009, 4 percent of students reported being a victim of a crime "at school." Crimes involving theft were reported by 3 percent of students. Crimes involving any sort of violence were reported by 1 percent of students, and less than half of 1 percent of students reported being a victim of a serious violent crime. There has been a steady decline in reported victimization in all crime categories between 1992 and 2010 (Robers et al. 2012, figure 3.1:15).

Schools remain remarkably safe places: Federal Bureau of Investigation (FBI) (2006) data show that only 3.3 percent of the more than seventeen million criminal incidents reported to the National Institute-Based Reporting System between 2000 and 2004 involved incidents that took place at schools. Moreover, the majority of incidents involved students who knew each other and most of the incidents—62 percent—did not involve violence of any sort. Where the incident was classified as violent, the data show that the violence was perpetrated not by guns or knives, but so-called "personal weapons," which were in fact arms, legs, feet, and hands.

School suspensions and expulsions have increased despite the rarity of violent crime or weapons possession in schools. Instead of consistent policy that is clearly focused on serious, violent behavior, the use of and reasons for suspensions vary by school district, school, and even by classroom. Suspension policies and practices encompass an eclectic list of misbehavior far more trivial than the emotionally charged rhetoric that implies that schools are sites of gangs and gun violence. Of course school shootings like those that occurred in Columbine, Colorado and Newtown, Connecticut are tremendously traumatic, but these events are exceedingly rare. Truancy, tardiness, forging out-of-school excuses, smoking, drinking, disruptive behavior, uncooperative behavior, and fisticuffs between kids are the more common reasons for suspensions rather than the possession or use of weapons or serious physical violence (Costenbader and Markson 1998; Adams 2000; Advancement Project and Civil Rights Project at Harvard University 2000; Dinkes et al. 2007; Robers et al. 2012). School disciplinary polices, however, have been shaped by the atypical incident, creating sweeping, universal approaches that leave little room for flexible responses to the variety of student misbehavior and for inquiry into the factors that underlie discipline problems.

Criminalizing Student Behavior

Beyond the empirically measurable ways that school failure directs young people to the prison system, that is, in-school arrests, schools themselves have become more reflective of the carceral culture. Student misbehavior is increasingly labeled as criminal and subject to law enforcement authority. For example, in many school districts, fighting among students is no longer termed "fighting" but rather "assaults," a term that carries with it law enforcement connotations. The arms, hands, and feet involved in the pushes, shoves, slaps, punches, scratches, and kicks in school yard fighting are now defined as "personal weapons" (Federal Bureau of Investigation 2006). The officious relabeling of kids' behavior was driven home to me several years ago when I was working on a project to increase alternatives to juvenile detention in Delaware. As part of this planning effort to reduce juvenile detention, I interviewed judges to learn their opinions about when and why detention was imposed. In interview after interview, judges noted the increasing numbers of youth being brought into court for school-based incidents and commented that there was a spate of charges termed "offensive touching." Assuming this was a form of sexual assault, I asked one judge to clarify what kinds of behaviors underlie this charge. I was amazed to learn that "offensive touching" typically involved snapping bras or slapping butts. Most of the judicial officers and counsel I interviewed voiced irritation about this influx of cases that, while perhaps distasteful or troubling, did not merit criminalization. These behaviors, once considered obnoxious but typical of adolescent males, are now criminalized, reported to the police, and processed in the formal court system. Kids were actually detained in the juvenile facility for this behavior, now redefined as a criminal offense: the data I collected showed that in 2002, "offensive touching" was the third most frequent charge for which youth were detained. Moreover, after eliminating cases involving violations of probation and failure to appear in court, that is, charges that do not reflect new criminality, offensive touching became the primary reason for the detention of children in this jurisdiction.

Delaware is not alone in defining what may be objectionable youthful behavior as criminal. In a widely publicized case in Oregon, two seventh grade boys were arrested and charged with felony-level sex offenses, charges that carried a ten-year prison and lifetime registration as a sex offender for similar butt-slapping behaviors (Goldsmith 2007a). While the charges were ultimately dismissed, the youth spent about a week in detention and were suspended from school for the remainder of the school year (Goldsmith 2007b).

The criminalization of student behavior exemplifies how the carceral culture is transferred from the prison to the school. As Simon (2007) and Garland (2001b) argue, criminalization of a wide range of behaviors reflects governance in late modern society. Complex social problems become reduced to criminal justice problems accompanied by enhanced law enforcement responses. The criminalization of student behavior is a result both of new criminal laws and application of law enforcement to behaviors previously addressed by other means internal to the school.

The definition of student misbehavior is, to a large extent, a social construction that changes over time based on public policy and public perceptions of danger. Behaviors can be classified in various ways, for example, as criminality, as a learning disability, and as health or mental health problems. The labeling of behaviors varies based on the source of reporting, the goal of reporting (e.g., to document the need for law enforcement resources versus mental health services) and the level of analysis (Small and Tetrick 2001; Adams 2000; Vavrus and Cole 2002). To justify the increase in police presence and law enforcement tactics, the rhetoric of school violence is broad, encompassing both physical violence committed by students against other students or teachers as well as verbal "assaults" and insults. Ignored, however, are issues of structural and institutional violence including racism and sexism, under-resourced schools, ill-prepared teachers, and inadequate curriculum (Henry 2000). The catchall category of "disruptive behavior," the basis of most school suspensions, is defined within the social context of the classroom that is influenced by both teacher and student backgrounds and experiences, and classroom status (Vavrus and Cole 2002). Even violent behavior, which one might assume would be consistently defined, is subject to the interpretation of principals and teachers (Skiba, Peterson, and Williams 1997; Nadeau 2003). In a survey of school administrators conducted for the New York Center for School Safety, Nadeau found considerable variation in what administrators considered to be violent behavior. For example, almost 6 percent of administrators classified weapons possession as "*not at all violent*" while another 6 percent of administrators rated pushing to be first on line to be "*an extremely violent act*" (Nadeau 2003, 1; emphasis added). These varied opinions translate into real life differences in how students are disciplined, with outcomes depending on the viewpoint of a particular school administrator.

Evolving Responses to Student Misbehavior

Punitive responses to student misbehavior have long been a part of the American school system. Corporal punishment, for example, was the most commonly used form of discipline in the past, and while it is still legal in almost half the states in the United States, it is less frequently used (Owen 2005). Since 1985, twenty-seven states have enacted bans on such methods of discipline (National Coalition to Abolish Corporal Punishment in Schools 2007), and the number of children subjected to corporal punishment declined from 1.4 million in 1980 to under 225,000 in the 2006–2007 school year (US Department of Education 2006). Corporal punishment had greater support as an effective deterrent to student misbehavior when schools were small (the one-room school house), and when cultural mores fostered greater parent and child subservience to authority figures. As schools grew larger and more complex, and as the culture changes of the 1960s countenanced student challenges to school authority, educational systems took up other forms of discipline. For the most part, these forms remained school based and school defined through in-school suspension, after-school detention, and out-of-school suspension to alternative schools (Adams 2000). However, the first police manuals guiding police management of "school riots" were published in the late 1960s and early 1970s (Rubel 1986, 3). Seymour Vestermark, one of the lead authors of these manuals, described the police role in schools as "similar to that of an American military officer overseas" and having the authority to supplant school administration policies and practices (quoted in Rubel 1986, 11).

The de facto and de jure criminalization of youth misbehavior in schools has been accompanied by significant changes in the methods of identifying and responding to school disciplinary problems. With zero tolerance came new technologies of surveillance and disciplinary policies that established mandatory punishments. Schools added police, undercover surveillance officers, metal detectors, surveillance cameras, and dogs, and subjected students to various types of searches, including strip searches (Hyman and Perone 1998). Spatial responses to student misbehavior include in-school suspension rooms, segregated sections of schools, geographically separate "alternative" schools, homebound instruction, and finally expulsion to the streets.

Alternative Schools as Progressive Education

The mission and purpose of "alternative schools" is also a reflection of sociocultural context that changes in time and place: there is no single definition of alternative school (Aron 2003). While earlier forms of alternative schools existed, they were popularized in the 1960s as part of the civil rights and/or counterculture movement. Freedom Schools associated with the civil rights struggle strove to improve educational opportunities for African American young people and experimental educational environments, and the "Free School Movement" typically attracted affluent children from the white intelligentsia or professional families of the counterculture movement (Lange and Sletten 2002).

The Freedom Schools were intimately connected to the civil rights movement, beginning on a small scale in a number of locales such as Boston and Prince Edward County, Virginia, and gaining momentum as part of "Mississippi Summer" in 1964. Student activists worked with community members to set up schools in an effort to compensate for Mississippi's poor public education system for African American children (Payne 1997; Perlstein 1990). Freedom Schools were not only an alternative to the poor education delivered to African American children, but also were a haven for the growing number of students expelled for asking provocative questions about the civil rights struggles taking place throughout the South: "There are Negro students who have been thrown out of classes for asking about the freedom rides, or voting. Negro teachers have been fired for saying the wrong thing. The State of Mississippi destroys 'smart niggers' and its classrooms remain intellectual wastelands" (Cobb 1963).

The Freedom Schools were intended to provide basic education using instructional methods that engaged and stimulated students rather than the traditional rote memorization. Freedom Schools had a political purpose as well, both in curriculum and as part of the burgeoning effort to create "parallel institutions" (Payne 1997, 6) to end reliance on mainstream institutions, which were unresponsive to African Americans. The Freedom Schools included academics, arts, and culture and political education and organizing activities (Perlstein 1990). The concepts that undergirded the Mississippi Freedom Schools resonated in other local community efforts that had concerns both about the education of African American children and political aspirations, including Black Panther Liberation Schools set up in California, and the Malcolm X Academy in Chicago (Potts 2003).

The Free Schools were also parallel institutions, albeit established by the advantaged, yet discontented members of the white counterculture movement. The Free School Movement had it roots in Summerhill, founded in 1921 by A. S. Neil and influenced by the works of Paul Goodman (1960), Ivan Illich (1972), John Holt (1964), and Jonathan Kozol (1967). Unlike Freedom Schools, which were an effort to compensate for the substandard education offered to Black children, Free Schools were focused on enriching and expanding the public education provided to the more privileged children of the white upper middle class. Miller (2002) estimated that between 400 and 800 Free Schools were set up in the United States between 1967 and the late 1970s. Despite the multicultural intentions of many of the founders and participants in these schools, they remained largely white and inaccessible to African American and Latino children. Kozol (1972) in fact came to criticize Free Schools for failing to provide the kind of educational structure that Black and Latino parents thought would ensure that their children would learn the academic skills needed to succeed. Nonetheless, Freedom Schools and Free Schools shared an emphasis on teaching students critical thinking, albeit differently focused, and experiential learning.

Educational reformers, along with social and political activists have been major proponents of Freedom School and Free School and related alternative school models. They argue that the traditional "one size fits all" educational model does not meet the needs of a diverse student population and is particularly ineffective for students at greatest risk of dropping out of school (Kerka 2003).

Alternative Schools Today

Ironically, despite the progressive antecedents of alternative schools, these schools have come to serve as warehouses for students considered to be disciplinary problems and for teachers who lack the skills or motivation to educate (Brown and Beckett 2007). The following statement included in the executive summary of the US Department of Education National Center for Education Statistics *Report on Programs for Students at Risk of Education Failure* reveals the use of alternative schools for a mélange of disciplinary problems:

> Concern among the public, educators, and policymakers about violence, weapons, and drugs on elementary and secondary school campuses, balanced with concern about sending disruptive and potentially dangerous students "out on the streets," has spawned an increased interest in alternative schools and programs. Many students who, for one reason or another, are not succeeding in regular public schools are being sent to alternative placements. In general, students are referred to alternative schools and programs if they are at risk of education failure, as indicated by poor grades, truancy, disruptive behavior, suspension, pregnancy, or similar factors associated with early withdrawal from school.
>
> (Kleiner, Porch, and Farris 2002, iii)

The use of alternative school settings to segregate students suspended (or expelled) from mainstream schools is largely a phenomenon of the urban school district (Aron 2003; Kleiner, Porch, and Farris 2002; Raywid 1994). With respect to student placement, many school districts use alternative schools for long-term suspensions or expulsions from mainstream school. Reliance on alternative schools varies by type of district: 66 percent of urban school districts had one or more alternative schools compared to 41 percent of suburban districts and 35 percent of rural districts. Other factors associated with the presence of alternative schools are minority enrollment and concentration of poverty (Kleiner, Porch, and Farris 2002).

There is considerable variation as to the location of alternative schools relative to mainstream schools: some alternative schools are schools within mainstream schools, others are separate schools that remain part of the school district, and still others are contracted out to other districts or even private companies. Alternative schools may be freestanding, housed within community organizations, organized as charter schools, or located in juvenile justice facilities. Alternative schools also differ on the criteria for student placement, the kind of programming offered, length of stay, and criteria governing a student's return to mainstream institutions (Kleiner, Porch, and Farris 2002). Raywid (1994) identifies three types of alternative schools: Type I, magnet-type schools, which are voluntary and open to all students emphasizing individualized learning; Type II, "last chance schools," which are involuntary, segregated, and punitive placements; and Type III, which are voluntary, and designed to be therapeutic.

The Syracuse City School District (SCSD or district) reflects the lack of clarity about the purpose and structure of alternative schools. Over the past decade and a half, the district convened several study groups, commissions, and work groups to tackle the problem of school suspension and alternative schools. As the director of the only organization in the city that focused on these young people, I was invited to participate in all of these groups. The contradictory expectations for alternative schools were reflected among committee members: some thought the district's alternative schools were established to carry out the consequences of zero tolerance, while others thought that alternative schools were venues to apply "restorative justice" practices (Syracuse City School District 2000). The ongoing discussion/debate over situating alternative education in the district conforms to the adage, "the more things change, the more they remain the same." Alternative schools were combined, re-separated, renamed, and, relocated, but the numbers of students excluded from mainstream education has not declined, nor has the link between suspension and school drop-out rates diminished.

Prisonization of Schools and Undermining Equal Opportunity to Education

Alternative school institutions in urban communities resemble prisons and jails in their racial composition. Blacks are 13 percent of the US population, but 41 percent of people incarcerated (Sabol, Minton, and Harrison 2007); black children are 17 percent of students enrolled in public school but 37 percent of students sent to out-of-school suspension (US Department of Education 2006). I have spent considerable time in both types of institutions, and at least in New York State, jails, prisons, and alternative schools look remarkably alike—filled with adults or children of color. I recall a day in the women's facility on Riker's Island. I looked out at a sea of black faces with one or two women who were light skinned. As I approached them, I heard that they were speaking Spanish. The same holds true for the alternative schools in the northeastern city—Syracuse—that is the location for this study. As I walk the halls of the two alternative schools, I see only black and brown children. This is represented in the voices of the young people interviewed; of the twenty-five youths, only one was white. SCSD data for 2011 through 2012 show that 25 percent of its student body was subject to out-of-school suspension and 82 percent were students of color.

Zero tolerance notwithstanding, much like the criminal justice system, the pathway to alternative school is subject to considerable discretion by authority figures: how a teacher interprets a student's behavior; how an administrator determines whether the behavior merits ISS or OSS; the value judgments made by hearing officers who determine whether a student can return to mainstream school or must be sent to an alternative school. In a frightening reflection of the criminal justice system, this discretion has resulted in racial disparities in the harshest form of school discipline—placement in an alternative school.

The prisonization of schools is particularly poignant in light of the long struggle for racial justice in education that has been such a seminal part of American history. Under slavery, blacks were forbidden an education. Those whites who taught black people were subject to imprisonment, and slaves who were discovered to have learned to read were subject to corporal punishment including beatings and amputations (Irons 2002). Education was a primary focus of reconstruction efforts that were undertaken in the immediate aftermath of the Civil War (Williams 2005). The Freedmen's Bureau established over 3,000 Freedmen schools in the South. Reconstruction broadly affected education, introducing a free public education system that was previously unavailable for white as well as black students.[2] Reconstruction also spurred the creation of the first black colleges—Howard and Fiske universities and Hampton College—whose main purposes were the training of black teachers. By 1870, 150,000 black children were enrolled in schools (Tyack and Lowe 1986). However, opposition to the education of blacks persisted even in the face of the expansion of educational opportunities. Poor whites, clinging to the culture of white superiority, feared a loss of status if blacks were to become educated. A general resistance to the taxes that would be needed to support a public school system was also a cause of opposition to efforts to expand education in the South. Whites did not want to pay any taxes to support the Reconstruction governments, which they considered illegitimate, and they were particularly opposed to being taxed to support the education of black children. This opposition to Reconstruction efforts at creating educational institutions for blacks (and poor whites) was expressed through violence that included the burning of schools, and the beating and whipping of students and teachers (Franklin 1994).

2. Prior to the Civil War, North Carolina was the only southern state to have a free public education system (Williams 2005).

The end of Reconstruction saw the gradual unraveling of education of black children in the south. The changes took place incrementally, propelled by the disenfranchisement of blacks, their removal from positions of public authority, the resurgence of white supremacy, the defunding of black public schools, and the formal resegregation of schools. Simultaneously, through the creation of schools supported by white philanthropists, the underlying purpose of education of African Americans was constricted to the instrumental goal of training for subordinate labor positions rather than a broader liberal education (Duncan 2000).

The US Supreme Court decision in a series of cases commonly referred to as "the Civil Rights Cases," 109 U.S. 3 (1883), ruled *unconstitutional* the Civil Rights Act of 1875 that codified protections against discrimination in private as well as public facilities, and ushered in the Jim Crow era. This decision opened the door to the passage of state laws requiring segregation in a multitude of domains across the South. The court in Plessy v. Fergeson, 163 U.S. 537 (1896), which involved a challenge to segregation in transportation, found that Plessy's civil rights were not violated by separate train compartments. The "separate but equal" doctrine introduced by the Plessy ruling directed institutional race relations in America until the decision in Brown v. Board of Education, 347 U.S. 483 (1954). By 1911, with segregation fully in place across the South, the majority of black children living in former Confederacy states were no longer enrolled in school. Jim Crow dismantled schools, cut off resources and left teachers underpaid, stripped schools of basic supplies, and in general injected terror and fear among the black population through lynchings and other acts of violence (Williams 2005).

De jure segregated education met its legal demise in 1954 with the US Supreme Court decision in Brown v. Board of Education. Justice Earl Warren, writing for a unanimous court, stated:

> Today, education is perhaps the most important function of state and local governments. Compulsory school attendance laws and the great expenditures for education both demonstrate our recognition of the importance of education to our democratic society. It is required in the performance of our most basic public responsibilities, even service in

the armed forces. It is the very foundation of good citizenship. Today it is a principle instrument in awakening the child to cultural values, in preparing him for later professional training, and in helping him to adjust normally to his environment. In these days, it is doubtful that any child may reasonably be expected to succeed in life if he is denied the opportunity of an education. Such an opportunity, where the state has undertaken to provide it, is a right which must be made available to all on equal terms.

We come then to the question presented: Does segregation of children in public schools solely on the basis of race, even though the physical facilities and other "tangible" factors may be equal, deprive the children of the minority group of equal educational opportunities? We believe that it does.

(Brown v. Board of Education, 347 U.S. at 493)

The full promise of Brown has yet to be realized. "White flight" from cities to suburbs created neighborhoods of de facto segregation, and enrollment in private schools were some of the ways that the intent of Brown was circumvented (Clotfelter 2004). Courts have been hesitant to fully uphold the Brown decision in subsequent court cases.[3] The Brown decision put an end to legal segregation, but fifty years after Brown, de facto segregation persists by virtue of segregation in residential patterns, classroom tracking, and the now pernicious disciplinary policies that exclude large numbers of minority students from regular education.

Racial Disparity in School Suspensions

Racial disparities in suspension have been documented by a large body of research (Costenbader and Markson 1994; Gregory and Mosely 2004;

---

3. As recently as 2007, the Supreme Court in a five to four decision invalidated voluntary desegregation plans: Parents Involved in Community Schools v. Seattle School District No. 1, heard together with Meredith, Custodial Parent, and Next Friend of McDonald v. Jefferson County Bd. of Ed., 551 U.S. 701 (2007).

Gregory 1995; Kaeser 1979; Lietz and Gregory 1978; Massachusetts Advocacy Center 1986; McCarthy and Hoge 1987; McFadden et al. 1992; Raffaele Mendez and Knoff 2003; Raffaele Mendez, Knoff, and Ferron 2002; Rausch and Skiba 2004; Skiba and Knesting 2001; Skiba, Peterson, and Williams 1997; US Department of Education 2000; Wu et al. 1982).

As of October 1, 2000, there were just over 600,000 students—representing 1.3 percent of all public school students—enrolled in public alternative schools or programs for at-risk students. A disproportionate number of those students were African American: the 2006 US Department of Education Elementary and Secondary School Compliance Report showed that African American students were almost 33 percent of those suspended from school, although they were only 17 percent of the total US student population. An earlier study by Gregory (1995) of the 1,524,241 cases of suspension during the 1994–95 school year showed that African American boys were twice as likely to be subjected to out-of-school suspensions as white boys. The American Academy of Pediatrics (2003) reiterated this finding almost ten years later.

A number of state and local level analyses demonstrate the racial disparities in suspension. In San Diego, youth of color are 53 percent of the student body, but 72 percent of students who are suspended and 76 percent of expelled students (ERASE Initiative 2002). Similar findings were identified in studies of suspensions in Texas (Fabelo et al. 2011; Texas Appleseed 2007; Reyes 2006). The state-by-state analysis of the relationships between school suspensions and race (Skiba et al. 2003) found disproportionate numbers of minority students suspended in thirty-seven of the forty-five states included in the study. Costenbader and Markson's (1998) survey of 620 middle and high school students found that 45 percent of black students reported out-of-school suspension compared to 12 percent of white students and 18 percent of Hispanic students.

The decision to suspend is the result of a complex set of prior decisions that often begin in the classroom with teachers deciding what behaviors merit out-of-classroom referral. School principals and other administrators then decide which behaviors and which students are referred to hearings that determine whether or not to suspend, and what type of suspension is to be imposed (Skiba et al. 2003). Teachers see and interpret behavior through the prism of race, culture, and class, which has resulted in suspension of students of color for less serious behavior than white students (Hosp and Hosp 2001; Townsend 2000; Adams 2000; McFadden et al. 1992; Shaw and Braden 1990; Skiba and Knesting 2001; Fabelo et al. 2011).

Teacher referrals for perceived disciplinary infractions and problematic behavior are the common triggers for school suspension. Minor infractions and violations of school rules constitute the majority of suspensions and expulsions and these sorts of behaviors are most vulnerable to individual teacher interpretation. Skiba, Peterson, and Williams's (1997) examination of sixteen middle schools in a Midwestern school district found differences in how these schools applied disciplinary practices, with some schools referring about one out of every ten students and others as many as four out of five students. Rates of suspension are more likely to be associated with factors other than student behavior, including student disabilities (Eckenrode, Laird, and Dorris 1993), and characteristics of the school, its teachers and administrators (Wu et al. 1982; Mukuria 2002; Advancement Project and Civil Rights Project, Harvard University 2000; Skiba et al. 2003). Verdugo's study (2002) found that while white students were suspended for violations that were more serious in nature and more clearly defined, such as weapons and drugs, African American students were suspended for minor violations, such as "disrespect" or "appearing threatening," behaviors that are more susceptible to subjective interpretation. A study of suspensions in Florida school districts (Raffaele Mendez and Knoff 2003) found that insubordination was the single most prevalent reason for student suspension, with 20 percent of all students suspended for this reason. Black students, who were 12 percent of the student population, were 28 percent of students suspended for disobedience and insubordination, 35 percent of students suspended for "inappropriate" behavior, and 32 percent of students suspended for disrespect, all behaviors that require subjective interpretation on the part of teachers (Raffaele Mendez and Knoff 2003). The study of school suspensions for all seventh grade students in Texas (Fabelo et al. 2011) found that 97 percent of school disciplinary actions were taken for behaviors left to the discretion of school staff, rather than state mandates.

Vavrus and Cole's (2002, 89) ethnographic study of classroom decision making examined the "moment by moment" interactions between teachers and pupils to deconstruct how behaviors become labeled as disruptive and meriting suspension. In contrast to commonly held beliefs that disruptive behavior can be identified by objective criteria, Vavrus and Cole (2002, 89) report that "disruptions appear to be highly contextualized social interactions whose interpretation depends on the sociocultural context in which potentially disruptive events occur." Students in the classroom with the greatest number of suspensions became disruptive when frustrated by their inability to receive individual attention or answers to their questions. In many of these classes, students, typically African American or Latino/Latina, assumed the role of spokesperson and challenged the teacher to respond to student questions. The teacher perceived these behaviors to be disruptive and responded by calling security guards to remove the students from the classes. None of the incidents observed by Vavrus and Cole involved overt physical violence; rather they were a series of verbal exchanges between the student and the teacher. Teachers and students were "co-implicated" (Vavrus and Cole 2002, 109) in the disciplinary event, but in the context of unequal power, the teacher's perceptions carry the day and determine the suspension.

With the advent of No Child Left Behind[4] policies, school suspensions also serve as a mechanism to remove students who are expected to fare poorly in standardized tests. Figlio (2006) found that in addition to assigning harsher punishments to low-performing students throughout the school year, schools increased suspensions immediately before the No Child Left Behind testing was scheduled. In almost 60 percent of the 41,803 cases analyzed, the longer suspensions were meted out to the lower-performing student even when the students' misbehavior was the same.

4. The No Child Left Behind Act of 2001 became law in January 2002 and established measurable goals in education assessed by standardized tests. Federal funding for education was made contingent upon state development of assessments in basic skills. These assessments have come to be known as "high stakes testing."

Consequences of Out-of-School Suspension and Expulsion

The consequences of school suspension are multiple, affecting educational experiences, educational planning, thinking about careers, and individual, family, and community psyche. As discussed in chapter 2, school suspension is a predictor of dropping out of school, which in turn is a predictor of one's likelihood of spending some time in prison. Skiba et al.'s 2003 study presented at the Harvard Civil Rights Project and Northeastern University School of Law's School-to-Prison Pipeline conference found correlations among rates of suspension, expulsion, and incarceration in forty-seven states that had data on these measures. States with higher rates of school suspension had higher rates of both adult and juvenile incarceration, and states with higher rates of African American disproportionality in school suspension had higher rates of disproportionality in juvenile incarceration. Martin and Halperin (2006) report that dropouts are 3.5 times more likely than high school graduates to be incarcerated in their lifetime. Fabelo et al. (2011) found that seventh grade students suspended or expelled in Texas were significantly more likely to become involved in the juvenile justice system in the year following their suspension.

The exclusion of youth from school through suspension and expulsion further fosters an attitude of self-defeat and cynicism on the part of students (Adams 2000; MacDonald and Marsh 2004; Costenbader and Markson 1998) and exacerbates their emotional and mental health problems (Krezmien, Leone, and Achilles 2006). Much like incarceration, suspensions are associated with recidivism, which for school children is reflected by repeated and escalating disruptive behavior (Atkins et al. 2002; Hemphill et al. 2006; Tolan and Gorman-Smith 1997; Lipsey 1992). Out-of-school suspensions stigmatize youth among their peers, teachers, and other school officials. In the school district that is the subject of this study, the negative connotation of alternative school placement was visible in the reassignment process in which my staff often participated. Informally referred to as "the round robin," a more appropriate name seemed to be "hot potato" as principals tried to push off students to another school rather than readmit them.

Zero tolerance policies affect the overall school culture and the ways that teachers manage classrooms and schools (Devine 1996). Reliance on punitive disciplinary practices thwarts teacher and administrative creativity in developing more constructive and nurturing ways of dealing with behavior issues and classroom conflict (Adams 2000; Atkins et al. 2002). It increases the isolation from pro-social institutions and opportunities for the very youth who may be most in need of such interactions. The young people in this study were exiled not only from their regular school and friends, but from their sports teams and other extracurricular activities. This sort of discipline reflects a type of "moral exclusion," a worldview that justifies "disparate access to opportunity and resources" (Fallis and Opotow 2003, 112). "Students are first seen as behaviorally, then as cognitively and finally as morally deficient and therefore outside the scope of justice and ultimately the cause of their own debilitation" (ibid., 114).

Engagement in the Question

Reflections on Setting and Method

In 1981, in the early days of the construction of the prison-industrial complex, I began work for an organization that focused on promoting alternatives to incarceration sentences. The essence of the work was "defender-based advocacy," that is, working with defense attorneys to design alternative sentencing options and to present these plans to the court and advocate for their adoption. The alternative sentencing plans typically included rehabilitative options (e.g., drug treatment), reintegrative elements (e.g., employment), and accountability measures (e.g., restitution, community service). I advocated for the imposition of these conditions as part of a sentence of probation in lieu of incarceration.

Within a relatively short time, I discovered that the juvenile justice system, much as the adult criminal justice system, was becoming increasingly punitive. My organization soon expanded its work to include youths in family court systems (juvenile delinquents) and introduced me to what would, twenty years later, become known as the school-to-prison pipeline.

Regular and obedient attendance at school was and remains a core condition of any alternative sentence imposed by family court. I soon came to learn that in addition to their delinquency charges, most of the young people with whom I worked also had problematic school histories characterized by truancy and disciplinary infractions. Many had been suspended from their mainstream school to the district's alternative school. Alternative schools are the automatic placement for young people reentering from juvenile justice facilities and students seemed to cycle between the alternative school and the juvenile justice system. I also observed how difficult it was for a young person to reestablish him- or herself back in a mainstream school once he or she had been suspended to an alternative school.

These practical experiences again led my organization to try to develop more effective ways to help youths negotiate the school system. Community support was focused on school advocacy, to run interference to keep youths in school on the one hand and, on the other, to encourage youths to attend school and to avoid circumstances and situations that could get them "in trouble." The interactions with the kids, their parents, their teachers, and school principals shaped my interest in how school suspension and alternative school placement prepare certain young people to become prisoners.

My personal contacts continued with youths both in alternative schools and in juvenile facilities. I was consistently struck by the wasting of human life and the similarities between youths in juvenile prisons and alternative schools. In both juvenile facilities and alternative school classrooms, young people were disengaged from typical youth pursuits. They spent their time in bleak, institutional settings. A visit to a juvenile facility for girls or a classroom in the alternative school would find girls braiding each other's hair, rather than reading or participating in athletics and arts activities or engaged in discussion with each other or caring, capable adults. My discussions with the adults who ran both schools and juvenile facilities revealed similarities in their assessments of the children's circumstances. Correctional counselors were not alone in their predictions that prisons were likely to be the end of the road for these kids: teachers and principals also conveyed the same sensibilities. Many pointed their fingers at the youths' families, expressing what seems to be a consensus that the dismal outcomes for the young people in their alternative schools and juvenile prisons lay with their "dysfunctional" families. An urban legend has grown up around the ability to predict the need for prison beds based upon the ability of a third grade child to master grade-level reading skills.

In 2003, almost three decades after I began my journeys to prisons and alternative schools, I attended the first national conference on the school-to-prison pipeline sponsored by Harvard University Civil Rights Project and Northeastern University Institute on Race and Justice. The presentations confirmed much of my day-to-day observations on the intersection between criminal and juvenile justice, and school discipline, yet none of the papers contained information about how young people themselves experienced the phenomenon of the increasing criminalization of schools. The school-to-prison pipeline conference spurred my interest in documenting how the young people with whom I work tell their stories about this relatively new and troubling phenomenon.

In considering the question of the role of school suspension in the school-to-prison pipeline, I challenged myself to focus less on the issues I faced as part of an organization that delivered "services" to students in the school, but as an explorer trying to discover how the youths themselves thought about their suspension and placement in an alternative school. However, I did not try to disregard or discount my work in the school; after all, my observations propelled this academic interest. I also engaged in this research as an activist. Over the years, I was involved in various community efforts to revamp alternative schools as they are presently constituted. I have worked to reduce, if not eliminate, out-of-school suspensions and challenged district and community messages that stigmatized young people who are suspended from alternative schools (Weissman 2008, 2009a).

I have done this work alongside the young people and their parents. For example, when faced with community opposition to relocate one of these alternative schools from its downtown location to a more residential, largely white neighborhood, my organization helped to organize students and parents to counter the negative image held by neighborhood residents, speaking out against stereotypes that propelled the "not in my backyard" protest and supporting youths in their efforts to represent themselves. At least for that moment, we were able to shame the opposition to the school relocation into demurring that they held no antipathy for the young people who joined the protest.[1]

I cannot and would not disavow my work as a practitioner or activist; to do so would be academically dishonest. Rather, I rely on a body of scholarship as described by Michelle Fine (1994, 15): "[Feminist] scholars

---

1. The district was ultimately forced to abandon the plan to relocate the school.

across disciplines, situate themselves proudly atop a basic assumption that all research projects are (and should be) political; that researchers who represent themselves as detached only camouflage their deepest, most privileged interests."

I consider my approach to fall somewhere between Fine's (1994, 19) classification of researcher as "voice" and researcher as "activist." This book is an effort to be a conduit for the opinions and experiences of the young people I interviewed. I never encountered any kid who was unwilling to speak with me, and while some of the young people (especially boys) often offered one-word answers to my initial questions, all of the kids warmed up and seemed genuinely animated by the opportunity to share their thoughts on suspension and alternative schools with an interested and seemingly authoritative adult.

Despite my best efforts to carefully listen to what the kids told me and not to hear in their responses what I expected to hear, I have to acknowledge a distance between my role as a researcher, as interpreter of stories, and the youths whose stories I tell. My years advocating to dispel stereotypes of young people and their schools as troubled and violent affected how I interpreted stories of school and community violence. I had to face the reality that relationships between peers were far more fraught with tension and danger than I realized.

My underestimation of the depth of challenges faced by the kids I interviewed shows how race and class defines space. I live in the city, in the fringe of one of the city neighborhoods that is considered one of the more deadly and dire areas. I live within walking distance of several of the mainstream schools that the kids attended, including the high school where the police officer decked the sophomore girl. I am committed not only to public education, but urban education in particular, and my two sons went to city schools for the whole of their lives. I claim no sacrifice in resisting "white flight": my children did quite well and, in fact, thrived in the very schools that the kids I interviewed struggled in and with. My children came with the "habitus" (see chapter 11) that reaps educational rewards. Because of my personal experiences, I often found myself defending city public schools and urging friends and colleagues not to flee to suburban or private schools.

My personal experience was reinforced by my work experience. For decades, kids from alternative school and the juvenile justice system were coming into my office. From this vantage point, what I saw belied the stereotypes of urban youth. Fights between the youths were close to non-existent. We have a fully open office and there was never any complaint about theft. I saw the kids work together to produce art, poetry, and to participate in a range of peer leadership activities. I spent two weeks with four of the kids, traveling to Geneva, Switzerland and back, a trip that left me amazed at their kind spirits, good hearts, and respectfulness. These settings, which were deliberately designed and carefully monitored to create an environment of unconditional care and support, shielded me from the crueler aspects of their environment.

While I knew that the young people in our programs were very poor and faced a bevy of challenges, I nonetheless underestimated struggles of the kids and the extent to which they lived on the margins of survival both physical and emotional. I was ill equipped to appreciate their sensitivity to perceived disrespect, and in the absence of adult guidance, the extent to which standing up for oneself often relied on physicality. I found myself asking and re-asking questions to get a better sense of what happened to provoke the suspension incident. I think I leave this work with a better understanding, but it would be less than honest to deny that the provocations that evoke suspension behaviors remain somewhat mysterious to me.

Race, class, gender, and age certainly had an effect on my ability to hear and interpret the voices of the study participants. The voices most critical to this study were those of young people of color, predominately very poor African American adolescents who make up the population of alternative schools. These young people most typically experienced women such as me—older, white, middle class professionals—as teachers and school administrators. I was concerned that my persona and its messages about age, social standing, race, gender, and power would make it difficult to connect with the young people whom I wanted to interview: Would these young men and women be willing to open up to me, and would I be able to frame the questions and understand the answers in a way that would contribute to my ability to answer the key research questions? Could I frame my questions in ways that would be accessible, and would I be able to understand the language that urban youth use to convey their ideas and opinions?

I believe that several factors enabled me to bridge, however imperfectly, the various divides of class, race, age, ethnicity, and culture. Circumstances that helped me overcome the possible skepticism of youths included my connection with my organization, its mission, and the staff who worked directly with the young people. The organization is trusted by young people who have seen us stand up for them at suspension hearings. Some of the kids knew that we had helped to represent their older siblings or parents—advocating in court to avert incarceration or mitigate the length of imprisonment. I was introduced to the youths through the staff with whom they directly worked—people who had earned their trust and respect. My staff was able to transmit some of that trust onto me. I took care in introducing myself and the study: I was willing to share with the youths some of my community activism and concerns. For example, I referenced my participation in a local and well-regarded campaign against police brutality. My acknowledgment of this community issue resulted in several participants literally taking a second look at me. I was able to refer to my residence in the city and familiarity with city schools that my sons attended in ways that surprised kids who, for the most part, came in contact with authoritative white adults who lived only in the suburbs. Also, my affiliation with my organization helped to break down barriers with young people and their parents and guardians, as it is known as one of the few organizations working on behalf of people caught up in the criminal and juvenile justice system.

"I Want to Move Out of Syracuse so I Won't Have to Worry about Trouble"

The above sentiment about wanting to escape Syracuse was echoed by many of the young people interviewed for this story. It reflects the absence of hope for a better life, which was typically described as a job, a home, and without the pervasive sense of violence and danger on the streets.

These anecdotal perceptions are confirmed by socioeconomic data. Syracuse, New York is a mid-size city in upstate New York facing challenges typical to many northeastern "rust belt" cities, including a deteriorating economic base, declining population, and high and concentrated poverty rates (Vey 2007). Census data from 2010 show the population of Syracuse to be 145,170, roughly a 4 percent decline since 2000 (US Census Bureau 2013). The city's minority population is 47 percent (compared to the county minority population of 29 percent). Census data show that 53 percent of children in Syracuse live in poverty, placing it tenth in the nation in terms of childhood poverty; 37 percent of the city's total population is classified as poor (Fiscal Policy Institute 2012). It is also among the ten cities with the highest rates of poverty among black and Hispanic children.

Declining employment opportunities in Syracuse reflect the loss of the industrial base that once made Syracuse known as a city with a diverse economy. One by one, industries moved out of Syracuse—Carrier Corporation (absorbed into United Technologies), Solvay Process (absorbed by Honeywell), General Electric, and even Syracuse China—taking with them good-paying blue collar jobs, some of which were even available to the black population. Even as the metropolitan area as a whole declined, the city of Syracuse was particularly hard hit as the remaining industry and white middle class moved to the suburbs. The city, which is home to 30 percent of the Onondaga County population, has only 18 percent of its taxable property (American Institute of Architects 2006). The limited tax base supports 60 percent of the low-income population in the county who are disproportionately minority and concentrated in neighborhoods characterized by abandoned and substandard housing, high crime rates, and a lack of neighborhood amenities such as grocery stores. Socioeconomic and health risks are prevalent in these inner city neighborhoods as well. The neighborhoods exhibit high rates of unemployment, the lowest [adult] educational levels, the greatest indices of health problems (HIV and AIDS, teen pregnancy, infant mortality, low birth rates, STDs, cocaine, and opiate hospital discharges), and other measures of social disorganization (New York State Department of Health 2000; Lane et al. 2004). While poor communities of color in Syracuse lack jobs and healthy public/social institutions, they are rich in social control reflected by high rates of juvenile arrests and adult incarceration.

"A Laboratory of Abolitionism, Libel, and Treason"

The above words were used in 1851 by Daniel Webster to describe Syracuse, New York, because of its bold and vibrant abolitionist movement. Syracuse's role in the anti-slavery movement, the suffrage movement, and the long unbroken history of Native American sovereignty, stands in sharp distinction from its present dubious distinction of being one of the poorest cities in the United States. Rather than a place that people want to run from, Syracuse was once a place that people ran to for freedom and opportunity.

Syracuse is home to the Haudenosaunee ("people of the longhouse") or Onondaga Nation, which is the center of the Six Nation or Iroquois Confederacy comprised of the Seneca, Cayuga, Oneida, Mohawk, and Tuscarora Nations. The Haudenosaunee is considered to be one of the oldest continuous participatory democracies in the world. Its territory, which once enveloped Syracuse, is now limited to 7,300 acres just south of the city. The Onondaga Nation operates as a sovereign nation within the United States. The nation maintains that New York State lacks civil or criminal jurisdiction over its people or territory and state and local police have agreed not to enter the Onondaga Nation's territory without approval from the chiefs. New York State honored this agreement in 1983 when Dennis Banks, a leader of the American Indian Movement (AIM), fleeing federal charges stemming from the 1973 incident at Wounded Knee, was granted sanctuary by the Onondaga Nation. Governor Mario Cuomo directed the state police not to enter the territory to seize Mr. Banks. Banks remained under Onondaga Nation protection for about a year until he voluntarily surrendered to the FBI under a negotiated agreement.

The central New York State area was a major stop on the Underground Railroad. Ironically, the most notable event in Syracuse's abolitionist history actually involved a jailbreak. In 1851, William Henry, who was known as "Jerry," escaped from slavery and made his way to Syracuse. He was pursued by federal marshals enforcing the Fugitive Slave Law, which had been enacted by Congress the previous year. The law made it a federal crime to interfere with a slave owner's right to recover his "property." After

Mr. Henry was apprehended by federal marshals, he was held in the local jail. A group of Syracuse citizens, including civic leaders, stormed the jail, freeing "Jerry." Henry was hidden in Syracuse for several days and then was helped to escape to Canada. The "Jerry Rescue" is now commemorated by a statue situated in a prominent downtown location.

The Syracuse and central New York area was considered to be the epicenter of abolitionist activities beyond the Jerry Rescue. The region's location along the Erie Canal and relative proximity to Canada made it an ideal station on the Underground Railroad. It was home to Harriet Tubman, who settled in Auburn, New York, about thirty miles outside Syracuse. In yet another ironic example of the history of the area, Harriet Tubman's house is within two miles—walking distance—of Auburn Prison, New York State's oldest prison and the venue of the state's first electric chair.

Syracuse's progressive history also encompasses the women's rights movement, including Matilda Joslyn Gage, an early leader of the movement who came from Syracuse. Syracuse was the site of the Third Rights Convention, the first such conference attended by Susan B. Anthony.

Syracuse was actually a prosperous city for much of its history. Its early wealth was due to an abundance of salt, which was a critical ingredient in food preservation before refrigeration. The Erie Canal and subsequent railroad development made Syracuse a significant way station between the port of New York City and the St. Lawrence River and urban centers to the west. Its role as a market center for surrounding central New York farms expanded to become a growing industrial community. Companies that were first established in Syracuse include the Franklin Automobile Company, Crouse Hinds (traffic signals), Stickley Furniture, New Process Gear, the Smith Typewriter Company, and Syracuse China. Industrial expansion during World War II brought steel and machining to the area. General Motors and Chrysler both opened major plants after the war, as did General Electric, and Syracuse became the headquarters for Carrier Corporation. The thriving industrial sector became a mecca for African Americans leaving the South for better opportunities in northern cities like Syracuse, particularly during World War I and World War II. Blacks settled in what was known as the Fifteenth Ward, which supported small business—barbershops, butchers, and grocery stores, among others (Black History Preservation Project n.d.).

The population of Syracuse peaked in 1950 at just over 220,000 people, making it the forty-eighth largest city in the United States. Between 1950 and 2010, the city lost both population and industry. Many home-grown Syracuse businesses became subsumed in national corporations that shut down factories and plants or relocated these industries to other parts of the country and international locations. By 2010, the typewriter industry had been usurped by computers, Carrier Corporation became United Technologies headquartered in Connecticut with its Syracuse location phased out, and General Electric, Allied Chemical, and General Motors also closed their local plants. With a 2010 population of about 145,000, Syracuse ranks as the 178th largest city in the country. The largest employers are now the State University of New York, Upstate Medical Center, and Syracuse University.

The loss of manufacturing jobs was especially hard on the city's black population, as industrial labor was one of the few avenues of employment that paid decent wages and benefits. Racism closed doors to public sector employment and higher paid service jobs, leaving only low-wage jobs such as maid services and fast food work.

Urban renewal programs of the 1960s destroyed the Fifteenth Ward—the center of the black community in Syracuse. The path of urban renewal in Syracuse was comparable to that of cities throughout the United States. The National Interstate and Defense Highways Act, combined with the housing acts of 1949 and 1954, enabled the razing of homes and businesses in the Fifteenth Ward and the replacement of the neighborhood with Route 81, the interstate highway that divides Syracuse into what one city council member and the former head of the local NAACP likened to the "Berlin Wall" (Seward 2012). The homes and neighborhood stores were eventually replaced with high-rise apartments, an art museum, and the local jail. Left standing near the highway was Pioneer Homes, one of the oldest public housing projects in the United States. The residents of the Fifteenth Ward relocated: The Jewish population moved further out to the East Side of the city or the eastern suburbs. Because white landlords refused to rent to African Americans, the black population moved to spatial concentrations on the South Side and, to a lesser extent, the Near East Side. These remain poor, black neighborhoods, and are home to most of the students suspended from Syracuse schools.

The School District

The demise of Syracuse's economic base has had a direct impact on the financial well-being of the Syracuse City School District. An estimated 58 percent of property in Syracuse is tax exempt, and additional properties, such as the Carousel Mall shopping center, is tax abated, stripping the city of revenues to support the school district.

The relationship between the district and the city have become more contentious as the city's finances have dwindled, the district's needs have expanded, and funding for public schools has decreased. Unlike suburban and rural districts, school budgets in New York State's "Big Five" (New York City, Buffalo, Rochester, Syracuse, and Yonkers) are not determined by direct citizen vote. Rather, the Syracuse City School District budget is first determined by the school board and then submitted to the Syracuse Common (City) Council for final approval.

Decreasing revenues have been only one aspect of the pressure on the Syracuse school district. The effects of No Child Left Behind (NCLB) and high stakes testing, the advent of charter schools, and most recently, Race to the Top, Common Core Standards, and new teacher evaluation systems have left both administrators and teachers scurrying to adjust to changes that dramatically impact school and classroom operations. Under NCLB, states are required to implement a school accountability system based on student test scores. Syracuse has consistently failed to meet NCLB requirements. As part of New York State's obligations to hold low-performing districts accountable, the state commissioned an audit, which found a number of deficiencies contributing to the SCSD's poor showing (Learning Point Associates 2006). Among the key findings were: inconsistent implementation of curricula; teachers feeling unprepared to address student needs; parent concerns that teachers spent too much time "teaching to the test"; and a lack of timely and accurate data to guide instruction.

The SCSD's inability to meet NCLB is not unique. The other Big Five cities in New York State also are underperforming. District administrators cite insufficient resources to undertake all of the tasks and reforms that would be required to reach NCLB goals. This explanation is buttressed by research that has shown that federal funding available through NCLB is insufficient to enable school districts, particularly high-need districts such as the SCSD, to meet high performance standards (Duncan, Mendenhall, and DeLuca 2006). Teachers complain that they are forced to spend most of their time preparing students for tests and testing itself, rather than using their professional training to create lessons that engage students in learning.

The failure of NCLB and the inability of Congress to make changes to the law prompted the Obama administration to create a waiver process for states. As of 2012, thirty-four states, including New York and the District of Columbia, have been approved for waivers and an additional ten applications were pending. However, these waivers are conditioned on continued standardized testing and teacher evaluation systems. Moreover, Race to the Top (RTTT), introduced by the Obama administration, while offering incentives for a commitment and plan for school reform, is considered by some educators to have a more profound impact on teachers as accountability is moved from the district and school level to the individual teacher, and requires evaluation based on the test scores of their students. New York State was a second-round winner of a RTTT grant in 2010. The grant award was just under $700 million, with the Syracuse City School District getting $3.9 million. In addition to teacher evaluation, the RTTT also increased the number of charter schools in the state from 200 to 460 (New York State Department of Education 2010).

The SCSD became one of the first districts in the state to put a teacher evaluation system into place. The process is considered time consuming, involving the evaluation of more than 1,700 teachers and principals. News reports quote district administrators as estimating the cost of the new system to be between $10 and $12 million.

Overlaying the changes in testing and evaluation are the revamping of schools designated as "priority schools," previously known as persistently low-performing schools. New York State was required to agree to revamp the lowest-performing 5 percent of their schools in return for the NCLB waiver. In Syracuse, this means that between five and seven schools in Syracuse will have to replace their principals and 50 percent of their teaching staff by the beginning of the 2013–14 school year.

The socioeconomic characteristics of the student population, combined with underfunding, the ever-changing landscape of high stakes testing, teacher evaluation plans, and school turnaround ideas make the alternative schools that are the focus of this study part of a school district that might well be characterized as under siege. The 2012–13 enrollment in the SCSD was just over 21,000 students; it is the one of the largest districts in New York State exclusive of New York City. Seventy-seven percent of students in the district qualify for free or reduced-price lunch (New York State Department of Education 2012) (compared to the New York State average of 45 percent). The racial and ethnic characteristics of the general student body are 28 percent white and 72 percent students of color (53 percent African American/black; 13 percent Hispanic; 7 percent Asian; and 2 percent Native American) (ibid.). Twelve percent of the student body was classified as having limited English proficiency in the 2010–11 school year (ibid.) and 20 percent were classified as special education students. Only 51 percent of students who entered high school (ninth grade) in 2006 graduated within four years (New York State Department of Education 2010, 2012). The graduation rates for youth of color are even more dismal, with only 50 percent of the black students and 37 percent of Hispanic students graduating. The SCSD reports an average daily attendance rate of 92 percent, and 22 percent of students suspended from school for one day or more (i.e., out-of-school suspension) (New York State Department of Education 2011). Data from 2011–2012 indicate that 25 percent of students were subject to out-of-school suspension, 82 percent of whom were students of color, and almost three-quarters were minority males.

In 2007, the Syracuse City School District became the first district selected by the Say Yes to Education Foundation to tackle district-wide improvements focused on improving graduation rates, increasing college attendance, and stemming the white/middle class exodus from the city (Maeroff 2012). The latter goal was initially incentivized by a commitment that any student graduating from a Syracuse high school would be guaranteed a free or very low-cost college education at one of more than one hundred public and private colleges participating in the Higher Education Compact. Among the private schools participating in the "Say Yes to Syracuse" initiative are Syracuse University, Columbia University, Tufts University, and the University of Pennsylvania. The "Say Yes to Syracuse" initiative is a community collaboration with heavy involvement by Syracuse University and support of the city and Onondaga County. The ambitious goals of Say Yes are expected to be achieved by a combination of instructional improvements and social supports. Results to date have been uneven: elementary student test scores in English and math continue to be well below state standards, but graduation rates have increased slightly (Maeroff 2012). By 2009, the guaranteed free tuition was limited to students from families earning up to $75,000 a year. While enrollment in the SCSD increased slightly, the increase appears to be attributed to an increase in the immigrant population rather than a reverse exodus from the suburbs to the city.

Alternative Schools

The Say Yes initiative has not directly addressed the problem of school suspension from city schools, and the initiatives' social, emotional, and after-school programs are not available to students who have been suspended from mainstream schools. While students subject to long-term suspension are among the most marginalized on every social measure, and would most likely benefit from the haven of schools and services offered by Say Yes programming, they are unable to find these opportunities and this support in their alternative placements.

Without support and attention from a school district and its special programs, it is all too easy for kids to stay out of school. The kids we worked with were often late to school either because there was no adult at home to wake them up (many parents worked graveyard or early morning shifts) or because they simply did not want to go. My staff was charged with making sure kids got to school, and each morning they would visit homes, wake kids up, and take them to school. It was sometimes hard to rouse the kids in time for the start of the school day, but our commitment was to make sure that the young people attended. Our staff would arrive at the school with the half-asleep, somewhat disheveled youth in hand, only to find the doors locked shut. Contrary to the district's policy that required that students be admitted entry to school without regard to the time of their arrival,[2] one alternative school principal's policy was to bar kids from entering the school ten minutes after the official start of the school day. My staff would knock and bang on the door hoping to gain access and cajole the door monitor into letting the student slip into class. We were often successful when the door monitor was from the community and seemed to understand that for these kids "better late than never" was the operative reality. Unfortunately, one day, the principal himself opened the door and suspended not only the youth, but also my staff for being "insubordinate" and trying to circumvent his rules. It took me a month to get the principal to allow our staff back into the school.

Over the years, I spent many meetings in largely fruitless conversations with central office staff in efforts to diplomatically alert them to problems in the school. Both kids and my staff would complain of physical force used against them by school police officers, teachers, and school administrators. These red flags would go unheeded. A friend, who was at the time a deputy superintendent, confided that there was little that the central office could do as there was a district-wide tacit agreement that the alternative school was a dumping ground for troubled kids. To make sure that the administrators did not push back about the overcrowding and lack of resources at the school, the district assumed a "hands-off" policy. This changed only when an incident garnered public attention, such as news of a principal smashing a kid against a wall or a police officer punching a student in the face. In the face of public scrutiny, the offending party would be removed. For the most part, however, alternative school staff were not accountable for their management of and teaching in the schools.

---

2. Permitting students late entry into a mainstream school did not necessarily mean an absence of consequences. Students could be sent to ISS or Saturday detention, or suffer other consequence.

It was not that school superintendents were not concerned about alternative schools. I recall introductory meetings with several new superintendents who would initially convey dismay at the condition of alternative education. Reforming alternative schools was often on a new superintendent's "to-do" list. I have no reason to believe that they were not genuine in their concern or intent, but the constant crises facing urban schools inevitably pushed efforts to address the problems at alternative schools to the bottom of the "to-do" list.

At the time of the study, the Syracuse City School District had two alternative schools, the Brig Alternative School, housing children in grades six through eight, and the Steel School, serving as the venue for high school students (grades nine through twelve). Until the mid 1990s, the district had one alternative school, Brig, to which any student suspended from mainstream school was sent. However, with the advent of "zero tolerance" policies, the configuration of the alternative schools changed on almost an annual basis, reflecting changes in policies and procedures and the increased use of school suspension.

Until 1994, students suspended from mainstream school were sent to the Brig alternative school, located in the "South Side," an inner city neighborhood in Syracuse. When the district needed the Brig facility to house students from mainstream schools that were being renovated, the alternative school students were moved out and relocated to a nearby, terribly dilapidated parochial school that had been abandoned for more than two decades. Alternative school students spent a year in this building with boarded-up windows and a ruined physical plant. They returned to their alternative school, itself an old, grim building, after the repairs to the mainstream school were completed. No improvements were made to Brig itself, but after a year in a quasi-abandoned building, Brig seemed almost inviting.

Brig was one of the older schools in a district where the overall condition of city schools was described as "in great need of timely, massive renovation of existing space" (Syracuse City School District 2007). It commanded almost a full block in one of the poorest areas of the city, where abandoned housing is commonplace. It was also in a neighborhood known for street violence. The parents of kids sent to Brig from other areas of the city often expressed concern about the safety of their kids because of territorial "turf" issues. While Brig was originally a neighborhood school, as an alternative school, it received students from all over the city and "beefs" between rival street gangs were a worry. The school library was bereft of books; the school had no computers and no after-school activities.

My first encounter with the district's alternative school came in the mid 1980s when working with youths in the juvenile justice system. As part of the court mandate that allowed them to avoid incarceration, the young people were required to attend school or else face violating their court order. In addition to their court-related problems, many of the young people in the program had been suspended from mainstream school and thus, in supporting their school attendance, I frequently interacted with alternative school administrators.

Even as an adult, I found the school depressing and institutional. A large brick building, it had dirty windows that blocked sunlight and several entranceways, all of which were locked shut ten minutes after the start of the school day. Some of the doors were shackled shut with heavy metal chains that were wrapped around door handles and secured with oversized locks. Ten years later, in the mid 1990s, little had changed. Alternative school administrators and I held a meeting in the school library with a group of program officers from the Office of Juvenile Justice and Delinquency Prevention, which was overseeing a grant awarded to the organization that I work for. The visitors were shocked to observe that the library bookshelves were bare, without a book or magazine in sight. To my chagrin, after many years visiting this school, I had ceased to notice that the so-called library had no books. I had indeed accepted that this was something less than a school, and in so doing, I tacitly accepted that these young people were not really students.

When I first became involved with suspended students, all were sent to Brig, most typically for chronic disciplinary problems in class or fighting in school. However, with the passage of the Gun-Free Schools Act in 1994, which held federal funding hostage to school districts' creation of zero tolerance policies that established mandatory expulsion for the possession of a weapon, the SCSD was forced to create a special "program," distinct even from Brig, which was classified as a school. Initially called Stop All Violence Everywhere (SAVE), the program moved from location to location during its initial three-year period, eventually landing in the former central library, the Steel Building, located in downtown Syracuse. In 2001, Brig was co-located into Steel and the building was renamed the Renewal Academy. The two names, "SAVE" and "Renewal Academy," were used somewhat interchangeably, but the Brig middle school and the SAVE program operated separately under one roof. Despite efforts to share resources, the two principals and the two staffs did not get along and there was little cooperation between the two. Brig was later returned to its home on the south side of Syracuse.

The almost yearly reconfigurations of the alternative school student body continued. SAVE became a high school, no longer a separate program for kids charged with weapons possession, and Brig was reserved for middle school. At some point, fifth grade and sixth grade students were also suspended to Brig. Public complaints about sending fifth graders—some as young as nine years old—to Brig caused the district to limit suspensions of fifth grade students to either home-bound or in-school suspension. An afternoon school that ran from 3 p.m. to 5 p.m. (known as the "three to five") was set up for students who were suspended from the alternative schools or students who were known to be "beefing" with another alternative school student.

Changes continue as I write this book. Several school board members toured Brig and were horrified by what they saw. Dropout rates of students who attended alternative schools were as high as 90 percent. The newest configuration places suspended students in self-contained classrooms housed in a mainstream school or in a community organization. My organization in fact hosted one such "program." Little has changed with respect to the quality of education. The alternative schoolteachers were simply reassigned to the various programs and remained unaccountable for their teaching methods and style. The kids whose programs were in mainstream schools were not permitted to interact in any way with other students. They were not allowed in the school cafeteria and instead were restricted to eat lunch in their classroom, the only space in the school that they were allowed to be in.

These spatial relocations were due to changing enrollments (the growing number of suspended students), personnel issues that arose when the two "buildings" were co-located, and dissent from certain segments of the community. For example, the Downtown Committee, a group comprised of local business and civic "leaders," had long lobbied the city and school district to relocate the students attending Steel to some other location, claiming that the presence of the school and its students were having a dampening effect on downtown commerce.

The effort to move the Steel School to a local, largely white neighborhood in 2008 was met with vocal opposition, causing the district to reverse its plan to leave the high school students in their current downtown location. While the Downtown Committee and community groups opposed the location of the alternative school in their area, they seemed not to consider how this rejection would be perceived by the kids, parents, and even school staff. District administrators were not alone in being aware that the alternative school was unwanted in either location. For these officials, the public disdain presented a logistical problem. However, alternative school staff, the parents, and kids themselves were also aware they were unwanted in either location and experienced this reaction as a psychic assault.

The current configuration for suspended students is to disburse them into small groups housed in community organizations in various parts of the city or in self-contained classrooms distributed among mainstream schools. These configurations are in constant flux; with plans made, revised, jettisoned, remade, and partially implemented. Even as this book was being written, the alternative programs are going through two significant changes. High school students (grades nine through twelve) were first left in the Steel building, eighth graders in the Brig school, and seventh graders placed in two self-contained sites located at mainstream middle schools. Then all alternative school students were placed in self-contained sites in mainstream schools and community organizations. These placements were insufficient to house the ever-growing numbers of suspended students, and so the homebound population burgeoned. These students meet with a tutor in very small groups in various locations, including public libraries, and receive at most two hours per day of instruction. With the arrival of a new superintendent and the release of US Department of Education data and attendant national attention (Losen and Martinez 2013), the district is undertaking its first major reforms to reduce out-of-school suspension, including contracting with an independent agency for hearing officers and revising its code of conduct. My organization has been selected to provide "student advocates" who will help parents and students to understand the suspension process, to present their "side of the story," and provide mitigation to avert long-term out-of-school suspension.

Between 2004 and 2012 (the years when federal data were released) it was difficult to access accurate data on the number and characteristics of and outcomes for students suspended to alternative schools. The schools were reclassified as programs and were not required to report on the characteristics of their students and the results of their standardized tests. Instead, students in alternative schools were counted in the mainstream schools from which they were suspended, making it difficult to track demographic and educational characteristics of alternative school students. The last available data posted on the New York State School Report Card website showed there were about 250 students a year placed in the alternative school. They were economically disadvantaged, with 100 percent qualifying for free or reduced-cost lunch. The school population was disproportionately male—65 percent—although more recent estimates indicate that almost half the population is now girls. The alternative schools were also disproportionately minority, with about 75–80 percent of students being students of color. Based upon my observation and the data that are collected by my organization's programs, there is little reason to believe that these characteristics have substantially changed, save for the increase in the numbers of students suspended.

The Alternative School Students

The young people interviewed are the most critical source of data for this study. They provide the firsthand perspective of how school suspension and placement in an alternative school affects their personal identity, their expectations of education, and future aspirations. Only the voices of young people subject to exclusion from school can illuminate whether suspension and alternative school placement dashes their hopes for their futures or whether being pushed from school is accepted with resignation.

I interviewed a total of twenty-five students (twelve boys and thirteen girls), all of whom had been suspended from school. Most of the kids were in the ninth grade, and many had been held back a year at some point in their school career. One young man was seventeen years old and in the ninth grade. He dropped out of school when he was sixteen just after he was placed in an alternative school, but decided to reenroll when he was unable to get a job. When he reenrolled, he was permitted to enter a mainstream high school.

The types of schools that the youths attended prior to their suspension differed because of the varied configuration of Syracuse city schools. Some were enrolled in a K–8 school, others a middle school (grades seven through eight), and a few had been in high school (ninth-grade freshman). The seventh and eighth graders were suspended to the Brig alternative school, and the ninth graders were placed in Steel.

Many of the kids had been suspended and placed in an alternative school on more than one occasion. This did not come as a surprise to me as one of the district committees that I served on heard from teachers, parents, and students that kids have a very hard time returning to mainstream school after alternative school placement. The mainstream schools do not want them back and they are "marked" once they return, subject to high levels of scrutiny, and readily re-suspended.

Most of the kids lived with their mothers in single-parent families, but 20 percent lived with both parents and several lived with their fathers and stepmothers. There were a few kids who were living with a grandparent, and one young woman was in foster care placement. Most kids had contact with their parents even if they were not living with them. All of the kids had a family member (father or older sibling) who was incarcerated and contact with that family member was typically limited or nonexistent during the time that the relative was incarcerated. The prevalence of incarceration in the lives of these young people illustrates the toll that mass incarceration policies have taken on communities of color. Rose and Clear (2004) for example found that two-thirds of their sample of almost 1,400 people in an inner city Tallahassee, Florida neighborhood either had been incarcerated or knew someone in that position. Table 1 summarizes the demographic and family characteristics of the youths included

Table 1 Demographic Characteristics of Youths Interviewed

	NUMBER	PERCENT
Gender		
Male	12	48%
Female	13	52%
Race/Ethnicity		
African American	19	76%
Latino	5	20%
White	1	4%
Age		
13	4	16%
14	10	40%
15	6	24%
16	4	16%
17	1	4%
Grade		
7th	6	24%
8th	6	24%
9th	10	40%
10th	3	12%
Living arrangements		
With both parents	5	20%
With mother	13	52%
With father	2	8%
With grandparents	4	16%
Foster care	1	4%
Contact with non-custodial parent		
Yes	12	48%
No	3	12%
Limited	3	12%
Parent deceased	2	8%

Table 1 Demographic Characteristics of Youths Interviewed (*Cont.*)

	NUMBER	PERCENT
Prior suspension		
Yes	16	64%
No	9	36%
Juvenile justice involvement		
Yes	11	44%
No	14	56%
History of family incarceration		
Yes	25	100%
No	0	0%

in this study (I discuss the family circumstances and community lives surrounding the young people in chapter 5).

Understanding School Suspension as a
Prelude to Prison: Reflections on Method

This study is based upon interviews with twenty-five students who were suspended to one of two alternative schools operating in the Syracuse City School District. Kvale (1996, 8) defines qualitative research interviews as "attempts to understand the world from the subjects' point of view, to unfold the meaning of peoples' experiences, to uncover their lived world prior to scientific explanations." Interviews with students allowed me to collect information about how young people interpreted their suspension experience. I used a semi-structured interview approach using prepared questions as a guide, but allowing for open-ended answers and divergence in how the questions are asked and answered. My approach most closely resembled the "long interview" described by McCracken (1998, 9) as a technique that enables the researcher to probe shared meanings that take one into the "mental world of the individual" and better understand how the person understands his or her experience. While several broad theoretical frameworks influenced the research, it proceeded along the lines suggested by Glaser and Strauss (1967), allowing themes and theories to emerge from the data.

I approached the interviewing process in ways that resemble Kvale's (1996) emphasis on interviewing as a craft, requiring instinct, practice, and dexterity. After years out of the academic mainstream, I was comfortable embarking on a study that relied on interviewing, as much of my work experience required me to interview defendants in order to construct a life history to help judges, prosecutors, and juries contextualize and interpret criminal actions. I knew that while it was important to prepare for the interview with questions and topics to be covered, interviews are more useful if they allow the listener to hear a flowing conversation that may take unexpected turns, rather than a series of mechanical questions and answers. In my work, I learned that it is best to start an interview with an introduction that conveys respect and participation, encouraging the interviewee to ask questions if I am not clear in my inquiry, reinforcing that the questions have no right or wrong answers, and spending time putting the interviewee at ease. I have learned to follow the lead of my informant: for example, in interviewing defendants I discovered that some people like to start right off talking about the criminal incident, while others are not comfortable disclosing information about this aspect of their life until much later in the conversation.

The youths were recruited from among youths who participate in a program for youths suspended from mainstream school that is run by my organization. I recruited youths with the help of my staff who had daily contact with students in the alternative school. The staff were known to and trusted by youths through advocacy in the schools and by their work in after-school and summer activities. I trained staff to assist me in recruitment efforts by explaining to them the nature and purpose of the study and by clarifying that youth participation was not a requirement of kids' enrollment in my organization's programs.

I followed fairly standard procedures to guarantee the confidentiality of the study's participants. The most significant difference was related to procedures governing confidentiality of youth, who as minors are considered a vulnerable population and therefore need parental consent to participate.

I obtained both a signed written consent and a separate signature indicating that confidentiality concerns were explained verbally and in writing and were understood by the youths, and obtained such consents from parents and guardians. The parents and students were promised that their real names would not appear in any written materials associated with the study, and pseudonyms are used in identifying their comments and stories here. The interviews were held in my office, which was a familiar location to the young people; they lasted on average about one and a half hours.

At the beginning of each interview, I explained the purpose of the interview and gave the person being interviewed the opportunity to ask questions before getting started. I also obtained consent to record the interview and all agreed, but in three cases there were technical difficulties with the recorder. In fact, having the youths help me check and start the digital recorder was itself an icebreaker as we chatted about the generational differences in being comfortable with technology. I also let the interviewees know that I would turn off the recorder if at any point in the interview they became uncomfortable speaking on "tape."

Once the introductory discussion was completed, the youths were reasonably at ease. I found them to be patient and in fact eager to share their opinions with me, and none asked to leave before I completed asking them all of the questions. For example, Damian jumped right in before I could even ask my first question to tell me, "Teachers, they don't care about us as long as they get paid." I had to ask him to "hold that thought" until we got situated.

Following the interview, I thanked the student for his or her cooperation and their willingness to speak about some uncomfortable topics. Many of the youths commented that they enjoyed the interview and the chance to tell their version of the events and their experiences.

The interviews with students were supplemented by a review of student records, including data maintained by my organization in a Microsoft Access database that contained socio-demographic and educational status information on each of the youths interviewed. I read through documents concerning school discipline, school rules, and regulations, student rights and responsibilities, and reports, including newspaper accounts written about the alternative schools. In the present volume, pseudonyms are also used in referencing any other individual described or quoted. I also spoke with my staff who work with the kids on a daily basis and reviewed materials such as memos, program reports, and reports from various committees on which I participated over the course of my professional career. These sources of information include descriptions of situations and circumstances based upon informal observation of the schools, conversations with parents, teachers, principals, and district staff, as well as minutes from community meetings that I participated in as part of my professional work and activist activities. In addition, to document the community setting and school district characteristics, I used quantitative data available from the US Census Bureau, the National Center for Education Statistics, and the New York State Department of Education.

Most of the youths were interviewed once. However, four youths were part of a delegation to Geneva, Switzerland that I helped organize for the United Nations' review of the United States' compliance with the International Convention on the Elimination of All Forms of Racial Discrimination. As I accompanied these young people, I had multiple informal opportunities to discuss issues related to the school-to-prison pipeline.

Most of the youths were still in their alternative placement at the time of the interview, but several had completed their "sentence" and were permitted to reenroll in a mainstream school. This allowed for a rich exploration of student perceptions of the suspension process—the incident, the hearing, and their entry and adjustment to the alternative school and in some instances, following their reentry to mainstream school.

I took some notes during the interview to underscore any point that seemed particularly interesting and made additional field notes following each interview. I also reviewed the recording of each interview immediately following its completion and made additional notes. The digitally recorded interviews were transcribed with emotional responses such as laughter or raised voices noted, reviewed, and then saved to a text-only file for coding using HyperRESEARCH, a qualitative software program. I augmented the coding process with notes and memos to help me capture and interpret ideas that appeared in the interviews.

I coded the transcripts with an eye to how the information provided by the youths addressed three main questions: (1) How do youths who are suspended from mainstream schools understand this experience? (2) What do they think about the suspension process? (3) What do youth think about the consequences of suspension from school?

My use of school district documents, newspaper accounts that covered alternative school issues, student records, and notes taken during informal observations at school-related meetings as well as informal conversations with program staff who regularly work with youths in the alternative schools provided me with other sources of data to compare and contrast the themes that emerged from my analysis of the interview data.

This study is obviously limited and involves a small number of young people. As such, it cannot be generalized to all students who are suspended from school, nor can it be considered representative of policies and practices across all school districts. However, those were not my objectives; my goal was to elevate the voices of youth as their opinions are rarely heard. I now turn to these voices as they describe their families and communities, which set the context for their school experience.

Backstories

The Lives of Marginalized Kids

[S]he's the only one who's been there for me. She been [there] since
I was zero age. . . . Like, if I need anything, she puts a roof over my
head. She's always asking me about school and stuff.
—Jose

THESE ARE THE WORDS of Jose as he explains the close relationship with this mother. Jalil affectionately refers to his mother as his "partner in crime." Tyrel tells me, "My dad was the only one who was always
there for me."

I typically began the interviews by asking the kids to tell me something about themselves and their families: whom they live with, whether
they have brothers and sisters, where they live, and information about their
friends and neighborhoods. I was especially interested in hearing about
how these adolescents described their families. Throughout my working
years, I would hear school district staff, law enforcement, and court officials denigrate the families of young people, citing parents as the source of
their children's academic or legal problems. In contrast, the young people
I interviewed describe their families mostly in positive ways and as critically important to them.

This chapter purposefully highlights what young people have identified as the strengths of their families. I deliberately do this, at the risk of
being criticized as a romantic, since these are the kinds of stories and
perceptions that are rarely considered. On countless occasions during
my years of working in family court, I saw kids sent to detention facilities
and juvenile prisons because judges and prosecutors considered these

penal institutions a better option than the kids' own families.[1] Research, practitioner commentary, and public discourse are replete with the dismissal of poor and often minority families as dysfunctional and harmful (Wasik 2004).

To be sure, the stories told to me by these young people caused me to rue their family circumstances. The stories of distended family connections, the movement between and among family members, and the family diasporas due to incarceration or addiction were jarring to my white middle class sensibilities. However, I was most struck by the burdens that fall on these young people who are barely more than children. The kids feel responsible for their families' well-being because, at a gut level, they are aware of the trials and tribulations of their parents, brothers, and sisters. Yet despite the hardships, the families are a source of support and joy for the kids with whom I spoke.

Family members are described as providing emotional support, guidance, love, and care. Jose, Jalil, and Rayquan express opinions typical of these young people: almost all identified family members who are essential to their sense of security and love. They also describe very difficult family situations created by poverty, health problems, violence, addiction, and the weight of the criminal justice system.

As I describe later in chapter 6, the behaviors for which the young people are suspended range from weapons possession (no guns), to fighting, to attitudes that offend teachers and other school staff. However, these behaviors, real or perceived, are contextualized by family and community issues that make these kids ripe for suspension. There are multiple dimensions to the backstories of their suspensions that include the circumstances of their lives, the ongoing interaction between school personnel and youth, and the way that street life seeps into peer relationships

1. This preference for jails over kids' families becomes almost obscene in light of the findings of the US Department of Justice on conditions in New York's juvenile justice facilities where abuse by staff has resulted in concussions, broken bones, and death (US Department of Justice 2009).

and eventually into the schools. In this chapter, I introduce these youths in the context of their families and their communities.

Family Connections

The youths describe extended and complex family relations that are impacted by multiple relationships, incarceration, and street violence. Jalil's description of how closely he is monitored by his mother flies in the face of the often-heard complaint by authorities that parents no longer supervise their children:

> If I ask her can I go somewhere, she'll ask me how long I'm going to be, and . . . I probably say I don't know or I probably give her a specific time and she'll say, "Make sure you'll be home at that time." And then she'll call me and check on me to see if I'm there, and if I'm not there she's going to come and get me.
>
> (Jalil 2008)

One of the many myths that I encountered in my work with kids suspended from school was the notion that the parents of suspended students did not even care enough to attend the superintendent's hearing, that is, the hearing that determined whether the child is to be readmitted to mainstream school or removed to an alternative school. Despite that common perception, virtually all of the kids were accompanied to the hearing by their parents, grandparents, or other guardians. It was often difficult for parents to attend, as they are employed in jobs that lack "family-friendly" personnel policies, and so a day or even an afternoon of missed work means lost wages and a black mark against your name. Moreover, the kids told me that their parents were concerned about the suspension and, depending upon the circumstances, were either angry at the child for misbehaving or angry at school personnel for their treatment of their child. When they believed their child was in the wrong, parents imposed their own punishment, usually grounding or removing a privilege. When parents thought that the charge was unfair, they tried to come to the defense of the child at the hearing. It was clear from my conversations with the kids that none of their parents were cavalier about their suspension.

Rosa describes a joyful, happy family, even though her parents do not live together:

> [I love] important events like when we all get together and stuff. Like on weekends, we do like watch movies for the whole weekend, or we go out and just do something like go out to eat or go to the mall [and] hang out. And then me and my sister, we have a good relationship; we talk all the time . . . [about] stuff I don't think I can talk to my mom about. And then she has a real good relationship with my mom. They talk about everything. And then she tells me on how I should talk to my mom and stuff like that. Like if I have a problem that I want to go to her with, I should also go to mom. And then my dad comes over whenever I'm having trouble or something or if I'm in trouble, he comes over all the time. My mom and dad have a good relationship. They always playin' around.
>
> (Rosa 2008)

Rosa's interview was filled with stories about family connections and family events. One of the most upsetting aspects of her suspension (caused by a fight with another girl outside of school) was that because it occurred right before the end of the school year, she was not permitted to participate in her graduation from eighth grade. She shook her head ruefully as she told me how her family felt when they learned they were not going to be able to see her "walk the stage" and follow that with the joyous celebration that was planned in her honor.

Family hardships alone do not prompt the teens to reject their relatives. As Malik explained to me:

> They [brother, father, and sisters] *all* been through the same thing I been through, and they really don't want me to be through it! And I'm understanding that now. It's like I got the grips on my future, and I don't want to be some bum on the street. I don't want to be out here, hustling, trying to make a living. I don't want to have 700 kids, three grandkids,

and all that. I want to be a young professional architect, who has everything he ever wanted.

(Malik 2008)

The young people do not see their families through rose-colored
glasses. They acknowledge the ways that their family lives are sources of
problems and trauma. Their narratives include accounts of the violent
deaths of brothers and other relatives, the incarceration of many family
members, the health problems of parents and guardians, community violence that takes a direct toll, and general life stress.

While almost none of the youths mentioned physical or sexual abuse,[2]
Kora is the exception:

We used to get abused at my grandfather['s], me and my sister, but we
left them. Like hitting [with a] belt; we get bruises. I showed people at
Maple [Elementary School]. They took a picture. I showed people at
Clark [Junior High School] and they called the lady [at social services].

(Kora 2008)

Janella's description of a family overwhelmed by stress and poverty is
the typical account of family life shared by the kids I interviewed. Janella
lives with both parents: her mother works cleaning rooms at a Motel 6; her
father is unemployed. In addition to her parents, an uncle and an older sister make up the household. Her sister's daughter is in foster care (kinship
care), placed in the custody of a niece who lives in Delaware; Janella is not
sure whether this is a temporary situation or whether the child has been
adopted. The New York State Department of Social Services, which is
responsible for ensuring family visitation, has not facilitated long-distance
visits. Janella explains:

2. I did not directly ask the kids about abuse issues. Kora is the only child who raised
this issue directly. I do not draw any inferences as to whether she is the only youth to have
been victimized.

She's [Janella's older sister] supposed to call them every second Saturday and get pictures and stuff. But they don't send pictures. She can't talk to them like on second Saturdays. Like, she can't ever be able to get a hold of them, so she can't talk to them and stuff. So that's really hard on her.

(Janella 2007)

Janella describes her older sister and her mother as sad and depressed, observations that in turn are shouldered by this young woman:

It makes me feel sad to see my mom working like that. She be doing it for me because I be wanting stuff, so she go to work for me. And that's sad. So that's why I'm about to get my own job so she can . . . , so she don't have to keep going to work. I know she be tired because when she gets home she got to clean up the house, and cook and stuff because my dad . . . and my uncle Jeff—they dirty up the house. So she having to come home and clean when I'm not there, but I don't get there in time.

(Janella 2007)

Family health issues are also common concerns for these kids. Poor health seems to be a major contributor to family poverty, an important reason for parental or guardian unemployment when such occurred. Jalil told me that his mother had to stop work because she was found to have tumors. At the time of our interview, his mother was in the hospital being prepared for surgery. Jena's father spent many years on disability and died of a heart attack a year prior to our interview. Zeke's father is in rehabilitation for drug addiction. Jayda cannot live with her mom because she is disabled by a stroke and cannot care for all of her children. Shayna ended up in foster care because her grandmother who was caring for her died of cancer. What is also striking in these stories of ill health is the relative youth of the parents and grandparents: most of the kids' parents are in their mid-thirties to early forties, and the grandparents are in their forties and fifties.

The family portraits painted by the young people are at odds with the mythological American family of a mom, dad, two kids, and a dog. Nonetheless, family bonds and connections are present in ways that transcend physical living arrangements and conventional definitions of what constitutes a family. Family members are most often present, but dispersed among different biological parents, grandparents, and other relatives, or living in their own households. Most kids who were interviewed for this study lived with only one of their parents. The custodial parent was typically, but not always, their mother. However, it was not uncommon for youths to be living with their fathers or grandparents.[3] One of the girls interviewed was living with a foster mother. However, save for the child in foster care, most had regular contact with their noncustodial parent. They frequently moved from one parent to the other parent, from parent to grandparent, and back to parent. Their families are transient, moving frequently from apartment to apartment, neighborhood to neighborhood, and occasionally from city to city. Their households are composed of siblings, half-siblings, cousins, nieces, and nephews, but the young people do not necessarily find these labels to define their emotional relationships and connections. There is frequent contact with other family members who live independently or with other relatives. Roland's situation is fairly typical of extended family relations and connections:

> I live with my father . . . on . . . the Northside. . . . My little brother lives with my mom. . . . I have five brothers and two sisters. I'm my father's only child. My two little sisters live with my mom and two of my little brothers live with my mom and one of my little brothers live with my grandmother and my other little brother lives with um his father and my oldest brother he's in Job Corps. My step mom she has kids, but not with my dad. Only one of them lives with me.
>
> (Roland 2008)

Marla lives with her mother and younger brother but has extensive contact with her father, whom she describes as more involved in her school life:

3. Of the twenty-five youths interviewed, one lived in a foster home, one lived with both biological parents, two lived with their fathers, four with grandparents, and the remaining seventeen with their mothers.

Because my dad was in the military, my dad helped me with school and stuff. But my mom, like, she don't know, like, because she didn't make it through high school like that. So she don't know what be going on like my dad.

(Marla 2008)

Marla has many siblings, including half-siblings in a set of complex but bonded relationships. She answered a series of questions about her siblings as follows:

M: So where is your sister now?

MB: She goes to Job Corps. Out in Rochester I think.

M: Does she like it?

MB: Yeah she likes it. She visited like last weekend.

M: How old is she?

MB: Seventeen.

M: Do you have any other brothers and sisters?

MB: Yeah. I got two sisters. One of them, my older sister, she's twenty-four. She lives in Binghamton. But she on her own, like she got her own house, she got a boyfriend. She doing good out there. She comes to visit once in a blue moon. And my sister Cee-Cee, she just be like, she don't work. She's nineteen and don't have a job. She just be all over. I don't know what she's doing.

M: Does she live with you?

MB: No, she live, like she stays with people. Like she lives with her mom, but she goes with like, she stays the night at her friend's house and party and all that stuff.

M: So is Cee-Cee your half-sister?

MB: It's my father's daughter. And I got a brother. He lives with my dad. I got another brother that lives with his mom, but it's my dad's son. He lives with his mom, but they live upstairs from my dad. It's my dad's girlfriend so they together, but they live upstairs.

M: And how old are these brothers?

MB: My little brother who lives upstairs is seven. Then I have a little sister—they brother and sister. Yeah, I have a little sister; they got the same mom. So they live upstairs with her and my little sister. She's two. Yeah, two I think. And like then my little brother that lives with me, he's five so there's like seven of us, seven or eight of us.

(Marla 2008)

Despite what seem to be extenuated family connections in conventional terms, Marla considers them all her sisters and brothers, and never uses the adjectives "half" or "step" to distinguish among these relations unless prompted by my questions. Instead of stereotypes of dysfunction, Marla experiences connections from her extended family. She reports happily:

Sometimes my dad, because he takes care of all of us, so my dad will want to get my little brother with us when he takes us places. He want to get him with us too. . . . He's been taking care of us like ever since we was like all born. Yeah. But when my mom and him broke up, he got a girlfriend now. . . . But my dad still takes all of the kids out some times out to dinner or places like that so he gets us all together. So he really like, he's a father to all of us like really. Even if my little brother don't see his [own] father.

(Marla 2008)

Rosa lives with her mom and her half sister (whom she refers to as "sister") but regularly sees her father and his wife who live in the neighborhood. She has a good relationship with all of them and describes her stepmother as "nice" and "cool." She has brothers on her dad's side who live with their mother in North Carolina. These brothers visit once a year during the summer.

Jalil also has many sibling relationships. He has a one-year-old sister, the daughter of his mother and her boyfriend. He has two older brothers and three sisters "on my father's side." He also has two stepbrothers related to his mother's former boyfriend with whom he once lived. Jalil said, "I call his sons brothers, they are like my brothers," indicating that his feelings about sibling relationships are defined in ways that are not determined by biological parentage. Physical proximity is important in maintaining relationships, and he has no relationship with a brother who lives in New York City and limited contact with his seventeen-year-old brother who is in jail. His relationship with his biological father is also limited, but not nonexistent. He talks to his father on the phone and sees him occasionally. Jalil, however, spoke with pride about his father's job as a cook in a local restaurant, mentioning his father's specialties and commenting "he's real good with food."

Kwame lives with his mother, two older brothers, two sisters, and one cousin. He does not have any relationship with his father; he does not know where he is and has not seen him since he was three years old. However, he turns to an older cousin and his grandfather for guidance and support.

Undeniably, several of the young people have faced more challenges in locating unconditional family support. Karla has had a hard time finding a safe haven. She has divided her time between parents in Puerto Rico and Syracuse. Born in Puerto Rico, her parents split up when she was young. When her mother and stepfather first moved to Syracuse, she remained in Puerto Rico with her father, her stepmother, two stepsisters, and one stepbrother. Karla reports that it was her choice to remain with her father in Puerto Rico, explaining:

> Because when my mom left Puerto Rico, I had many problems with my sister that be aggravating everything. I started getting tired of this. So my mom said, "You want to go live with your father?" and I'm like, "yeah." So she was like, "Take your clothes and go live with your father."
>
> (Karla 2008)

However, when Karla's father went to jail, her relationship with her stepmother, which was never strong, deteriorated: "She kicked me out of the house like four times. I got to go to my aunt's house or my uncle house and everything" (ibid.). Karla was then sent to Syracuse to live with her mother and stepfather and three half-siblings (two sisters and a brother).

Shamiya did not know her father for many years, as he was in prison when she was born, and after his release he moved to California to live with his sister. Despite these rather tenuous ties, Shamiya reports that when she was in the fifth grade, she and her brother moved to California to live with her father. She told me that she returned the next year, in the middle of sixth grade, explaining, "I missed my grandma." At the time of her interview with me, Shamiya was living with her mother and three younger brothers. She has an older sister who lives on her own. She also has siblings on her father's side, but she is not close with them.

Zeke, Jayda, Norah, and Shayna were primarily raised by their grandparents. Shayna moved to Syracuse from Atlanta, Georgia with her mother and family. Her mother then moved to New York City, leaving Shayna and her siblings with her grandmother and grandfather. However, her grandmother fell ill and was unable to care for the children, causing the brothers and sisters to be split up. Initially Shayna was placed in a group home, but following her grandmother's death she was placed in foster care. Her brother remained with the grandfather and her sister was sent to live with an aunt. Shayna is pleased that she is able to see her siblings daily, as they live within walking distance of each other.

Zeke seemed most troubled by his family situation. He was raised by his maternal grandmother and her husband and described his relationship with his mother and step-grandfather as often strained and beset by fighting and arguments. Zeke has almost no relationship with his father. In speaking about his family situation, he often resorted to quasi-Biblical references and seemed to define himself as the family peacekeeper:

> We need to keep it in control . . . , just arguments and fights, that's how I can break it down to you with arguments and fights. How do I survive that? Just speak the truth and you know, just be like the just. You just got to make those moments go by and in good timing pattern. You just got to be on that pattern. You got to be ready. Don't hesitate to love that person at that time. Just a lot of things we need to fix as a family and as friends. People need to start preaching that Gospel. It's like, bless those who curse them . . . ; it really is a spiritual thing. Like if you believe in the spiritual realm, that's the only way you're going to survive in this world faithfully.
>
> (Zeke 2008)

At the time of the interview, Zeke's mother and younger sister moved into the flat upstairs from his grandparents, and he said, "You know, I'm trying to build this nice relationship between everybody now."

While Zeke and Shayna are adrift in these extended families, others like Norah and Jayda are grounded, despite not living with a biological parent. Norah and her older brother live with their paternal grandparents. She has lived with them for her entire life and calls them "Ma and Pa." Her father lives with his wife and two children in Puerto Rico; Norah says she visits her father every summer. She has a tenuous relationship with her mother who lives in Boston, and Norah briefly lived with her. While living with her mother did not work out, in this case, it was Norah's affirmative choice to return to her grandparents with whom she has a strong and loving relationship: "I came back because I don't like living with her [Norah's mother]. I like . . . , I'm used to my grandma already. I never lived with her [Norah's mother] before." Her grandmother, or "mom," is the person who accompanied Norah to her hearing, and disciplines her with care: "to her [Norah's grandma], I'm not a bad girl." Grandma is the adult that Norah looks up to and does not want to let down:

Well, I told my grandma, I promised my grandma that I was going to behave after this [the suspension]. And that I'm going to finish my school no matter what, no matter how many times I fail, and no matter what happens. And I'm going to go to college and get my degree and my diploma.

(Norah 2008)

Jayda also has been back and forth among parents and grandparents, but unlike Zeke, feels supported by all of them. At the time of our interview, she was living with her grandmother, but at various times has lived with her mother or father. Jayda's brothers and sisters "live with my mom and some live by themselves" (ibid.). Jayda is unable to live full time with her mom because she is partially paralyzed as a result of a stroke and thus cannot care for all the kids. She describes the custodial arrangements this way:

My dad—he had custody of me. He was trying to get custody of me. My dad—he was fit, but he didn't have a place to stay at the time. So my grandmother took me in so that I could have a place to stay 'cause she thought since I'm a girl, I need my own personal space. So she took me in and got custody of me. Her and my dad and my mom share custody.

(Jayda 2008)

I spent considerable time with Jayda as she was one of four young people who accompanied me to Geneva, Switzerland to testify before the United Nations Convention on the Elimination of All Forms of Racial Discrimination. Her close ties with her family were apparent from their efforts to help Jayda prepare for the trip by finding the various documents needed for her passport, and as the family chipped in to buy luggage and a cell phone from which she could make international calls. Jayda was eager to stay in touch with them, and the family wanted to hear her day-to-day accounts of this unusual adventure. Jayda and the other young people on the trip were attentive to shopping for gifts for their family members—parents, grandparents, brothers, and sisters—making no distinction between "step," "half," and biological relatives.

When we returned from Geneva, I wrote a letter to Jayda's adult family members—father, mother, and grandmother—thanking them for allowing us to take Jayda with us and sharing with them her stellar behavior and insightful, well-honed testimony. Shortly after, I received a call from Jayda's grandmother thanking me in turn, and telling me that they had never before been complimented about their daughter. Several months later, when my organization arranged a celebration of the youth's success in Geneva, many of the family members, including Jayda's grandmother and father, showed up to honor their children.

These complicated but rich relationships are poorly understood by those of us who have come to see the world with eyes that accept the mythical family construction. An alternative understanding would see these families as quintessentially American, with antecedents in a family mosaic that was constructed under slavery yet survived even the selling of family members to parts unknown or situations where a biological father could own his own children (Gordon-Reed 2008). The stories of kids' family connections are more multifaceted than is often acknowledged by teachers and school administrators. While it would be an error to discount family problems, it is equally problematic to fail to distinguish sources of family strength and bonds or to ignore the structural factors that contribute to family dispersion. One of the ubiquitous causes of family separation among the young people included in this study was the criminal justice system itself.

Families Inside and Outside of Prison

For poor children of color, prison has become a significant cause of family dissolution. One in 15 black children and 1 in 42 Latino children have a parent in prison, compared to 1 in 111 white children (Glaze and Maruschak 2008). Virtually all of the youths included in this study had a parent or other close family member who was at the time of the interview incarcerated, or had been so in the past.

Some of the kids knew where their relative or relatives were imprisoned, and some had even visited them while they were incarcerated. Other youths knew less of the details of family members' incarceration or were reluctant to speak about this aspect of their family life.[4] Jose was one of the young people who spoke freely about the members of his family who had been in prison: his father, a brother, two uncles, and a cousin. While Jose sees his father every day since his father was released from prison, he is critical of his father and their relationship: "He ain't no good father because he don't buy me nothing. He say cares about me. But if he cared about me he won't want to be back in and out of jail all his life" (Jose 2008).

Another young man, Damian had this to say in response to my question about his father's whereabouts: "He's in jail . . . somewhere in New York" (Damian 2008). Damian adds that he has a good relationship with

---

4. Secrecy is one of the hallmarks of children of incarcerated parents. They are told not to speak about their incarcerated parent to protect family reputation or to avert further intrusion by government into their families' lives (Johnson and Waldfogel 2002).

his father, but has not visited him and does not know exactly where he is incarcerated since he was transferred from one prison to another. At first, Damian seemed to be disinterested in his father's circumstances and their lack of contact. However, he visibly perked up when he learned that he could look up his father's whereabouts on the department of corrections website. My notes from that interview describe him as popping straight up in his seat and asking questions about how he could find out where his father was incarcerated so he could write him a letter.

Unlike Damian, many of the young people I interviewed did visit their incarcerated family members. The location of the prison or jail was a significant factor in the youths' ability to visit. Almost all the youths had visited their relatives or friends if they were incarcerated in the local jail or penitentiary. However, visitation was far more problematic when the site of incarceration was a state prison. In New York State, as in most states, prisons are located far from the urban centers that are home to most inmates. Although Syracuse is located in what is considered New York's prison belt, these prisons are located in surrounding rural areas that are still some distance from upstate urban centers. Even the state prison that is nearest to Syracuse requires an almost two-hour drive to reach it and is not accessible by public transportation.

The experience of visiting loved ones in prison and hearing family members recount their life in prison gave many youths a basis for comparing their school setting with a jail environment. These comparisons emerged when we began to discuss their perceptions of school security. The kids commented on the pat downs, police presence, highly regulated environments, and even the physical appearance of drab institutions. Ironically, one young woman (Donela 2008) reversed the comparison. Her first visit to a prison came after her placement in an alternative school. She found it difficult to visit the jail because it reminded her of alternative school, an experience that she wanted to forget:

> I went with her [sister to the prison] like three weeks ago and I said I feel like I'm walking into SAVE. Because they pat you down and do the wand and then you walk through the metal detectors and that's what I felt like when I was going to SAVE. They pat me down, wand me,

then walk through the metal detectors. And I just say no, I feel like I'm going back to SAVE and I don't like that. I told her I'll see him [sister's boyfriend] when he get out of jail because I can't walk through them. That made me feel like I'm in SAVE and I don't want to think about that school no more.

(Donela 2008)

I share more examples of the kids' comparisons of school and jail in chapter 7.

Despite the growing awareness of the problems faced by children of incarcerated parents and the data that suggest that family incarceration is commonly experienced among urban school students in general and alternative school students in particular, the school district has no structured means to identify children going through this traumatic experience. Tyrel's story gives a sense of how disruptive and confusing parental incarceration can be. To Tyrel, the incarceration of his father played out somewhat like a disappearing act: "here today, gone tomorrow." He last saw his father about two years before I sat down with him for our conversation:

> T: Actually the last time I seen him [his dad] was for Christmas. We were all at his house and he was giving us presents and stuff. And then the next day, I know my mom told me my dad was in jail.
> M: And how did that make you feel?
> T: I was like mad because my dad was the only one who was always there for me. He took me places. He knew how to calm me down. He was somebody I could talk to. And I felt like I was losing something when he went to jail.

(Tyrel 2008)

The stigma and secrecy that surrounds incarceration discourages children and families from seeking help, which contributes to the social isolation of the entire family and deprives children of normal outlets for grieving that are available to children who lose a parent through death, military service, or divorce (Sack, Seidler, and Thomas 1976; Sack 1977; Jacobs 1995). As I saw from my interviews, children may be deceived or ill-informed about their parent's incarceration or, even when informed, may be directed by their caretakers to maintain secrecy because of real or perceived threats to the family's well-being (Sack, Seidler, and Thomas 1976; Chaney, Linkenhoker, and Horne 1977). Yet, save for a handful of youths who are involved in services provided by my agency, there were no school-sponsored efforts to attend to the way that parental incarceration can affect student behavior and performance.

"I Saw People Shot Right in Front of Me": Living with Omnipresent Community Violence

Prison is one source of family destruction common to the young people I interviewed; community violence is another. Street violence, increasingly defined as a public health problem (US Department of Health and Human Services 2001), looms large in the lives of youth who are on the school-to-prison track. The stories of death or injury of a family member resulting from street violence are particularly disturbing and poignant. One of Rosa's closest teenaged friends is serving an eighteen-year sentence for murder; other friends have been wounded by guns and knives:

> . . . I have a whole bunch of friends, because of where we grew up at, like, I know who got shot at and stuff and who seen people get shot and stuff like that. I live in that type of area.
>
> (Rosa 2008)

She herself has dodged bullets:

> Me and the girl I'm really close to, like we were coming home from a party one day, like we seen it. There was another one when we was all on the porch. It was during the summertime. Everybody was out. We was, like a whole bunch of us on the porch and stuff, people across the street. We was all just playing around. It was nighttime, like getting nighttime, and there was people in the car they was trying to shoot at people across the street. So we all tried to run in the house and stuff but the gun was jammed, so they just pulled off. I was scared because

like we was close to the people that was getting shot at so it could have hit any one of us.

(Rosa 2008)

Kwame (2008) has also been directly affected by street violence:

M: And why do you think so many people are getting shot and stabbed and hurt like that? Like, what's that about?
K: Like people, they just do stupid things for no apparent reason. Like they just shoot anybody or try to hurt anybody. And it happens . . . it seems like that it happens to my family.
M: Has anybody ever been killed?
K: My aunt died and my two uncles died.
M: How's your mother dealing with that?
K: Like she tried not to think about it sometimes and all this stuff.
M: And how about you?
K: Like every night I like pray and like of all this stuff and I try not to think about them so that I won't try killing myself or something like that.

(ibid.)

Kwame worries about his mother's health because of the violence that has consumed his family:

Because like every day, like mostly every day my mom she gets calls early in the morning. My mom, she gets a call early in the morning saying that either one of my family got shot or stabbed or one of them in the hospital or they either getting hurt or something like that and I just don't want my family someplace where they going to get hurt.

(ibid.)

While Kwame's experience is an extreme example of the impact of street violence on families, having lost one aunt and two uncles to murder, he is by no means alone. Jena knows her mother is constantly worried about dangerous streets. One of Jena's brothers was shot to death while he was attending a community "Stop the Violence Rally." Her surviving brother is addicted to drugs and has been in prison; her mother worries that she will lose this son to violence, as well. While Jena described this, her voice was unchanged and seemingly without emotion, but the tears welled up and streamed unchecked down her cheeks:

> J: Yeah, it's [her brother's incarceration] really stressing my mom out. And an older brother of mine died and it's like he's the only son living, you know, and she worries about him so much.
>
> M: How did your older brother die?
>
> J: He was at a "Stop the Violence" party for his friend that had passed away and some guys came in and they were shooting and he got shot.
>
> M: Oh my God.
>
> J: Yeah.
>
> (Jena 2008)

Some of the interviewed youths have themselves been victims of serious street violence. Damian lifted his shirt and showed me a long scar, the result of getting jumped on the street. He was also stabbed in the head and had me feel the lump in his head that resulted from the six staples that were used to put his head back together after the stabbing. He also said the attack resulted in his having his knuckles broken (showing me his swollen knuckles) and his arm broken.

Damian explained that he was jumped by a group of kids, several of whom he knew, for being in "the wrong place at the wrong time." However senseless this may seem to white middle class people, it is these long-standing feuds that make the streets dangerous places to negotiate. These are the fights and feuds that arise over ephemeral issues of respect that consume so much of the lives of poor youth of color. They become embedded in blood feuds focused on retaliation for increasingly serious incidents. Here is Damian's description of what boys fight over:

> D: [Fights start] from different gangs and they don't like each other. That's what I got jumped for. Because I got jumped a few

months back. I got my knuckle broke and somebody stabbed me in my head. And somebody kicked me in my eye and my eye, I got a busted blood vessel in my eye. It was red and swollen for a week, like a week and a half. My knuckle was broke, you see. I knew all of them. I knew most of them. [They jumped me] because I live, used to live over there over around the 10th area. They used to think I was from there. I am not with nobody. I don't claim no set, no gang, no nothing, but I was walking over in their area in their turf. . . .

M: All you did was walk where they didn't think you belonged? I don't get that.

D: I don't get that, neither. That's what I be talking about gang violence. Like gangs, they don't like other gangs. For example, you know the Rocks, right, and the Easters. They beefing. Because they don't like each other. And the 18th and the Rocks used to be beefing. Now the 18th is beefing with the Cribs. And Easters and the Rocks beefing still. And now some other gang, the Block, beefing with North Ave., and North Ave. and the 18th right next to each other. At first they was beefing, now they cool because they right next to each other. And you know the Homes and the Rocks is right across the street from each other and they was beefing. And they still beefing. And the Rocks and the Easters still beefing. And the Cribs and the 18th still beefing and the Block and North Ave. still beefing. They don't know them and just because they don't know them, that means they don't like them. . . . They just fighting over the top gang. Because a guy from the Block got killed by the 18th and they still beefing from that.

(Damian 2008)

Damian tells me that even though his uncle was killed in gang fights, he still resists joining a gang. But he draws the line at his "no retaliation policy" if an incident were to involve harm to a member of his immediate family:

My uncle, he was my uncle and I'm still not with a gang. I don't care what family member's in the gang unless it's my brother unless they got killed. If it ain't my brother, I ain't got nothing to do with it. If they [a brother] get killed, then I got something to do with it.

(Damian 2008)

Celia also spoke of how street violence surrounded her life:

I saw people get shot right in front of me. I saw Boo get killed. Like over the summer. Yeah, that was my boy. It was crazy. And two days before that, my buddy Terry got shot. And we was all sitting in front of my house. It was just crazy.

(Celia 2008)

I asked Celia if she thought anything could be done to stop the killing and violence. She looked at me for a long time, somewhat puzzled, and said, "I don't know. It's just something that happens." But as she added details, a story emerged that is common to street violence in inner cities—blood feuds that arise out of seemingly minor insults and escalate into homicide. Celia explains the shooting of her friend:

Boo got killed because he killed Nicky. But he didn't mean to. It was an accident. And when he killed Nicky and he went to jail for it. Then they let him out. Like a month later, he left his mom's house and came to our house. We was all standing out front. We was down the street from my house. We was all standing on the porch and then the boys came. Freddy got out of the car and was like, "What's up, bro?" He was like, "You hot." And he started laughing and pulled a gun out and said, "That's for my cousin." And they got in the car and left. They shot him [Boo] twice.

(ibid.)

Celia goes on to explain that the source of this violence is a murky "beef" with a long history.

It's just a beef that's been going on for years and it's not never going to end. And then they get disrespectful. Like they saying words to the man's family that died. Like say you from the Northside and you came to the Rocks being funny like, "Ha, ha, ha, you the L7, we the cap, we the OJ."[5] You're going to get messed up straight like that. You're being disrespectful and then you have the nerve to come to the 'hood. . . . That's just not right. You're not just going to get away with it. Like you know how the boys is? It's the same way with the girls. It don't matter if you're a boy or a girl. Like literally, the boys from the Northside don't care, they'll fight a girl. Like you a girl from the Rocks and you being disrespectful that boy from the Easters, he is going to fight you. They going to do what they got to do. Like literally.

(ibid.)

In response to my question about why being disrespected is so significant, Celia responds:

It just is. Like how would you feel if someone just came in and say your mother died right? How would you feel if somebody, just, you already had a problem with them and they just word to your mother? How would you feel?

(ibid.)

Celia and other young people have come to accept the violence as something that "just is." The practices of revenge prevalent among marginalized youth provide a roadmap of relative power and social place. The use of violence is perceived by young people to vaccinate them from being marked as prey. Revenge becomes the tool of justice among youths who lack confidence in the fairness of the criminal justice system.

I was left drained after hearing these stories of loss and violence and I remained bewildered. The deaths happen literally on the streets that I walk on daily, the roads that I drive through, the parks where my own sons played. The events do not take place in some strange land, they happen around the corner. Kids carry with them these traumas, but they are at best superficially addressed. When street violence claims the life of a student, schools will muster together "grief counselors" for a day or two.

---

5. Slang terms used by kids: "L7" is nerd or square, "cap" stands for shooting someone with a handgun held sideways, and "OJ," to kill by violent slashing.

But when Jena gets suspended for fighting a girl in school because she was "at the end of her rope," no hearing officer stops to consider whether the rope was frayed by the recent murder of her brother or premature death of her father.

Yet despite the dreadful violence that permeates the lives of the kids that I spoke with, I end this chapter reiterating my opening theme. That is, difficult family circumstances notwithstanding, the young people's narratives of their family lives preclude the facile dismissal of poor, minority, families as wholly dysfunctional. Extreme poverty, instability, incarceration or the tragedies of street violence do not negate family connections, and as the report from the US Department of Justice (2009) on conditions in New York's juvenile justice facilities shows, institutions do not necessarily offer better protection from murder and mayhem.

The family-level risk and protective factors identified in the literature (Shader 2004) cohabitate in the lives of the young people who shared their family situations with me. To be sure, there are examples of absent fathers and ineffective mothers, but the portrait that emerges is a complicated picture of family life of very poor families. The comments by the youths provide a glimpse into the structural barriers that stand in the way of successful school experiences. The persistence of family support in the face of these barriers belie teachers', school administrators', and law enforcement's often-voiced criticisms of parents as solely responsible for the failure of children to behave properly in school. Instead, the youths describe their parents' work in arduous, underpaid jobs. They long for parents who are absent because they leave town for jobs in other areas or are incarcerated in prison. They are concerned about their parents' health problems. Contrary to stereotypes about "welfare queens" or "deadbeat dads," almost all of the youths reported that one or more of their parents and guardians worked as home healthcare aides, nursing home aides, hotel workers, restaurant cooks, retail store stock clerks, in data processing, and in other very low-wage jobs. Almost all of the young people spoke with love and admiration for many of their family members, and with respect for their efforts to persevere despite challenges. And while most of these adolescents also spoke of troubled family members, relatives in jail, or step-parents with whom they had difficult relationships, these detrimental experiences were not cast as the sum and substance of their family relationships. Unfortunately, the external authority figures in the lives of these children are often far less nuanced in their judgment of their families.

Families are important to the well-being of children and there is much educational research and practice that posits that parents and families are essential partners in the educational success of children. Yet schools take shortcuts when dealing with children who are considered to be disciplinary problems. In my experience, I have found school administrators and teachers are often critical and dismissive of students' families, whom they blame for the children's behavioral problems. Trauma and stress that students experience due to family factors—parental incarceration, violence, and grueling poverty—are not considered as mitigating factors in evaluating misbehavior or meting out sanctions. As I discuss in the next chapter, the suspension incident is viewed in isolation and measured against zero tolerance standards without consideration of the larger circumstances that contribute to misbehavior.

"Bad Decisions"

The Suspension Incidents

CARLOS SITS across from me munching on a granola bar that I passed him before we started the interview. I ask him to tell me how he came to be suspended to Steel alternative school. He swallows, shakes his head and says "bad decisions," adding:

> I went with my friends and they didn't tell me nothing. They was like, "Oh, we going downstairs." So I followed them downstairs . . . and the next thing I know I'm at the stairs and there's a fire alarm. So they pulled the fire alarm and the next thing I know they were like, "Carlos, run!" I went upstairs with them and they catched us on camera. So that's what I was suspended for.
>
> (Carlos 2008)

As I chatted with Carlos, I became increasingly saddened and enraged that this young man spent a year wasting away in alternative school. His backstory displays the precise kind of complexities that are overlooked by stereotyping kids as "bad" and coming from "bad" families. While his uncle was in prison and some cousins were allegedly dealing drugs on the street, Carlos had heretofore escaped the underground life. As we chatted, we developed rapport over the fact that I, like his parents, came from Brooklyn (he recognized my accent). The Brooklyn roots somehow led into a discussion of baseball (before his suspension, Carlos was on his high school team) and I reminisced about the Brooklyn Dodgers and how my first lesson in property rights came when I learned that the Dodgers were in fact owned by one person who could summarily move them to

Los Angeles, and were not communally shared by the people of Brooklyn. (Our rapport was solidified when I said I was a Mets, not a Yankees fan.)

Baseball was not just a frivolous icebreaker: Carlos and his parents were heartbroken that suspension to alternative school meant he could no longer play on his high school team. His parents, though divorced, dutifully and enthusiastically turned out for all his games. His father, he proudly told me, had a two-year college degree and his mom worked for a local agency that advocated and served Syracuse's small Latino population. The richness of his story and the promise of his future were not considered when Carlos was kicked out of school.

Suspension is a multistep process that begins with an incident that sets in motion the school's disciplinary system. This chapter focuses on how youth describe and explain what I call the "suspension incident." In subsequent chapters I explore the ways that the students interpret the events that follow—in Carlos's words—their "bad decisions." I painstakingly dissect these incidents, since they are the trigger for school discipline and thus are important for evaluating whether the response to perceived and real misbehavior is sensible and for considering whether less punitive approaches might be more effective.

While some students get suspended from school for behaviors that clearly cause physical harm, most suspensions are for relatively minor disciplinary infractions (Raffaele Mendez and Knoff 2003; Brooks, Schiraldi, and Ziedenberg 1999; Skiba, Peterson, and Williams 1997). With respect to the most serious types of suspensions (out-of-school) and expulsions, National Center for Education Statistics data (Dinkes, Cataldi, and Lin-Kelly 2007) show that 32 percent were for fighting, 31 percent for behaviors related to drug or alcohol use or possession, and 21 percent for insubordination. The research generally identifies gender differences with respect to the incidence of and reasons for suspension. The data clearly show that boys are more frequently suspended than girls, and African American boys are the most frequently suspended compared to white and Latino youth (US Department of Education 2012; Skiba, Peterson, and Williams 1997; Raffaele Mendez and Knoff 2003; Costenbader and Markson 1994, 1998). African American boys are more likely to be suspended for more trivial behaviors compared to their white counterparts (Skiba et al. 2000;

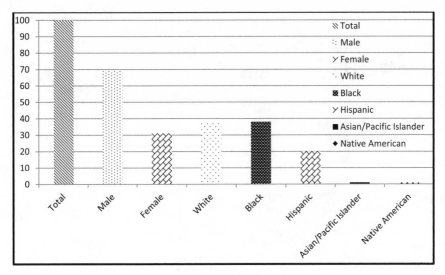

1. Percent of elementary and secondary school student suspension by sex, race, and ethnicity, 2006. Source: US Department of Education, Office of Civil Rights Data Collection 2006.

McFadden et al. 1992; Shaw and Braden 1990). Figure 1 shows how suspension rates vary by sex, race, and ethnicity, with black children suspended at higher rates than any other group.

The number and percent of girls suspended or expelled from school has risen in recent years. In 2000, girls were 28 percent of suspended students; by 2009, girls comprised 34 percent of those suspended out of school (US Department of Education 2000, 2012).

Nationally, by the 2009–10 school year, among middle school students, black girls were second only to black boys in terms of the percentage suspended out of school. Eleven percent of black middle girls were suspended compared to 20 percent of black boys, 9 percent of Hispanic boys, and 7 percent of white boys (US Department of Education 2012). All other girls of color were suspended at lower rates than boys.

The Center for Civil Rights Remedies analyzed the US Department of Education (DOE) civil rights data on a school district level (Losen and Martinez 2012). The Syracuse City School District was identified as one of the "high suspending" districts. As shown in figure 2, males with

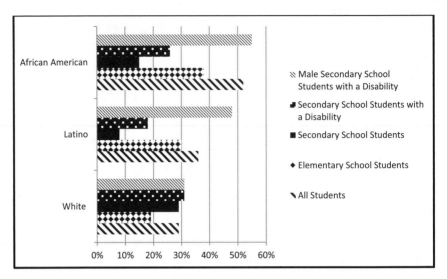

2. Risk for suspension at the elementary and secondary levels by selected subgroups. Source: Losen and Martinez 2013; for full report visit www.civilrights project.ucla.edu.

disabilities were at highest risk of suspension, particularly African Americans. Losen and Martinez's analysis showed that the majority of SCSD secondary schools suspended at least one subgroup at a rate of 25 percent of their total enrollment, and four secondary schools suspended at least one subgroup at a rate of 50 percent of their total enrollment.

In 2013, in response to public outcry about high suspension rates, the district released its own data showing an increase in suspensions between the 2010–11 school year and the 2011–12 school year (SCSD 2013). There were almost 10,000 out-of-school suspensions in 2011–12, representing 4,210 students. Forty-six percent of seventh grade students and 40 percent of eighth grade students were subjected to OSS in the 2011–12 school year. While middle and secondary school students were most likely to be suspended, there were high rates of OSS in the district's elementary schools as well, with 14 percent of elementary students suspended. Twenty-seven percent of students suspended out of school were African American or black.

The SCSD data also broke down suspension rates by schools. There were four elementary schools out of a total of fourteen that had rates of suspension that were just below or just above 25 percent; two out of seven K–8 schools had such rates. With the exception of one small, specialized middle school, the remaining five middle schools had suspension rates that ranged between 37 and 51 percent. All five high schools had suspension rates of around 20 percent.

The SCSD data did not report the reasons for suspension. However, the young men and women interviewed were suspended for different types of behaviors. Unexpectedly, the girls were all suspended for fighting and the only youths to actually use a weapon (knife) in a fight was a young woman. None of the boys were suspended for fighting, and although two of the young men were suspended for having a weapon (knives), these charges related to simple possession rather than actual use of a weapon in a fight.

"So We Decided We Was Gonna Fight": Girls and Fighting

I was surprised to discover that fighting and overtly aggressive acts were the reasons for the suspension of the young women I interviewed. The few studies that have looked at gender differences in suspension-related behaviors found that girls were more likely to be suspended for truancy than disruptive behavior (Skiba et al. 2000). The limited research on girls and violent behaviors has focused on girls in the juvenile justice system rather than girls in school. A meta-analysis of forty-six research studies published between 1991 and 1999 concluded that aggression by girls is both physical and relational, with gossiping, rumors, and arguments featuring prominently in fights among girls (Leschied et al. 2000). Zahn et al. (2008, 12) found similar causes for fights among girls, but noted that boys also fight for similar reasons and concluded that overall, girls are "not frequently violent in schools." Thus, my finding that fighting is the predominant reason for the girls' suspensions is unusual.

The young women freely admitted that they were suspended for fighting and gave detailed descriptions about the fight—whom they fought, why they fought, where the fight took place, and who stopped it. While acknowledging their involvement in physical altercations, the young women were upset that their reasons for fighting were not considered when principals and other school staff made the decision to suspend them from school.

The description given by Karla reflects how the girls often explain the suspension incident:

> K: I had a problem with a girl. So a boy came to me and say that she said that I don't know how to fight. So I get mad and go to her face and punched her and I broke her nose.
> M: And what kind of problem did you have with the girl before you had the fight?
> K: Well, the first time she came to that school, nobody liked her. Me neither.
> M: And why didn't people like her?
> K: Because she talks with an attitude and people don't like that about people like that.
> M: Ok. And so what happened, like did you have the fight in school? Were you in school when you fought?
> K: Yeah.
> M: And who broke it up?
> K: The teacher and the police, I think.
>
> (Karla 2008)

Karla was not the only girl to describe a fight with vague antecedents. Rosa, an eighth grade student who was suspended from a K–8[1] school, describes a long simmering feud of sorts that culminated in a fight at the end of the school year.

> M: And tell me a little bit about how you got to be suspended.
> R: I got into a fight at the end of the school year with this girl named Chakala in seventh grade. She was in seventh.

---

1. K–8 schools are schools that start at kindergarten and end at the eighth grade. The school district that is the locale for this study is replacing middle (6th–8th grade) or junior high (seventh and eighth grade) schools with the K–8 model.

M: Tell me a little bit about why you fought and what happened?

R: Like during the whole school year, we just kept arguing. And then finally at the end of the school year we both just had enough and so we decided that we was going to fight. And then I got in trouble because my friend jumped in to fight, because she didn't like her either. So I got suspended and sent to SAVE and then my friend got sent to Brig.

M: OK. Now why didn't you like the girl?

R: We just never liked each other since we was young. We always knew each other. We always went to the same center.

M: But what didn't you like about her?

R: We just never got along because we started arguing over stuff like simple stuff, little stuff. And we would, like, always look at each other like we didn't like each other.

M: So give me example when you say simple stuff, little stuff that you would argue over.

R: Like, if I would have an opinion, she would have something to say against it. Like, if I liked something, she would say she doesn't like it. I would say, "Okay, you don't have to like it; that's my opinion." She'll just start a little argument, or I would start an argument.

M: OK. So did you two mutually agree to fight? Like, did you just say enough?

R: Yeah. She said, "I'll fight anybody out here," and I said, "What about?" And she said, "Okay, we're going to fight." And I said, "Okay." I got in the fight because we was arguing through the whole school year and that we both decided that we should just get it over and done with.

(Rosa 2008)

Fighting looms surprisingly large in the lives of these middle school girls. For the most part, the fights are over "he said, she said," or more accurately, "she said, she said." Donela's explanation of the animosity between herself and the girl with whom she fought illustrates this:

The girl I fought was . . . , I was friends with her and she then started talking behind my back and stuff about me, and people started telling me. So I asked her and she said no at first. And then I kept telling her that people keep telling me otherwise—that you are talking about me and if you talking about me, you supposed to be my friend and that's not cool.

So then she started acting different when she got around her other friends. So I stopped talking to her and then she had her friends coming up to me asking why I don't want to talk to her no more and why I'm not cool to her no more. I told them and they said, "Yup, she was talking about you." Even her friends told me that she was talking about me. So I told her, "Well, don't talk to me if you going to talk about me behind my back." I guess she took it offensive. I was with all my friends and none of my friends like her neither because she was two-faced. She was always talking about somebody and none of my friends liked her neither.

So one day me and my friends was walking down the hill, and I guess she thought that because we was behind her we was about to do something to her. And she called her family and her family came up to the Shane hill and they jumped out of they car and we started fighting all of them.

(Donela 2008)

I remained puzzled about how and why the rumors and ill feelings got started, and I continued to prod Donela for a reason that would make sense to me. She traced the feud back to one incident, which seemed to me to be a simple misunderstanding that quickly escalated into name-calling.

Yeah, because she was a cheerleader and we go to the games. This is how it first started. We went to her game and she was cheering and then they get a break where they can get a Gatorade, juice, all that. And we was like, "Oh girl, you cheering, you good, da, da, da, da."

(Donela 2008)

What was meant as a compliment was misinterpreted and the rumor mill went into high gear. Donela continued:

I guess someone told her that we was talking about her, but we was telling her that she could cheer. She was like, "I don't care what they say, they all dirty[2], they all this, they all that . . . ," a whole bunch of stuff. Then everybody started telling us that she said that. And I said, "How she supposed to be our friend and she talking about us?"

(ibid.)

Donela eventually decides to confront her former friend:

So nobody wanted to ask her, so I asked her. At first she was denying it, then she just came out and told me, "Yeah, I was talking about you." I said, "What made you think I was talking about you? Because if I had something to say to you I could say it to your face." She was like, "Well, I do believe you was talking about me," basically not believing that I was telling her, that I wasn't talking about her. And she didn't believe me and she said, "Well, you was talking about me and you going to have to fight me," and calling me all sorts of "B's" and "F'ers" and everything. So I told her, "Well, you not about to call me out on my name and if you want to fight we can fight."

But we didn't fight in school; we left and she waited to call her family. That was the whole thing. I really wasn't going to fight her, but she called her family and her family got out of the car and started fighting, so we fought.

(ibid.)

As I listened to Donela's, Rosa's, and Karla's stories, which were repeated by virtually all of the young women I interviewed, I was struck by the banality of the issues that sparked the arguments. I did not find the triggers significantly different than my recollections of the fights that dotted my junior high years, when crowds would gather after school to see two girls fight over the "she said, she said" about boys, reputation, power, and social position. Like Donela, these fights typically took place outside of school right after dismissal. However, it does seem that fights between

2. "Dirty" was defined to mean slut.

young women are more common today, at least this is what the young men and young women told me. Moreover, there is little tolerance for what was once thought of as school-yard scraps. Instead, zero tolerance policies virtually ensure out-of-school suspension for any student caught fighting.

Like much of the debate around violence, it is difficult to tell whether violence among girls is actually increasing, whether we are more conscientious about reporting these behaviors, or whether we are more prone to fearmongering around what has long been typical adolescent behavior. What does seem clear to me is the response by school authorities to the banal violence. As the youths' stories reveal in chapter 7, school authorities do not try to learn about what caused the fight, nor do they offer interventions that might quell gossip or help the young women find other ways of dealing with perceived slights and insults.

Jayda's and Kendra's stories illuminate the consequences of school staff failure to attend to simmering disputes between students. Jayda and her male adversary had a history of bickering and disputes that were pretty much ignored by the teacher until it exploded into fisticuffs. Kendra's suspension for fighting was also preceded by harassment from other girls. Both she and her mother complained about the situation and she was annoyed that school officials discounted her prior complaints:

> I was telling administrators. I was telling principals, the vice principals. I was telling the teachers and nobody believed me. When I was coming to school with bloody noses or bloody lips, bruises, I would come to school crying every morning because they [other girls] would beat me up and they [school authorities] thought it was just an act.
>
> When the first year that I was there, in sixth grade, my mom and dad would go in there and talk to the sixth grade principal and she would just sit there and be like, yeah, like she wasn't even paying attention. And then the seventh grade principal, he would just sit there and listen and write stuff down but he wouldn't do anything about it.
>
> (Kendra 2008)

I find parallels in the young women's behaviors and school authorities' reactive responses that both convey an acceptance of fighting as inevitable. Rosa's statement—"Finally at the end of the school year, we both just had enough and so we decided that we was going to fight"—seems to sum up the girls' expectations. Zero tolerance policies of school authorities also communicate a sense of hopelessness about finding alternatives to violence other than the exclusion of students from school.

"They Were Tired of Me": Boys and Suspensions

In contrast to the girls, the boys were mostly suspended for behaviors that are more subject to teacher or administrator judgment. This is consistent with the extant research. Skiba, Peterson, and Williams (1997) and Verdugo (2002) show that black males tend to be suspended for infractions that are highly dependent upon teacher interpretation, such as disrespectful attitudes or insubordination, whereas white students are suspended for behaviors that at least have objective measures, such as drug or weapon possession. Ferguson's (2000, 83) study found that the behavior of black boys is more likely to result in their exclusion from schools because of how their behaviors are interpreted by school staff. She concludes that the behaviors of black youth, compared to their white counterparts, are assessed as "sinister, intentional, fully conscious . . ." (ibid.). Townsend (2000) attributes the higher rates of suspension of African American boys to the dissonance between the culture of Caucasian teachers and cultural and physical styles of African American adolescents. The stereotypes of African American males as dangerous or threatening also lead white teachers to overreact to minor challenges to their authority.

The boys I interviewed describe their suspension behaviors in ways that comport with the research, that is, as incidents that were misunderstood or misinterpreted. Unlike the girls, the boys' incidents are reactions to immediate situations and events. In contrast to the girls whose behaviors are enveloped in long-standing, interpersonal melodrama of gossip and rumor, the boys respond to situational circumstances they encounter when traveling the halls or fooling around in classrooms. Once called out by the teacher or other school personnel, including school police, the misunderstanding escalates into arguments that find their way to the principal's office and suspension. Often the boys were considered "threatening," as depicted in these narratives, first by Damian and then by Jalil.

D: The officer at Shane [his mainstream school] and a few other staff members claim that I threatened them, and cursed at them and stuff.

M: And where did this supposedly take place?

D: At Shane . . . , outside and in the hallway.

M: OK, and what happened?

D: One of the staff members was getting disrespectful to me and I got disrespectful back and the officer was escorting me from the premises. I told him he don't got to escort me, I'm going to leave, myself. And he said, "I'm going to make sure that you don't do nothing." And I said, "I'm not because I'm leaving the premises. You can watch me leave the premises." And he said, "Just leave the premises." And I was like, "Why don't you go back into the school and be the officer of the school?" And he said something like, "You don't wanna make me angry, because you don't want to make me angry." And I said, "Go ahead and get angry."

M: What did the officer do?

D: Claim that that was a threat.

M: And who was the school staff person who was disrespectful to you?

D: Mr. Petrie and Officer Savage and one of the other staff members. Mr. Nelson and another guy.

M: Are they teachers except for the officer?

D: They like vice principals.

M: And what were they doing that was disrespectful?

D: They like threaten to kick me out and say, "Oh, you ain't tough" and all that kind of stuff. Because I be having passes in the hallway. They don't think I have passes, they think I be skipping class. Like I was getting a pencil for class. The teacher can send you to the office to borrow a pencil and you go down to the office and get a pencil. And then that's what happened. They just told me to get my coat and leave.

(Damian 2008)

Jalil tells a story that begins with him being a bystander in a fight between two girls and ends with having his behaviors misinterpreted.

> M: Why did you get suspended to Brig?
> J: Because there was two girls fighting and one of them threw a chair, and I picked up the chair and put it back because the teacher asked me to. Then a teacher in the hallway said that I shot a chair at somebody. But I told her that she was lying. And she went and told them that I was yelling at her and stuff and she told them that I pushed her when I didn't push her.
>
> (Jalil 2008)

Jalil elaborated about his suspension incident event, explaining that he was walking by the teacher during class transition in a crowded hallway:

> It was during that [transition] and there was a lot of kids in the hall. I tried to walk by her because she was talking to somebody. I was like, "Excuse me," and I went between them and she said that I bumped into her and I almost made her fall.
>
> (Jalil 2008)

Of all the boys I interviewed, Kwame's comments most clearly echo the findings of the many scholars who have looked at the suspension of African American boys:

> I was suspended from Buchanan [his mainstream school] because I was charged with persistent disobedience. Like, getting in trouble too much and having teachers complain to the principal that I get in trouble too much, and they were tired of me and all that stuff.
>
> (Kwame 2008)

The boys' stories resemble the experiences of young men of color and the racial profiling by police that takes place in cities across the United States (Ramirez, McDevitt, and Farrel 2000). In contrast to the girls whose fighting behavior is overt and less subject to interpretation, the boys are charged with more subtle behaviors that are adjudged in the worst light. The girls more freely admit to violating school rules that prohibit fighting, while the boys describe events and behaviors that are less clear cut. The girls feel that their reasons for fighting are discounted, while the boys believe that they are unfairly accused.

The distance between teachers and other school personnel and police and black youth on the streets is similar and yields similar results. On the street, young people of color are stopped under the vaguest of suspicions, or simply because behavior such as hanging out on street corners is considered threatening. Youth object to such police actions and wind up getting charged with nebulous offenses such as disturbing the peace or resisting arrest. Such racial profiling has undermined minority community trust in social institutions in general and the criminal justice system in particular (Rose and Clear 2004). The distrust erodes the efficacy of the criminal justice system as more and more young people refuse to participate, whether they are witnesses to or victims of a crime. The legitimacy of the system is compromised and has a destructive effect on its continued institutional capabilities.

I see parallels reflected in the mandatory, excessive school zero tolerance disciplinary policies. Students who are most directly affected by zero tolerance disciplinary policies believe they are stereotyped even when they are not directly involved in an incident, as Jena's observation suggests:

> Like, sometime it seems like they [teachers] have favorites and stuff like that. And sometimes, you know, it's like that with some teachers. Like some kids, they [teachers] kick kids out for like stupid stuff like coming to the classroom and as soon as you say something, as soon as you say one thing, like you're out. It could be a silly thing, like you laugh or something and they kick you out.
>
> (Jena 2008)

These experiences, whether direct or observed to be inflicted on other students, undermine young people's confidence in the educational system. They believe that schools are complicit in their inability to learn or keep up with their schoolwork. Carlos thinks about dropping out, and Zared does so as soon as he turned sixteen. Roland sees himself as being set up by teachers, much as kids on the street believe they are set up by the cops:

> . . . I would literally walk in class and sit at a desk and just cooperate and not say nothing, and a teacher, they would find any small thing, any little teeny tiny thing, just to go off on you. They would say, like, get out of the class or you can go down to the office or you know, just things that get you mad because teachers know, they know how to literally press your buttons. And they know how to get you mad and they will push you and push you and push you until the point where you get mad at them and then you start arguing.
>
> (Roland 2008)

If students believe that they can be suspended unjustly, their commitment to education is eroded. Manifestations of student alienation from school is conveyed in lackadaisical attitudes, such as Donela seeming to be unconcerned about being late for school when she needs more time to take care of her hair, or when she thinks it's too cold for her to walk to school, or Stash, who often does not bother to finish his tests. Giroux (1982) would classify these behaviors as forms of resistance to a school system that does not seem to care whether students are in class or not.

In the Syracuse School District, the distrust of school officials, including school police, boiled over after a police officer punched a female student in the nose for being insubordinate. This triggered widespread criticism of school policies and practices that went beyond the incident in question. In the meetings that I attended, I heard parents say they were losing confidence in the ability of the public school system to educate their children and to treat them fairly or with respect. Many of the parents expressed frustration about being trapped in the Syracuse city public school system by suggesting or wishing they could pull their kids out and send them to parochial school, private school, a charter school, or move to the suburbs. This loss of confidence helps to fuel the abandonment of public schools in general.

Safety Tools: How Weapons for the Streets Wind Up in Schools

Of the twenty-five youths interviewed for this study, only three were suspended for possession of a weapon, specifically some type of knife. The low incidence of weapons possession did not surprise me: it is in keeping with data on school suspension that show most suspensions are for nonviolent and non-weapons related offenses.

Much of the rule-breaking around weapons possession is a response to the danger that youth feel on the streets, and not fear of violence in school. Celia is one of the three youths interviewed whose suspension involved the possession of a weapon. She readily admits that she regularly carries a knife for self-protection on the streets, but she knows that the schools do not allow knives in school and she does not feel that she needs that form of protection in school. I asked her about how she negotiates the world of the streets and the world of school. She answered, "There wasn't really no reason to keep a knife in school because schools are on the safe side. Literally." Nonetheless, Celia did bring a knife to school one day, describing it as one of the few times that street violence penetrated the school:

> [You know] how you got one group of girls and boys from the Northside and one group of boys and girls from the Rocks, whatever. I'm from the Rocks and we beefing with the Northside. So in school, there was a lot of the boys and girls from the Northside ganging up on me. So one day, this other girl from the Rocks had started the school. So there was just us two in school and all the girls and boys from the Northside just kept coming up to us saying, "You all from the Rocks, you all from the Rocks." And we was like yeah. And they started talking mad junk. Like you know how people die and stuff, and you be like where the L, whatever. That's just what we say because that's somebody that died or whatever. And then they was just being funny. They was like, "Where the L, where the Cap, where the OJ?" swearing on us and stuff. So Layla had a knife and I had a knife and then they came at me like they was about to jump me. And I had put my knife out and I was trying to stab the girl and then they all started screaming for the cops. And when the

cops came, I was refusing to let them search me and then when they
searched me they had found it and stuff.

(Celia 2008)

While Celia was the only youth interviewed who was suspended for
the actual use of a weapon, there were two other students interviewed
whose suspensions also involved possession of a weapon, again knives.
Like Celia, they told me that the knives were for protection against violence on the streets rather than any direct fears about school. Rayquan
says simply, "I came into the school and there was a weapons search and
I remembered I had a knife on me so I just gave them my knife." I asked
Rayquan why he had the knife on him and he answered:

R: I just had it from a previous day. I was with my cousins and stuff; I
just had it.
M: But why do kids carry things like knives?
R: I really don't know but everybody has their own reasons. Some
people just use it as, you know what I mean, a safety tool. It's just
like you could say it's just like a screwdriver, you know what I
mean? People carry screwdrivers around, I mean, because something might happen. Or it can be a hammer, like a handyman
weapon. Pretty much like a handyman thing.
M: Do you feel safer when you have a knife on you?
R: Not really. It don't really help too much, you know what I mean.
It's just a weapon, anything can be a weapon. They just see a
sharp object as a weapon. Because like if it was that serious, like
anything they come to school with could be a weapon. It more
like, what I'm trying to say is, if a knife is a weapon when you
come to school with it and you get suspended for that, you may
as well say anything you come to school with is a weapon. May
as well say all the kids at SAVE and Brig [the alternative schools]
for anything they come to school with. Like their sneakers can
be a weapon. A schoolbook can be a weapon. Chairs, too.
M: So it's not what you have, it's how you use it?

R: Yeah. Pretty much. Because anything can be a weapon. Because anything that you got can be a weapon. You better just come to school with a pencil or a pen; they may as well suspend you for that, too, because you could stab someone with a pen.

(Rayquan 2008)

Roland, on the other hand, was suspended when he took his brother's knife away from him in an effort to break up a fight and avert serious injury:

Well, it was all an incident on a bus where my little brother, um, he actually brought a knife on the bus. And him and another student got into a disagreement, which turned into a physical fight, or whatever. He, my little brother, pulled out the knife and um he pulled out a knife and he attempted to try to cut or stab the student. So I literally broke up the fight and tried to take the knife away from my little brother. And the knife was in my possession, which, like, they literally had no choice but to send me to Brig because it was in my possession.

(Roland 2008)

Roland offered that most kids did not bring weapons to school with them, and those who do, like his little brother, are fearful of attack:

Not a lot of kids, certain kids who ya know, like my little brother, and they the nervous type. Nervous, they haven't, ya know, they're not used to being around a whole lot of people. Ya know, it's just certain kids, but I don't think like it's a whole lot of them.

(Roland 2008)

The kids' analysis of the issue of weapons is more nuanced and sophisticated than the adults'. They understand that weapons can be dangerous and do not condone even their own possession of them. However, they have the insight to understand that a weapon is a response to fear and intimidation, and that in fact, if pushed against the wall, as Rayquan explains, literally anything can be used as a weapon. While kids make an error in judgment in resorting to weapons and carrying them on their person, the authoritative adults make perhaps a more egregious error in judgment in neither diverting their resources and efforts into changing the conditions that leave kids fearful or in responding in ways other than suspension, which is likely only to contribute to youth estrangement.

With the exception of three students, none of the youths were suspended for weapons. Rather, the suspensions came down to what Carlos refers to as "bad decisions," that at times involved fighting to protect one's reputation and retaliation for insults and gossip, being disruptive in class, or even being in the wrong place at the wrong time. Once accused of a behavior or rule violation, the young people are immediately suspended from school and sent home for a week to await their hearing. The students object to this dismissal, as they are left to spend the week at home, bored, and without schoolwork to do. They worry about falling behind, as Jayda explains:

> I don't think it makes sense because, why should a child be suspended for five days. If they was suspended for five days, at least the teachers or somebody should get work together and have somebody then do probably homebound [an option where teachers meet with students in their home or community location, such as a library] for the five days so you can get caught up on work. Because you're suspending a child for five days, they losing out on five days of work and that's basically failing them.
>
> (Jayda 2008)

This is just the beginning of their exile from regular school and age-appropriate curricula. In the following chapters, I explore, through the kids' words, bad decisions made by school administrators as they apply zero tolerance policies. In chapter 7, I look at the actual suspension decision-making process through the eyes of young people.

"They Never Want to Listen to Us"

The Process of Being Suspended

> They [the hearing officers] said, "What happened?" But when you go
> to stuff like that, you got like tell them what they want to hear. Like
> you got to tell them that you really did it and you are guilty, because
> they don't want to hear, "Oh, I didn't do it." They want to hear that
> you did it, and now you got to be punished for it.
> —Janella

THIS WAS Janella's assessment of the process of suspension that cul-
minates in what is called a "superintendent's disciplinary hearing," where
guilt or innocence is determined and the "sentence" meted out. Her opinion eerily resembles those of defendants in the criminal justice system
who feel compelled to take a plea.

The inability to listen to kids, to inquire about the background of the
suspension incidents, or to use discretion in discipline results in the suspension of youth for reasons that might simply be viewed as nonsensical
were it not for the tragic ramifications for the youths' lives.

Janella's suspension story is illustrative. I asked her why she was suspended and she told me that she spit on another girl, an image that, while
disgusting, did not seem to merit suspension and placement in an alternative school. The backstory of this event reinforced what for me seemed like
an unnecessary, if not unwarranted suspension. I followed up, asking why
she spit and again heard a story of rumor, misunderstanding, and a quick-
ness to retaliate in the face of perceived insult or slight:

> She [Janella's "victim"] got mad friends and I didn't have any friends that
> go there [her school]. My cousin just went out of town and it was just me

132

by myself, and her and her friends tried to gang up on me and stuff. And I felt, you know what I mean, that I had to protect myself, but I didn't do nothing. But she pushed me and of course, if someone pushes you, you are going to act mad quick. And my reaction was, the first thing to do was to spit on her, because she was whistling [at me]. I turned around and I was eating sunflower seeds and she pushed me, and I just like reacted. I just turned around and spit. And I was talking and I was about to say something and spit just came out. The principal was just going by and he seen the spit fly. So he broke it up and took her to the office and called her mom and sent her back to class, but suspended me.

(Janella 2007)

According to Janella, the principal did not ask what prompted her behavior. She described her feelings about being so dismissed:

I was mad because he didn't ask me what happened. You know what I mean? He just kicked me out for nothing—just send me there [the alternative school] for the whole school year.

(ibid.)

Janella, like many of the young people I interviewed, feels confused and betrayed by her one-year suspension from school. These emotions do not stand alone—they are entwined with the emotions associated with the larger context of her life. As I learned and described in chapter 6, Janella's experience in foster care, her estrangement from a niece who remains in foster care, and the effect of this family diaspora on her mother and older sister all affect her view of the world and how she behaves. Her one-year suspension for spitting was piled on top of these more significant family tragedies. Janella was fearful that her suspension would prompt the department of social services (which she referred to as "CPS," for child protective services) to again insert itself into her family's life.

I be stressing about a lot. Like I be trying to do good. But like, the things that I be stressing about, I be worrying about them more than school. And it just makes me off track. [I worry about] My mom. I be trying to make sure that my mom happy and my sister happy, because she's depressed. . . . I go to school, then come home check on my sister and cook her something to eat. And then I talk to my friends and go outside and stuff. And I just be coming back home and going to sleep. . . . I don't talk to people about this stress because they will probably try to get the white CPS in our business and I'm not trying to leave my mom for nobody.

(Janella 2007)

Janella is a young woman who needs to be included, not excluded; embraced, not pushed out; and encouraged to speak about her life, not silenced. Instead, she was removed from her regular high school and exiled to an alternative school for one year for the offense of spitting.

In this chapter I consider the themes of institutional (school) disrespect and lack of fairness that emerge from the young people's responses to my questions about school authorities' reactions to misbehavior. The young people I interviewed often feel that they have not been treated fairly and that the school disciplinary system, particularly in the era of zero tolerance, is unwilling and increasingly unable to consider mitigating factors. Sadly, the young people feel they are powerless to create a different outcome. The deck is stacked against them: the opinions of professional adults are privileged over their voices and also the voices of their parents, who are equally disempowered. A sense of fatalism emerges from the comments of these young people.

The initial response to student misbehavior sets in motion what seems to be the inevitable exclusion from regular school. The meeting in the principal's office could be an opportunity to hear the kids out, and to look more closely at the actual behavior and circumstances and situations surrounding their disruptive behavior. Instead, at least according to the youths' stories, administrators neither ask for explanations nor do they consider alternative responses.

"You Just Got to Go": Initial Responses to Suspension Behaviors

The process of suspension has multiple steps that can be likened to criminal justice system processes: *the arrest*—the breaking up of the incident;

the interrogation—the meeting in the principal's office; *the arraignment*—
including contact with parents/guardians, the preliminary disciplinary
response; *the trial*—the "superintendent's hearing," where the final *verdict*
is rendered; *the sentence*—placement in a disciplinary alternative school;
and *reentry*—return to mainstream school.

The first step in the suspension process takes place immediately after
a youth is caught or called out for the misbehavior (i.e., wandering the hall
without a pass, being disruptive in class, fighting). The youth is sent (or
escorted) to the office of the principal or other school administrator, where
a discussion may or may not take place about the child's alleged misdeeds.
Official school policy expects, but does not require, that the administrator
call the parent or guardian if the child is to be immediately excluded from
school, that is, sent home. The initial telephone call is to inform the parent or guardian of the problem and ask the parent to come to pick up the
child. The administrator will at that time notify the parent that the child
has been suspended for five days and will not be allowed back into school
until after the superintendent's hearing, at which time the final disciplinary outcome is determined.[1] The parent is told to call the district office to
set up a date and time for the hearing.

The students' stories of their experiences with this initial step in the
suspension procedure often varied considerably with official policy that
articulates a calm, professional, and somewhat informative approach. Surprisingly, not all incidents for which the students were suspended even
took place in school or on school grounds, demonstrating yet another way
that the once-separate spaces of street and school merge. There were four
such off-campus incidents among the kids I interviewed: one took place in
a park and the three others took place down the block from the school, but
off school property, per se. More disturbing were the stories where youths
were summarily sent out of school without a meeting in the principal's

1. These outcomes include a student's return to home school, his or her placement
in an alternative school, placement in a three-to-five program (typically a small group led
by one teacher that takes place in an alternative school after the regular school day is over,
hence the term "three to five"), or homebound. Homebound consists of a meeting with a
teacher off of school property in locations such as libraries or community organizations.

office or where such meetings sounded more like street brawls than disciplinary sessions. In general, these initial disciplinary encounters left the young people feeling disrespected either because of the treatment they were subjected to or because their version of the incident was disregarded.

Kendra's description of her immediate suspension from school was shocking and graphic:

> Well, I was walking back from dropping a notebook off from another class and I was going back up to one of my classes. . . . I had a pass and the officer took my pass and would not give it back, and he told me to go call my dad so I can go home. So I went into the sixth grade office and I called my dad. Then the principal—he's 6'2", 200 and something pounds, like 275 pounds, at least, so he's a big dude—so he comes in. He yells in the phone and tells my dad to get off the phone and stop calling and then hangs up on my dad. Then, they put me in handcuffs because I was throwing a fit because they hung up on my dad. They had the actual police officer come down and put me on the ground and put handcuffs on me. But then after he had me in the handcuffs, the principal came and sat on my back . . . so it made me cry even worse.
>
> (Kendra 2008)

Dissection of Kendra's description of the first step in what would become her yearlong suspension reveal subjects that are repeated by other youths. The first is the role of the school police in school discipline for what, at best, would have been a minor infraction of school rules. It is the police officer who stops Kendra and makes the decision to send her home. Second is the lack of credence given to the student: Kendra is not believed when she insists she has a pass. A third issue is the role of adults in escalating the situation. By disrupting Kendra's call to her father, the principal, expected to be the authoritative adult, enflamed the situation by adding to the thirteen-year-old girl's frustration. Kendra becomes emotionally distraught and in her own words, "throws a fit." The response to the child's out-of-control behavior is handcuffs and physical force applied by both the police officer and the principal.

Roland's story provides another example of the way that school administrators do not always follow school policy in their initial response to the suspension incident. Roland, who was suspended for trying to break up a fight on a school bus, was initially detained on the bus and questioned by two administrators. After the questioning:

> They [the administrators] took us [Roland and his brother] into the school. They talked to us both. They asked us to write a statement about what happened and how did everything happened. So after that they just sent us home.
>
> (Roland 2008)

I then asked whether the school had contacted anyone to pick them up. Roland responded: "No. They actually gave us bus vouchers to catch the bus home."

Other youths also said they were summarily sent home from school without any parent or guardian notification or opportunity to be picked up. In a few cases, the parents were either unavailable or had no working phone. In those instances, the administrator asked the student if he or she had another adult to contact. Rahsheem, for example, gave his aunt's number to call and then was sent home on his representation that it was his aunt on the telephone.

Damian's suspension is another example of how school authorities can escalate what might otherwise be a minor incident. Damian, too, was accused of wandering the halls without a pass and cursing at the school police officer who stopped and questioned him. He said he was never given an opportunity to tell his side of the story. Damian asserts that he had a pass, but before he could pull it out, the encounter with the police officer deteriorated into a standoff around notions of respect, which turned a minor incident into the more serious allegation that Damian threatened the cop.

Damian says that the school cop told him to "get my coat and leave [the school]." This is a violation of school policy, which requires that a school administrator (not a police officer) impose the initial suspension. Nonetheless, Damian was in the process of complying, but became angry when the officer followed him to make sure he was leaving the school. Damian's report (quoted in the previous chapter) suggests that he and the school officer became embroiled in a war of words, with the police officer challenging Damian and Damian responding in kind, as the culture of the streets seems to require. However, in facing down a police officer, Damian confronted an authoritative figure with the power to redefine his tit-for-tat response as something more sinister. As a result, Damian was charged with threatening a police officer.

The day after the incident occurred, Damian and his mother were called by a school who informed them of the five-day suspension and the hearing. He believes the school authorities (administrators, teachers, and police) treated him this way because of personal animosity, "I don't think they liked me. They don't like me." The opportunity to use discipline as a "teachable moment" is lost when the incident degenerates into a power struggle between Damian and the authority figure, in this case, school police.

Jalil, who was accused of pushing into a teacher, also said that he was never brought to the principal's office, but rather was just told to go home by the teacher. He then left the school, went home, and told his mother what happened.

The off school grounds incidents all involved fights between girls and all were broken up by police. One example of such an incident involved Donela, who was involved in a fight in a park area about a half-mile from her K–8 school. It involved other students and their adult family members. The fight was broken up by police officers assigned to the high school adjacent to her K–8 who were likely heading back to police headquarters at the end of the school day. Donela's description sounds very much like any street-level police encounter:

> Officer Savage [the school police officer] had us by the cop car. There was three—there was me and my two cousins, and the girl and her mother and father came by that time. And she was talking to [Officer] Thorne and Thorne was writing down her statement, and we was talking to Savage and he was writing down our statement.
>
> So we called my aunt and my aunt came to get us because my aunt only lives down the street from school. And my aunt came. . . . Then they took down our statements. My aunt was asking them what was

going on [and] asking us what was going on. We let her know because Savage was not paying us no attention. He wasn't even trying to hear what we had to say.

(Donela 2008)

Not being heard or listened to is a common complaint voiced by the youths interviewed. Even when the youth admits his or her involvement in the incident, they are dismayed that no school authority will listen to the contextual background of the situation, and so the opportunity to address the issue without a formal hearing is missed. Marla, at the time a high school freshman attending a west side school, was suspended for an out-of-school fight that took place near a middle school on the east side of town. At the root of the allegation was the assumption that Marla deliberately traveled from her west side high school to the east side solely to fight with another girl. Marla explained that she was considered the aggressor, since school officials believed that she purposefully went to the east side to provoke the fight. With annoyance and frustration, she tells me that she lives on the east side and in fact was returning home. Marla was not successful in her efforts to explain the circumstances surrounding the fight to any school authority:

They thought I went over there. . . . They thought I went from [my] school to that school and fought somebody. I'm like, "No, it didn't happen like that because I go over there every time I come from school. I get off the bus and go pick up my friends and we walk home together. . . ." I tried to tell them [the school administrators involved in her suspension] and they kept saying, "No . . . , we heard this and that." They just said, "You got to go." They wasn't even trying to, like, talk about it.

(Marla 2008)

Marla admitted she fought with the other girl; her admission was contextualized by the "she said, she said" background common to the fights between girls. According to Marla, the girl with whom she fought used to be her friend, but the two had a falling out when she heard that Marla was spreading rumors about her.

There may be many reasons that school administrators do not take into account the factors underlying student behavior. The personal authority of principals and teachers have been eroded with the advent of zero tolerance rules, automated disciplinary procedural requirements, and the increasing presence of law enforcement in schools (Devine 1996; Schwartz and Rieser 2001). It is not uncommon for teachers and administrators to believe certain students are bound for jail and therefore are not worthy of efforts to unravel what is really going on with them (Ladson-Billings 2001; Wacquant 2001; Ferguson 2000; Noguera 2003). Zero tolerance rules and the transformation of schools into high security environments discourage teachers and administrators from learning about the emotional lives of their students (Casella 2001; Robbins 2008). Given the powerful role of schools as social institutions, it is appalling that the new educational paradigm of zero tolerance dictates the pushing out of kids rather than creating opportunities and initiatives that would productively engage young people. Through the superficial and hasty initial responses to student misbehavior, schools instead keep pushing kids further down the pipeline.

"They Were Just Going to Tell Me Where They Were Going to Put Me": The Disciplinary Hearing

At [the hearing], they were just going to tell me where they were going to put me. I thought they were just going to let me go back to school at first, and then they told me, "No, you're going to Brig." When I heard that, I had, like, all the rumors that I had heard about Brig, like Brig's the worst school. Like at Brig you have to know how to fight. You got to fight people everyday, which had me worried . . . and in the hearing, I broke down in tears because I didn't want to go to Brig.

My dad tried to ask them to give me a chance to go somewheres else. He say, "I don't want my daughter going there. My daughter, can she go somewhere else?" And then I said, "Well I'm going to deal with it."

(Kendra 2008)

This statement was made by Kendra, the young woman whose suspension incident was precipitated by an accusation by school police that she was

traveling the halls without a pass. She ended up handcuffed and physically restrained by her principal.

The superintendent's hearing is the event that determines whether a
student can return to his or her home school, or will be placed in an alternative school. The process itself has many of the attributes of the criminal
justice system. It is governed by a hearing officer and takes the form of a
quasi-adversarial process. The hearing room was, at the time of this study,
located in a middle school on the outer fringes of the city and far from the
neighborhoods that account for the majority of suspended students. To
get to this location by public transportation typically requires at least two
buses and a short walk.

The accused youth appears with his or her parent at the hearing.[2] The
charges are presented by the principal or another school administrator.
Witnesses are called, usually limited to the adults who were involved in
the incident, such as the teacher, school police officer, or hall monitor.
None of the youths interviewed presented their own witnesses or character
references. The proceeding is formal and is tape-recorded. The process is
frightening to youth and reminiscent of their perceptions of police procedures, as revealed by Tanza's description of her suspension hearing:

> It [the hearing] was crazy. I was scared because I had never been to a
> hearing before. They closed the door and they got you speaking on this
> mic and they talking like you was in jail or something . . . because the
> lady, she got this big old thing. It's like a confession like when you see
> on TV, like when they have a confession tape. They have one of them.
> And I was, like, oh my God.
>
> (Tanza 2007)

The youths have varying expectations about the formal hearing. Some
expect that the hearing will finally provide them with an opportunity to

---

2. Youths can be represented by an attorney, but this is a rare occurrence. However,
youths can and do bring more than one family member and/or other person in their support system. For example, youths who participate in the Center for Community Alternatives program bring their "youth advocate" to the hearing.

tell their side of the story. They suppose or hope that their parents and guardians will advocate for them. Instead, they find themselves in situations where their voices are not heard, where their parents do not know what to say or do, and where they may not even fully appreciate what is happening to them. Marla says:

> So I go [to the hearing] the next week. My mom went and she don't know how to talk to people when it's in a situation like that. She don't know how to talk, so she just let them tell me where to go. She just say, "Okay, that's where you got to go."
>
> (Marla 2008)

Marla's statement about her experience is fraught with echoes of courtroom defendants who feel intimidated by the court actors—the judges, prosecutors, and even their own lawyers. Rayquan, who had been to court with family members, was explicit in comparing the superintendent's hearing with court procedures. In recounting his inability to get his side of the story considered, he said:

> It's just like court, once you go in there. The hearing is just like court. Pretty much you go in there, they overrule you, and they give you your time.
>
> (Rayquan 2008)

The youths in suspension hearings, like defendants in the criminal justice process, face powerful, authoritative figures who are typically from a different class and race. They are enmeshed in a system governed by complicated rules and impersonal bureaucracies over which they have no control. Like criminal defendants, the young people have little opportunity to speak for themselves in their own day-to-day language and do not think to call witness or character references. Donela, too, describes a formal and unfriendly process that quickly moves to its inevitable conclusion:

> Yeah, they put on a tape recorder and you talk about the situation that happened, and then at the end they tell you the end result and what's

going to happen. You either go back to your old school, or you take three to five for one semester, or you go to an alternative school. And mine was I went to an alternative school.

(Donela 2008)

Zeke, who had been suspended for talking back to a teacher, also expressed frustration and fatalism when I asked him if he was able to speak up for himself at his hearing: "Yeah. I got my little words in, but they still wasn't, they wasn't trying to hear that" (Zeke 2008).

Some of the youths thought that the decks were stacked against them in the hearing. Kendra and her mother just viewed the hearing as an event where "they were just going to tell me they where they were going to put me." Similarly, Carlos's mother wrote a statement trying to explain her son's behavior (he was involved in pulling a fire alarm) and asking that he not be suspended. Carlos concluded that that effort was futile:

> My mom wrote a statement and sent it back to them saying, like stuff that happened. Because I explained it the same way I did to Bovo [the police officer who caught the students]. But they had everyone else's side of the story.

(Carlos 2008)

Carlos, who was involved in the prank with the school fire alarm, continually asserted he was a minor player, a lowly participant with his group of friends, but not directly involved in pulling off the alarm mask. His reaction to being suspended is a mix of emotions—fear, shock, and anger:

> Well, I was really scared at first because I didn't want to get kicked out. I wanted to stay at Fordham [his mainstream high school] and do my stuff at Fordham and graduate. So when they told me that I would be kicked out of Fordham and go to Steel, I was like, "Wow. Why should I get kicked out if I didn't do something?" They was like, "No," because the other students (my friends) said that I was the one that pulled the mask and I really didn't do nothing.
> I said, "Why should I get in trouble if I didn't do nothing? I didn't pull the mask." They was like, "Because one person accused you." I said,

"I spoke to Officer Toro [pseudonym] and he understands." They was like, "Well, we don't know what's happening because they [the students] wrote a statement or a report and that's what happened." They said they had me on tape but I never got to see the tape. They just said they saw it on tape. They said they had pictures, but they only had pictures of me walking up the stairs and down the stairs. I asked to see the tape, but [the] officer said they didn't have the tape with them.

(Carlos 2008)

Carlos's story has many elements of a run of the mill criminal case: a police officer enticing leniency in exchange for cooperation, friends who become "snitches" in return for a more lenient sentence, prosecutorial evidence not made available to the defense, and inadequate advocacy. Carlos was accompanied to the hearing by his mother and grandfather, but when I asked him if they had spoken up at his hearing he simply said, "Not really."

Like Carlos, Jalil also felt that the hearing officer discounted his account of the incident for which he was suspended: "I was mad because teachers always believe other teachers over the child and they never want to listen to us" (Jalil 2008).

Jena, who was suspended for fighting with another girl, sounds like she was at sea during her hearing and was not able to effectively communicate her explanations about the suspension incident or advocate for the outcome she hoped for. She described her hearing experience with a nervous giggle as:

Kind of scary. I'd never been to one before. It was just . . . it was just like I was in there. The lady was nice, and then they had like a recorder and they recorded everything and asked why everything happened—why it happened and "Did I want to go to an alternative school?" Of course I didn't, but you know.

(Jena 2008)

Whether due to fright or the generally alienating process, Janella was disconnected from what was happening to her:

I'm not too sure. I don't remember much. I know she asked me if I did
want to go and I told her that I didn't. And I'm not sure what happened
next. I don't remember too much.

(Janella 2007)

When I asked her if she understood why she was placed in the alternative school, Jena initially said, "I'm not sure," but later hypothesized that an overall negative judgment about her, rather than the fight, was the cause of her suspension:

I think the reason why I got suspended, I think why they sent me to
SAVE was because, like, they looked at my attendance and, like, it was
my first year and I skipped a lot. And so they looked and said, well, she's
probably not a good kid.

(Jena 2008)

What is striking about Jena's story is the lack of consideration for her personal circumstances. Her entry into high school and increased truancy took place shortly after her father's death and coincided closely with her brother's murder. As with many of the young people I interviewed, Jena concluded that her exclusion from mainstream school was a rejection of her as a person, her humanity, and not just a response to a particular behavior. I talk more about the phenomenon of rejection in the next chapter.

The young people's description of the hearing process once again suggests missed opportunities. If the purpose of suspension is to teach kids the consequences of misbehavior, it seems that a quasi-legal proceeding is not the best setting to teach such lessons. Adolescents especially have difficulty in comprehending official proceedings (MacArthur Foundation Research Network on Adolescent Development and Juvenile Justice n.d.). The reasons are multiple: the developmental capacities of adolescents, the stressful nature of the processes, a lack of knowledge about their rights, challenges in communicating with their advocates, and advice or the lack thereof from their parents (Viljoen, Klaver, and Roesch 2005; Hazel, Hagell, and Brazier 2002). Matza (1990, 133) captures the essence of the situation: "Like

Camus' stranger, he [the delinquent] is frequently a mystified observer at his own trial. But he is aware of the outcome, the disposition."

Courts and the criminal justice system are forbidding systems indeed, but for the thirteen- and fourteen-year-old young people, a formal school hearing that determines their educational future is an intimidating experience as well. Suspension from school can have a profound impact on a child's future—his or her educational opportunities, employment prospects, and loss of freedom. With so much on the line, it seems critical to ensure that a child have an advocate to help make his or her case. While the school district policy does allow for an advocate of one's choice, few families in the district have the wherewithal to retain an attorney, and unlike the criminal justice system, this is not a right afforded to children based upon indigence. The young people I interviewed were all accompanied to the hearing by a family member (parent, stepparent, grandparent) who ostensibly served as the child's advocate. In a few instances, a caseworker from a community agency or probation officer was also present, but those were the exception. In no case was a child represented by an attorney.

Although most of the young people told me that their parent tried to speak up for them, they observed that their parents and guardians were no more effective than they were in representing their side of the story or preventing them from being suspended. This is not surprising given the parents' lack of social or political resources to challenge school authorities and the stereotypes that color schoolteachers' and administrators' view of parents of troubled children. In my work with the parents of the young people sent to alternative schools, I often noticed that parents react to school authorities based upon their recollections of their own marginalized and usually unsuccessful school experiences. These memories are compounded by their continued marginalized status as adults based upon race and class. In their school encounters, be they routine parent-teacher conferences, meetings prompted by some problem, or the more formal suspension hearing, they are often intimidated as well as angry, frustrated, worried, and confused. Karla's description of her mother's efforts to try to convince school administrators not to send her to Brig captures what often happens when parents try to advocate for their child:

Well, the hearing was like, I said to the principal, I was scared [to go to the alternative school]. She was like, "You don't have to be scared." So my mom told her that I used to have problems in Puerto Rico, too, with my father and he was in jail and at the same time they kicked me out of school. The principal, she was like, "I don't care." So my mom just said, "Okay."

(Karla 2008)

Damian was also accompanied to the hearing by his mother, who did not ask any questions during the inquiry. He said his mother attended the meeting so that she could "know what was going on," implying that neither of them thought they had any influence over the decision-making process and were instead present just to learn the verdict, which turned out to be quite confusing to Damian.

They didn't even call it SAVE. . . . They called something else. Umm . . . Institution Learning Center[3], or something like that. I don't remember what they called it. They said that it was going to help me.

(Damian 2008)

It was not clear to Damian that he was being sent to an alternative school until he arrived at the door. Although he was familiar with SAVE because his sister had been sent there, the hearing officer's use of the school's new name left Damian unaware that he was in fact getting placed in SAVE: "At first I was happy. I thought it was going to help me. But as soon as I got there and saw it was just SAVE, I knew it wasn't good." Damian felt betrayed when he learned it was SAVE, and based upon his sister's experience, he knew he would not get the help he was hoping for.

3. As noted in chapter 4, SAVE has been referred to by several names. SAVE and Steel are in the vernacular of students and parents. During one of the many reconfigurations of the alternative schools, the district renamed SAVE "the Renewal Academy at Steel." I speculate that this was the name that Damian heard during his hearing.

"They Don't Treat Them the Same": Kids' Views of School Rules and Fairness

> I was crying because I didn't understand that the fact that I was trying to help and do the right thing. But I still got to be suspended for five days and a formal hearing and serve time in Brig for just trying to do the right thing. It really hurted me because, you know, I was just trying to, ya' know, help. And it really hurted me that I really have to serve time just for my little brother.
>
> (Roland 2008)

This is Roland's response to my question about how he felt when he learned he was going to be suspended to an alternative school for what he believes was an effort to keep his younger brother from using a knife. It is one example among many about how the suspension process leaves young people with a profound sense of unfairness. A few of the kids felt that they were singled out for punishment while other compatriots or instigators escape sanction. Some of the kids believe they are victims of racism on the part of teachers and other school authorities. Still others, such as Roland, think zero tolerance policies themselves create a school system incapable of fairness.

Roland was aware of the district's zero tolerance policy that bans weapons of any sort from all school property, including the bus on which he was riding. He was at once resigned to his fate, but still confused by a system that could not understand the nuances of behavior:

> They literally had no choice but to send me to Brig because it [the knife] was in my possession. They [school administrators] said to me that they know I didn't do nothing wrong, but if my hand touches the knife then they have no choice but to send me to Brig, and that's how I got to Brig.
>
> (Roland 2008)

Despite this seeming acceptance and resignation about zero tolerance rules, Roland thought that his acceptance of responsibility coupled with his explanation about how he came to possess the knife would mitigate his punishment:

Well, no I, personally myself, you know I'm an honest person. I mean I'm respectful. . . . When we were talking [during the hearing], I actually thought that, you know, okay, thinking to myself, like, just stay calm, just talk, get it over and done with. But when they said that they were gonna, ya' know, suspend me, that's what had got me upset. I started crying because I didn't understand the fact that me getting suspended just for taking the knife away from him, because if I didn't take it away from him, it would have been, ya' know, a dead student.

So actually I thought that, ya' know, personally myself, I thought that I was doing the right thing by taking the knife away from him so the other student wouldn't be hurting, ya' know. . . .

I understand the fact that, you know, they said that, you know, if it's in my possession, if my hand touches it, then they, you know. I understand that, but I mean still it's the simple fact, I was only taking it away from him so he wouldn't use it on the other student. And if I didn't, understand, like I said, if I didn't take it away from him there would have been a dead student. So I think that personally, I shouldn't really have gotten, ya know, really, be serving time in Brig or shouldn't really have gotten suspended for something that, ya' know, I really was, I thought that I was doing the right thing. But to them, they told me that, ya' know, they knew I was doing the right thing, but still it's the simple fact that the knife was in my possession.

(ibid.)

There are several ways that youth perceive that the disciplinary and suspension process is unfair. A central theme, articulated by Roland, is school authorities' disinterest about the circumstances surrounding their behavior and their unwillingness or inability to adjust the punishment to comport with the underlying facts of the situation. The youths are usually willing to accept responsibility for breaking school rules, fighting, and other forms of misbehavior, but they also think that the disciplinary response should take into consideration what precedes the suspension incident. Their descriptions of the suspension process show that they do not believe they are given an opportunity to explain the entirety of the incident. They also resent the discounting or dismissal of their explanations. Because contextual factors are not considered, youths at times believe that the other parties involved in the incident escape without punishment, which also offends their sense of fairness. Punishment seems arbitrary and capricious. Karla, for example, does not understand why she was suspended while the other girl involved in the fight was allowed to remain in school:

> They didn't do nothing to her. They didn't send her to Brig. Nothing. She just went to school regular, like that. Because my friend told me that this girl still be in school. And I'm like, that's not fair. Why did I get suspended for five days and they don't do nothing to her? My mom said that wasn't fair.
>
> (Karla 2008)

Marla said much the same thing:

> I think they should have gave us the same thing. I don't think they should have gave me more days and the hearing and all that stuff, because it wasn't my fault. So they put it on me when it was supposed to be her. I didn't start nothing. She started it, so they should have just had her. I think it should have been the other way around.
>
> (Marla 2008)

Carlos's story expresses another way that young people find the application of suspension to be unfair. Carlos was suspended from school for breaking into a school fire alarm with a group of his friends. He admits to participating in the prank, but says he was not the student who pulled open the alarm box. He felt misled by the school police officer whom he thought had promised him lenient treatment if he cooperated.

> I think it's not fair because I didn't do nothing, but I had gotten in trouble for what other people said. And then I think, what I don't understand is why would I get in trouble? Because . . . Officer Bovo [pseudonym] told me if I was to cooperate that I wouldn't get in trouble, and I was just thinking about that the whole time. So when he said I wouldn't get in trouble, "The most you'll get is a suspension and a formal." So I thought

about it when I was suspended at home for those five days. Thinking about what happened to me. Did I get kicked out because a lot of people got kicked out? So when they told me that I would get kicked out and I would be sent to Steel, that messed me up right there. I didn't feel the same about school. I was thinking about dropping out and stuff.

(Carlos 2008)

Carlos said he was "horrified" to learn he was being sent to Steel (ibid.).

Jayda's story provides a good example of the youths' exasperation that accompanies administrators' inability or unwillingness to consider the circumstances of student behavior. She was suspended for fighting with a boy during her Spanish class. Jayda places this fight in the context of racial discrimination on the part of the teacher (whom she identified as a Cuban woman), as well as the ongoing dispute with the boy, and in the specific argument that preceded their fight:

The Spanish teacher—I just felt and other people felt she was prejudiced. So we had a lot of people in the classroom [who] felt like she was prejudiced towards us blacks, the Hispanics, and some of the Caucasians. So it was always a problem with me and that teacher. And then one time in that classroom, this Hispanic boy came into class late and I was sitting in his seat. We never had assigned seats. [But he said] I was sitting in his seat, so he got mad at me and she [the teacher] sent me out.

Then one time, the same boy, he always came to class late, he sleep in class, and he came to class one day and he told me get out his seat. I wasn't in his seat; it was the seat behind him. He just picked on me and this other girl, so I moved out his seat. He left the binder, his binder in the seat I was in, so he thought I was cheating on his paper. I asked him, "How could I be cheating on your paper? You're asleep. I'm writing down the notes from her classroom." So he got mad and he started calling me a black b and started disrespecting me saying, black girls are disgusting and they like to have so much kids and just was basically putting down black ladies.

(Jayda 2008)

Jayda said she told the teacher, but the teacher did nothing, instead responding: "'Senorita, just let him be' ('cause that's was what she used to call us, 'senorita')." In a moment, the simmering dispute became a fight:

> Then he like took a paper, like, and tried giving me a paper cut on my face. So I pushed the paper out of his hand and he punched me in my mouth and busted my lip. So, quick reaction, quick reflexes, I started fighting him back automatically. He punched me, so I started fighting him back and she kicked us both out. I got suspended for five days; I don't know if he got suspended for five days, too, but I'm the one who got kicked out to Steel alternative school and he stayed in Fordham [high school]—and he hit me first.
>
> (ibid.)

Jayda concluded that her suspension was unfair for many reasons:

> I thought it was unfair because he's a boy. I come to her class all the time, he always comes to class late and he's always sleeping and he don't participate and I always participate in her class. And I'm not Hispanic and I always try to learn it [Spanish]. So I felt like he'd come into class all the time, sleeping, and he don't do his work. I hand in my work. I do my work. Why should I be suspended? Plus, he's a male putting his hands on a female.
>
> (ibid.)

Jayda's sense of fairness is violated because she considers her behavior justifiable self-defense. She also believes that the teacher shows favoritism in allowing the boy to violate other school rules without repercussion while her efforts to conform to classroom expectations go unappreciated. Finally, she believes that the boy's violation of expected gender roles should have resulted in the boy being found to be the aggressor.

Jayda is not looking to avoid her own responsibility in the classroom fight. She does, however, expect the blame to be equally shared.

> I knew I was in wrong . . . and I knew that I could have handled myself in a different way. So I take blame in every part I did because if not, I

wouldn't be in that situation. So I took all the parts, every little thing that I took the blame for. But when I knew that I wasn't wrong, I didn't take the blame for it.

(ibid.)

Jena is also puzzled that she was the only party to be suspended. She thought it unfair and attributed it to teacher favoritism:

I think that we both should have got the equal thing. We both should have went to a hearing and, you know. . . . Like sometime it seems like they have favorites and stuff like that. And sometimes, you know, it's like that with some teachers, they kick kids out for, like, stupid stuff like coming to the classroom and as soon as you say something, as soon as you say one thing, like, you're out. It could be a silly thing, like you laugh or something and they kick you out.

(Jena 2008)

Karla had a similar complaint because the girl she fought with was not disciplined:

They didn't do nothing to her. They didn't send her to Brig. Nothing. She just went to school regular like that. Because my friend told me that this girl still be in school. And I'm like, that's not fair. Why did I get suspended for five days and they don't do nothing to her? My mom said that wasn't fair.

(Karla 2008)

I asked Karla what she attributed this unfairness to and she responded: "I think because she was white. . . . Yeah. Because most people are racist sometimes. It was Mr. Donahue (the principal), he was racist" (ibid.).

Karla's fight is unusual, since most of the fights between girls are same-race fights, which is not surprising given that the district is predominantly African American and that the fights take place between young women within the same social circle. However, almost all of the youths interviewed complained that the suspensions were one-sided, and that their adversary escaped punishment while they were suspended from school. As Donela's comments suggest, this perceived unequal treatment offends young people's sense of fairness. She asked the hearing officer:

> And why should I get sent to a bad school? (By that time he [the hearing officer] had told me that the girl [with whom she fought] wasn't going to that school.) Her's worked out so that she could go back to Shane in September. And I was asking why, when she started everything, when she called people up there to fight. Why can't she do three to five, at least get some consequences that I got?
>
> (Donela 2008)

Confusion about the hearing and the lack of effective advocacy contribute to a sense of unfairness about the suspension process, the outcome of the hearing, and ultimately undermine respect for school disciplinary policies. The kids' stories support prior research on the myriad reasons that zero tolerance policies are not effective (Skiba et al. 2006). Despite the intent of zero tolerance to mandate consequences for identified acts, the young people believe that it is inconsistently applied. They observe that their adversaries are not punished, that some students are suspended for minor infractions while others get away with similar deeds, and that some students are singled out.

As I listened to the young people, I was struck by how much their experiences were descriptive of a system that lacks the basic elements of procedural justice. In contrast, when defendants or plaintiffs believe that the system is fair and just, they are more likely to accept and respect a decision even if it goes against them. They are also more likely to abide by rules in the future (Tyler 1990, 2008). Thus, harsh suspension policies and procedures undermine long-term compliance with school rules. The suspension process as experienced by the young people interviewed seemed to teach them a counterproductive lesson, what Woolard, Harvell, and Graham (2008) have termed "anticipatory injustice," which engenders distrust in authorities and lower levels of rule compliance. Adolescence is a particularly important period for legal socialization, and negative experiences encountered during the suspension process have the potential of influencing future relationships with rule-making and enforcement authorities and institutions (Fagan and Tyler 2005).

In contrast, studies of restorative justice programs in schools show that they can more effectively manage school discipline problems by providing a space for both "victims" and "offenders" within the school community, by focusing on direct remedies to the harm caused, and by offering constructive ways of holding young people accountable. As all of the youths in this study acknowledged some measure of inappropriate behavior and recognized that they should not have behaved in such a manner, restorative justice could have been a mechanism to turn these incidents into learning experiences.

The zero tolerance culture that eschews consideration of contextual factors has not made school discipline any fairer than removing judicial discretion via mandatory sentencing has reduced disparity in the criminal justice system. It has, however, left young people frustrated that authoritative adults will not hear their explanations. Punishments that are perceived to be inconsistent and harsh undermine youth trust in teachers and connections to school. Rather than engendering norm conformity, youths who feel unsupported by teachers and school administrators are likely to reject and resist a disciplinary system that is believed to be arbitrary and unfair.

The suspension process is teaching young people that they live in a "black and white" world. Adults are in fact role modeling behaviors that show neither mercy nor wisdom. They are also perpetuating attachment to punishment. A good number of the youths were less concerned that they were suspended from school, but were outraged that their counterparts were not similarly punished.

The suspension process has come to resemble criminal justice system operations through the adoption of an incapacitation model, an approach that prioritizes removing and isolating so-called troublemakers to avert further problems, the racial profiling aspects of zero tolerance, and decision making that casts hearings as prosecutorial (American Bar Association 2001). The impersonal and formal enforcement of school discipline becomes another aspect of the "not-so-hidden curriculum" (Robbins 2008, 47) that inculcates students in poor, urban schools in the carceral culture.

As we will see in the next chapter, the carceral culture is made even more visible as the kids walk through the alternative school door.

"It's So Non-Regular"
Going to Alternative School

When you first walk in, you got to take your shoes off, you got to take your coat off. And a lady or a man searches through your coat and then you getting patted down by the other one. You get patted down just to be able to go upstairs to the metal detector. Then, at the metal detector you got to take your belt off, you got to take your shoes off, you got to take your coat off, and all your jewelry. And then you go through the metal detector and then you get wanded. Then they check your shoes and coat again. And then you put your shoes back on. And you're not allowed to wear nothing with no zippers like a hoodie. You can't wear a hoodie; you can't wear nothing with pockets except for your jeans. And you can't wear nothing with no hood on it. And your coat, you can't wear no coat.

—Celia

ALTERNATIVE SCHOOLS maintain discipline and order in ways that Foucault (1979, 141) terms "the art of distributions," which encompass physical, social, and administrative mechanisms. Urban schools have become spaces of domination and surveillance that shape students' perceptions of their own and their fellow students' dangerousness and otherness: "School space, then, can be read as strategies of (spatial) inclusion and exclusion" (Gallagher and Fusco 2006, 307). This well describes conditions that I have encountered over years of working with students in alternative schools: doors locked to late students, interested parents, and community members; extensive surveillance and security technologies; and chaotic school halls. As Gallagher and Fusco note: "Yet these practices and technologies are normalized, naturalized, and literally come

157

under the radar" (309), in essence describing the way that I and others had come to view a library bereft of books as unremarkable.

The kids were less inured than I and were more keenly aware of alternative schools as abnormal. Jayda recounted to me her impression when she first arrived at her alternative school:

> Well, it was an old, old building. It looked so old. I never knew it was a school. Then when I walked in and I see, like, this is the only floor. Then I didn't see no children in the hallway. I'm like, wow, nobody go here.[1]

Most of the students were wary about having to attend alternative school. Rumors about the school—its physical plant and lack of academics—left the kids frightened and nervous. Ironically, the youths had also heard stories warning them that alternative schools were filled with "bad" kids. However, several young people interviewed dismissed the characterization of their fellow students as violent or bad because they had friends or family members who attended these schools. My exchange with Celia shows how the youths rejected the stereotypes of their alternative school mates:

> I heard that the little rumor, the little stories: "Oh, the girls at Brig, they do this; they do that. . . . You look at them, they going to hit you." But, like, I wasn't worried about it because my sister went there, like my mom went there, my dad went there. Everybody went to that school. I already knew the people that was going there, so there was nothing to be scared about. Like, because at the time, my cousins was going, all the kids that live around my house go there. So I just knew everybody there already.
> (Celia 2008)

The kids were equally if not more concerned about having to acclimate to a new school, rather than the reputation of the students, themselves.

---

1. Celia's description was accurate: her alternative school was the former city library. While it was a beautiful building with an ornate entrance and large, impressive, high-ceiling rooms, it was ill-suited for classroom purposes.

These concerns are not misplaced: research on student mobility, a phenomenon of urban poverty where poor families change residences and therefore schools several times a year, shows that student transience negatively impacts academic performance, peer relationships, and school behavior (Smith, Fien, and Paine 2008; Kerbow 1996). Urban school districts, including the SCSD, have attempted to address these deleterious consequences by limiting the number of school transfers within a current year (Smith, Fien, and Paine 2008). The SCSD limits school transfers to three per year and justifies this policy as follows: "It has been determined that numerous moves at the elementary school level have serious negative effects on student achievements" (Syracuse City School District 2006, 35). However, assignments to alternative school settings are excluded from this transfer limitation policy. Nonetheless, the kids themselves recognize the disruptive impact on their lives as a result of the forced transfer to an alternative school. Shayna, for example, explained, "Like, the first day, I was scared 'cause I didn't know what it was going to be like and it was my first time there at a new school and I didn't really know nobody there" (Shayna 2007). Similarly, in response to my question about how he felt on his first day at Brig, Jalil said, "I was scared the first day . . . new school, different students. A lot of stuff. You don't know nobody there" (Jalil 2008).

Comments about being nervous about starting a new school and encountering new students were repeated by many of the kids. Jena explained that she was anxious "[b]ecause I was going to be at a different school. I wasn't with my friends anymore" (Jena 2008). Rosa says, "The first day, I was scared because I didn't know where to go" (Rosa 2008). Carlos describes how he felt: "I was really nervous because it was like starting the whole school year over again. So I didn't know who I was going to meet" (Carlos 2008).

Kids who were less familiar with alternative schools were worried about the overall environment. Donela explains it this way:

> The first few days I went to SAVE, at first I was like, "Oh, I can take it. I can take it, I'm tough. I ain't going to be worried about no kids." But when you get there, kids always got something to say. At first you brush them off. Then you get sick of hearing it all the time. And then you get,

like, "Oh my God, it's so cold in here. Are they ever going to turn on the heat? Never no heat."

[I heard] that it was a bad school, that you get checked every single day. The food is a mess.[2] The school is always cold and you can't wear a jacket. When I went there, that was the truth—everything I heard was the truth. Never nothing to do. It's so boring in that school and it's so non-regular. It's non-regular.

(Donela 2008)

"Ain't No Way Out": Space, Security, and Surveillance in the Alternative School

As Donela articulates, it is daily experience and not just the schools' reputations that cast alternative schools as prison-like institutions. For alternative school students, the school day begins with the penetration of a fortress-like institution, guarded by multiple layers of school security, including technology, personal intrusions, and constraining rules and regulations. Celia is not alone in complaining about the extensive searching that she undergoes at the beginning of the school day. The youths' comments about security levels reflect, on the one hand, the extent to which surveillance and control have been normalized in urban school settings (Gallagher and Fusco 2006), and, on the other, how levels of security and control in alternative school are considered excessive and likened to jail settings.

As students in an urban school district, the young people I spoke with have become accustomed to a certain amount of school security. All high schools in the district have metal detectors and these devices, as well as periodic random searches, were accepted by many of the young people as ways to ensure safety. Shayna even endorses metal detectors as "a good thing because, like, with a metal detector you can't have nobody like

---

2. One of the alternative schools, the refurbished central library building, lacked a cafeteria. One of the former reading rooms was transformed into a place where kids could eat, with food trucked in from another building. The kids often complained that by the time the food arrived it was cold.

bringing in weapons or nothing like that, so you won't have to be scared about nothing happening to you." Roland simply accepts metal detectors as "a part of life." Like the public in general, Shayna and Roland have internalized the message that schools are dangerous places even if this flies in the face of empirical data regarding conditions in their Syracuse schools. Metal detectors are intended to guard against weapons, particularly guns.[3] Only three of the youths interviewed were suspended for weapons possession, with one incident involving a youth who, when he realized he had neglected to leave his knife at home, turned it in himself at the start of the school day. Rather than weapons, the arguments between and among peers involved verbal taunts and fisticuffs.

The metal detectors do not prevent the kinds of violence most commonly experienced by these young people in school—fistfights between peers. Neither do the school metal detectors affect the more deadly violence that occurs in the streets or the structural violence attendant to the grueling poverty and marginalization of their lives. The young people are quick to tell me the kids who carry weapons (knives) do so for self-protection, and typically stashed these weapons outside the school. Yet these young people also accept the rudimentary security technology as "part of life." Metal detectors are part of the "meticulous rituals of power" (Staples 2003, 192) that allow for the routine and unquestioned acceptance of techniques of discipline and control.

However, when the youths reach the alternative school, they face tighter and multiple levels of security. These additional layers of searches

---

3. The New York State Department of Education includes the following in its definition of weapons: firearms (rifles, shotguns, pistols, handguns, silencers, electronic dart guns, stun guns, machine guns, air guns, spring guns, BB guns, and paint ball guns); knives (switchblades, gravity knives, pilum ballistic knives, cane swords, daggers, stilettos, dirks, razors, box cutters, metal knuckle knives, utility knives, or any other dangerous knives; clubs and related (billy clubs, blackjacks, bludgeons, chukka sticks, metal knuckles, sand bags, or sand clubs); sling shots or slung shots; martial arts instruments; explosives; firecrackers; deadly or dangerous chemicals (strong acid, mace, or pepper spray); imitation guns; ammunition; blank cartridges or "any other deadly or dangerous instrument" (New York State Department of Education 2008a).

are not accepted in the same way that many of the kids have come to tolerate the comparatively limited metal detectors of their regular schools. Instead, they describe the alternative school security measures as excessive and intrusive. It came as somewhat a relief to me to learn that the youths were affronted by the multiple layers of security in alternative schools even as they seemed to accept the relatively more constrained surveillance in mainstream schools.

Damian complains that in the alternative school, surveillance and security pervade every aspect of a student's life:

> Like, wear jackets—your coat with pockets. Like, in SAVE you had to take your shoes, take off your belt—they had to check you. You went through a metal detector, then they wanded you.
>
> (Damian 2008)

In response to my question about how that level of security made him feel, Damian responded, "Like in jail, like I was in jail" (ibid.).

Other students complained that even after they were searched and told to remove their jackets, they were followed to their lockers to make sure they locked up their jackets. Youths also complained that they were not allowed to carry book bags. The loss of jackets, sweaters, and sweatshirts were particularly troubling to alternative school students because the school was not well heated,[4] a significant problem in the cold winters of upstate New York. Donela's recollection of the school clearly captured the physical discomfort of being without a sweater or sweatshirt in the poorly heated building: "Then you get like, oh my God, it's so cold in here. Are they ever going to turn on the heat?" (Donela 2008).

---

4. Again, the refurbished library had large, lovely, high ceilinged rooms that were appropriate for reading and book stacks. This architecture did not translate well into classroom space: the rooms were large, making acoustics problematic, and it was very difficult to heat the building. I routinely kept my coat on during my winter visits to the library when it was still a library, and continued to need my coat when I went over to observe after school activities sponsored by my organization.

Donela's opinions about the level of security in the alternative school had a decidedly gendered aspect. She complained about the routine components of school security: "You had to take [off] your shoes, take off your belt. They had to check you. You went through a metal detector, then they wanded you" (ibid.). She went on to describe how this daily experience was demoralizing and uncomfortable for her as a young woman:

Every day you walk through there. As soon as you walk through the doors, you take your shoes off. They got to check your shoes and I'm like, what am I going to put in my sock? What am I going to put in my shoe? You take your shoes off, then you walk to the lady guard and she pats you all over. I don't like to be patted. I feel so insulted when I had to get patted down.

I told her, "Miss, please don't touch me because I don't like to get patted." And she talked to me. She had to probably talk to me every day because I always used to tell her, "Please don't pat me. I don't want you patting me." I could just walk through the metal detectors, but she had to pat you to make sure you had no cell phones. You can't bring nothing in that school and she had to pat you to make sure. I did not like that at all.

(Ibid.)

Several other young women I interviewed also made a point of telling me how much they disliked the pat down aspect of school security. Jayda repeated Donela's description almost verbatim:

At Steel, when you first walk in you got to get searched. Then when you walk, you got to take your shoes off. They pat you down. Then you walk up, then you got to walk through the metal detectors. Then after you walk the metal detectors, they got to wand you. I used to feel uncomfortable when they pat me down and go through this. I used to feel very uncomfortable when they touch me and stuff 'cause I don't like people touching me. . . .

(Jayda 2008)

The daily searches serve to actualize the metaphor of the "school-to-prison pipeline" for the young people sent to alternative schools. The kids well understand that they are in a jail-like setting. Here is what Jayda has to say:

> They treat you like you in jail. At Steel, they treat you like you in jail. When you walked through there [you go through] three searches in one day. That's not called for. When they pat you down, then you have to walk up through the metal detector and even if you don't go off, they still wand you. So I just feel like, wow, we're in jail.
>
> (Ibid.)

The layers of checking—the shoe and sock searches, the removal of jackets, jewelry, book bags, and hoodies, the metal detectors, the wanding, and the pat downs—make many of the young people angry, as reflected in this comment by Rosa:

> I was mad because all that just for nothing. If they search us, we don't have nothing there. Then we walk through a metal detector. Even though it don't go off, you have to have the wand go against you. That's too much checking.
>
> (Rosa 2008)

Janella describes even more intrusive searches that kids are subject to if the wand is set off:

> J: SAVE is like jail. You got to take off all your stuff when you get in there. You got to take your shoes off and get searched. Then when you go up the stairs, you have to take off all of your clothes, all your, like jewelry and stuff, and put it in this big old box. And then take your shoes off again and put them in the box. And then walk through the metal detectors and then you get wanded down. Then if you beep, they are going to take you in the bathroom and tell you to empty out all of your pockets. And then they move around and unzip your pants and all that stuff.
> M: Have you ever had to go through that?
> J: Yeah. It made me feel uncomfortable.

M: Why?

J: Because they had a lady touching on your butt and everything. They empty out your bra and stuff to see if you have any weapons.

(Janella 2007)

Janella's description of school security came close to resembling strip searches that prisoners are often subjected to. It also left me wondering how much instruction time—in an already shortened school day—was lost to these searches.

Donela explains that she "counsels" her peers to avoid behaviors that might get them into alternative schools because of the unpleasant nature of security, telling them:

[School police] officers [are] checking you every day. You don't want to get searched everyday you go to school. Why can't you just go to school one day and not get searched? At Shane [her home school], when we searched, all we got to do is bring our bags and put them down, walk through the metal detectors, and go ahead. At SAVE you got to get patted down, [and] walk through the metal detectors. [You] can't bring no gum, no candy, no nothing.

(Donela 2008)

Kwame said the security process in the alternative school made him feel "like they don't trust me or nothing" (Kwame 2008). Rayquan thought the security process was

[a]ctually setting kids up to go to jail and stuff. Basically, you don't really got no rights. Especially when you get to SAVE, because they make you take off your shoes and everything when you come through the metal detector. They don't just tell you to go through the metal detector, they wand you down. You got to take off your sneakers. Then, if they think you got something, they make you take off your socks and all that other stuff. And that's just like going to jail. Once you in there, you in there and there ain't no way out.

(Rayquan 2008)

Several of the young people were able to compare their alternative school to jail or prison because of their personal experience visiting relatives in these institutions, such as Jena, who visited her brother who was incarcerated in a juvenile facility: "He was at Louis Gosset, Jr. [the name of the facility] in Ithaca. And I visited him there. It's like being at school, going through a metal detector. You can't bring any food in there either" (Jena 2008).

Donela is even more explicit in describing that she finds jail visits distasteful because they remind her of the alternative school that she loathes:

> I went with her [Donela's sister] like three weeks ago and I said I feel like I'm walking into SAVE because they pat you down and do the wand, and then you walk through the metal detectors, and that's what I felt like when I was going to SAVE. They pat me down, wand me, then walk through the metal detectors. And I just say, "No." I feel like I'm going to jail or I feel like I'm going back to SAVE and I don't like that. I told her, I'll see him when he gets out of jail because I can't walk through them. That made me feel like I'm in SAVE and I don't want to think about that school no more.
>
> (Donela 2008)

The levels of surveillance and security applied in alternative schools affront even young people who have become inured to metal detectors in school entrances. The multiple levels of searches and the bans on typical student attire and accoutrements prisonize the alternative school in ways that are obvious to young people.

"I'm Scared": Perceptions of Police

Contrary to my expectations, the kids did not find police presence in alternative schools to necessarily be any more problematic than police in mainstream schools. My observations from interactions with various schools, both mainstream and alternative, reveals the role assumed by the officer, particularly with respect to traditional law enforcement versus counselor roles, to be largely a function of the individual personalities of the school principal and the police officer rather than the designation of the school.

The presence of police in schools has dramatically increased over the past decade. According to the National Association of School Resource Officers (2012), school police are the fastest growing area of law enforcement. According to the US Department of Justice, the number of school resource officers increased 38 percent between 1997 and 2007 (US Department of Justice 2007).

Yet, there is no standard definition of school resource officer (SRO) roles and responsibilities. Rather, the SRO function varies by district, and even within district by individual school. In general, SROs may perform four roles: traditional law enforcement; teacher (e.g., drug prevention curriculum); quasi-counselor; and public relations (e.g., "Officer Friendly"). A 2005 assessment of SROs conducted by the National Institute of Justice found that SROs spent about twenty hours per week on law enforcement activities, ten hours on counseling-type activities, five hours on teaching law enforcement-focused curricula such as D.A.R.E. (Drug Abuse Resistance Education), and the remaining six on "other" activities (Petteruti 2011). Along similar lines, in 2012 a "Triad Model of SRO" was articulated, which describes SRO roles to include "educator, informal counselor, and law enforcer" (National Association of School Resource Officers 2012, 21).

The factors distinguishing a police officer serving as an SRO from a "civilian" SRO may be clear within individual school districts, but are blurred with respect to using data to understand their impact. A review of the literature suggests that districts that employ SROs who are in fact police officers are more likely to have higher arrest rates. For example, in 1998 the New York City Department of Education (NYC DOE) ceded control of school security to the New York City Police Department. Parents and advocacy groups argue that this has displaced school administrator authority over school discipline and has increased school-based arrests (New York Civil Liberties Union 2007).

An even clearer example is the initial and subsequent response of school districts in Colorado in the aftermath of the Columbine tragedy. Colorado schools added more police as well as other forms of security and surveillance in school. The result was an increase in the number of students arrested in school, with most of the arrests associated with minor offenses. The Denver School District saw a 71 percent increase in school referrals to law enforcement, with most referrals to police for behaviors such as obscenities, disruptive appearance, and destruction of non-school property (Advancement Project 2005). After six years of effort, parents and youths in Denver who organized under the umbrella of "Padres y Jóvenes Unidos" were able to push for policies that rejected and abandoned the post-Columbine zero tolerance policies and limited the role of police in Denver schools.

The SCSD's articulated policy assigns the school principal the role of chief executive officer of the school. However, in some instances, principals seem more than happy to allow school police to operate without any accountability to them. In a meeting among the district superintendent, parents, community members, school police, and school administrators that followed the incident in Shane High School where a police officer punched out a fifteen-year-old girl, the superintendent was shocked to learn that the principal did not insist upon at least weekly reports from school police. The school police officers readily acknowledged that they routinely pull kids out for questioning about non-school-related issues going on in neighborhoods or tell kids to leave the school if they believe they are acting improperly (including wandering the hall without a pass). They believed it was part of their responsibilities. A school guidance counselor felt no compulsion against calling the police into her counseling sessions with students, believing that the officer could offer cautionary admonishment or help advise kids on family problems in ways that she could not. She did not consider that she was inadvertently violating student confidentiality or that she was putting the police in a position where they might be forced to make an arrest or further investigate the student or his or her family. Nor did she consider that the presence of a police officer in a counseling session might have a chilling effect on a student's willingness to confide in the counselor. Again, the superintendent was dismayed to hear these stories, but the principal seemed to be equally surprised that his deference to school police was not considered acceptable and pragmatic.

In the Shane High School case, the principal was willing to cede authority, particularly over student behavior, to the school police. However, another principal (actually the principal of one of the alternative schools) told me that she was sometimes uncomfortable with police behavior in her school and she tried to limit a particular officer's interaction with students. She bemoaned that she was powerless to do anything about it because she was herself intimidated by the officer assigned to her school. Wincing, she added that she would not want to meet up with him on the street.

While most kids interviewed eschewed police presence in school, this was not a uniform position. The kids' opinions about school police were colored by their experiences with cops on the street as well as their daily interactions with the officers in their respective schools. The variation in student opinions were not linked to the type of school (i.e., mainstream or alternative), and so I include youth opinions of their experiences with police in both types of school settings in this section.

Kendra's story shows the thorny issues entwined in school discipline: what school administrators do and don't do, what police do and don't do, and what the kids need. Kendra was initially suspended by the school police officer. She was aware that the officer was usurping the role of teachers or administrators. When she told me that she had been sent home by the school officer, I asked her how that was possible; I thought that suspension could only be ordered by the principal. She responded, "It should have been [the principal]. The administrator should have told me" (Kendra 2008).

Nonetheless, she was happy to be sent home to escape harassment from other girls in the school. Kendra and her mother had complained to the school administrator about the problems, but nothing was done to alleviate the situation. So she found the police officer's order to leave the school to be a relief: "Because what all the girls have been doing to me, like, going home was something to get away from the drama" (ibid.).

Shayna is another kid who feels that the police are the ones who respond to young people's needs:

Because, like, with a police officer, like, he was like different from the principals and stuff. Like, you could go to him and tell him a problem, then, like, he would do whatever he had to do to get rid of the problem. He make home visits and stuff, and make reports and stuff like that, and notify your parents and get your parents to come in and tell them the problem and meet with the other parents. So, like, the Officer, he was like a peacemaker.

(Shayna 2008)

The personality of the police officer influenced the opinions of youths and affected their interaction with the police in their school. Some kids felt more comfortable talking with a friendly, chummy school officer than with a teacher or guidance counselor. In these instances, the youths believed that the police officer was more aware of the real dilemmas of their lives. Jayda found the police to be caring and helpful:

But they on top of you. Like, if they see you skipping class or if you're going to the office, they don't be up on you, but they make sure that you're getting your education. Like that one cop at Steel, I like him cause he's, like, the person, if you're not disrespecting, he's gonna look out for you. And at Helmsley [her mainstream school], the lady cop . . . , she stay on top of you. Like, she always tell me and my friends, "I'm gonna see you guys walk the stage. I'm gonna see you graduate. I'm gonna be right here and I'm gonna see you guys graduate. And if you're not at Helmsley, I'm gonna make sure I see you guys graduate and encourage you."

(Jayda 2008)

Roland, too, felt that he had a personal relationship with school police that left him with a positive opinion:

It's like I know most of the security guards. Because I know most of them, ya' know, they cool. They just make sure that everyone is safe, that everyone gets to class and do what they supposed to do, that's all.

(Roland 2008)

However, not all youths are so receptive to police presence and do not see them as counselors or mentors. Again, this had much to do both with their experience with particular police officers in school and their more general experience with the police in their neighborhoods. My interview with Kora certainly exemplifies this. Kora was a student who was upset by the more extensive police presence in the alternative school. She explained:

> I'm scared. I'm scared of the policeman because at school, it's just so weird, it's not right. Ms. Wyatt [the principal] told them that I was scared of them. She came and found me. I was a little bit nervous when they [the police officers] came, but Ms. Wyatt and the hall monitors was holding my hand so they could talk to me. I didn't run. I was just very scared.
>
> (Kora 2008)

When I continued to probe about why the police frightened her so much, Kora explained that she had witnessed her mother being arrested:

> [It was] horrible, horrible because it was my mom that got arrested. We watched her get arrested. I was outside watching her in front of the apartment building. It was sad to see my mom get arrested.
>
> (Ibid.)

Kwame's opinion of the police in his alternative school was also influenced by his experience on the streets. I asked him what he thought of the police officers in Brig. He responded by describing what has happened to him both in the streets and in school:

> Like bad. Because you could be just messing with somebody and they acting like they arguing and stuff, and then a cop just come out of nowhere and grab you and grab you and stuff and start making slamming you on the ground and put their knee in your back and stuff.
>
> (Kwame 2008)

Rayquan did not distinguish between police in alternative school or mainstream school, but concluded from his experience with police on the streets that police presence in any setting is rarely helpful. He described a situation where his extended family was embroiled in an argument outside his house; a dispute that he thought was likely to be resolved by family members themselves. But, because everybody was out there, everybody gets caught up by the cops. Cops come out there and there's a big riot. Cops start shooting. I'm not for all that.

(Rayquan 2008)

Other youths pointed to the school police as having played a major role in the incident that resulted in their school suspension. These situations took the form of verbal or physical confrontations or, as Carlos described, being "set up" by police. Carlos believed that the police officer in the school entrapped him into a confession in exchange for a promise of leniency that was never received.

Officer Bova [pseudonym], he was talking to me about stuff. He told me if I told them stuff about the thing [pulling the mask from the fire alarm], he's not going to have to put my name in it. He said if I told him what happened, I wouldn't get in trouble, but I ended up getting kicked out of Fordham.

(Carlos 2008)

Karla is less critical of the police in school, but nonetheless, spoke about experiences that seemed to cross the line of propriety:

The policeman, he be talking mad Spanish, like bad words. I'm like, "Mister, where you learn that?" I'm like, "That's bad." He knows what he's saying because one time, I was opening my locker, he was like, "Move your *culo grande.*" That means move your "big ass." I'm like, "Mister, what's that?" He be like, "I don't know," but he then started laughing. He play with us like that because we show him, like, new words in Spanish, but not bad words. I don't know where he learned that. He thinks he's funny.

(Karla 2008)

There is a tremendous gap in how the kids and parents from inner city neighborhoods see the police, and how teachers and school administrators view them. Again, the meetings following the police-student altercation at one of the city's high schools starkly set forth these demarcations. The parent group, mostly African American mothers, complained that their kids were being criminalized in the streets and in school. While careful to acknowledge that not all police were racist or out of control, parents argued that police profiling and misconduct were commonly experienced by their children. The predominantly white school staff disagreed. In contrast to the parents who pointed to historical and structural problems in police relations with African American youth, school staff thought that police misconduct was an exception representing just "a few bad apples." The superintendent expressed his opinion that since 9/11, school boards, parents, and students across the country support giving police wide latitude to quell potential violence. However, the next superintendent of the district complained that school police heightened teacher fears and encouraged profiling of students by sharing gossip and innuendo about certain students and their families. She noted that a police officer in one school would tell teachers and school administrators stories about certain students being involved in street crimes, including shootings that occurred over the weekend. The superintendent found herself having to reassure school staff that if there was veracity to these allegations, the kid or kids in question would have been arrested.

One officer's name repeatedly came up during my interviews with youth. Prior to my conversations, the name meant nothing to me. However, the frequency with which this officer was identified as a problem made me remember his name—Savage (again, a pseudonym). It was surprising how many of the kids mentioned Savage either as directly responsible for their suspension or simply as a bully in the school. Janella complains that Officer Savage is "in her business": "But to that Officer Savage, he think I am just so bad and he got me all wrong." Damian told me that Officer Savage was always reminding him that, "Any wrong thing I do I'm getting kicked out and sent right back to SAVE" (Damian 2008).

Donela identified Savage as the officer who reported her off school grounds fight that resulted in her suspension, and who disregarded her explanation of the factors that precipitated the fight, i.e., "her side of the story." She concluded that Savage stereotyped her. Despite years of complaints about Officer Savage by many kids, it took the breaking of the nose of a fifteen-year-old student to get him removed from the school.

I subsequently learned two particularly interesting pieces of information about both the placement and removal of Officer Savage. I was describing the events to a local civil rights attorney who had undertaken many local police brutality suits; he was amazed to learn that Officer Savage had been placed in a school setting at all, since he was frequently a defendant in those police brutality suits. The second piece of interesting information was told to me by the superintendent himself, who shared that his relationship with the Syracuse Police Department was in jeopardy since he demanded that the department remove Officer Savage from the school in question.

"You Really Wasn't Learning Nothing": Student Views of Alternative School Curriculum

> They really don't do nothing in Brig. Like, we all used to just walk out of the class, go play through the hallways, run up and down the stairs, and we never used to get in trouble. So nobody really cared. And in Brig, they was passing you anyways. So, like, nobody really cared, but you wasn't really learning nothing.
>
> (Celia 2008)

Celia's description of her alternative school experience unveils a fundamental abdication of the schools' responsibility to educate. While many of the young people commented positively about the smaller class size in the alternative school, none thought they were learning much. Most considered the academics to be "easy" and worried that the lack of a rigorous curriculum would set them back when they returned to mainstream school. Jena contrasted the academic work in alternative school with regular school, saying, "It was different. It was easier. We didn't get a lot of homework. Like maybe a couple of worksheets. It wasn't a lot to do. I think it was pretty easy the work" (Jena 2008).

Carlos appreciated that the smaller classes in alternative school allowed him to get help with his work, but, like Jena, thought the alternative school curriculum was easy and boring:

Well, I think the work over there at Steel is very easy. I think one thing that's good at Steel is that it's a small school. There's not that many problems or nothing like that. But everybody gets their undivided attention. Like, if they ask for help the teacher comes to them and helps them. That's the good thing. The bad thing is, like, it's too dull. Like, nothing happens there. It's what I've already done in regular school.

(Carlos 2008)

Rosa told me that the word among students was that alternative school was not about education, it was about behavior. She found this characterization to be true based upon her experience:

My sister's friend, she told me about how it was like, you don't got to do the work, really. Teachers just want you to sit down and be quiet and stuff. . . . When I went there [Brig], it was like we didn't learn anything, just like she said. . . . Math was the most place that we didn't get work. He'll [the math teacher] teach us stuff that we learned in seventh or eighth grade. And not high school level like you're supposed to be learning. He'll just, like, do this or then mostly we'll do Sudoku puzzles or stuff like that.

(Rosa 2008)

While Kendra also liked the smaller classes, she was no longer able to participate in the college preparatory program that was available to her in her mainstream school. She rued the loss of this opportunity:

I think it's better than a regular school because I like the smaller classes. You get that one-on-one attention and the teachers understand you. But we don't get advanced classes there [alternative school].

(Kendra 2008)

When the kids commented favorably on the alternative school, it was in appreciation of the small class size and not the curriculum. Donela, for example, compared the attention she was able to get through the smaller alternative school classes:

[At] Shane [her mainstream high school], the teachers—you have to understand that they have, they can't pay attention to only you because, like I told you, they got nineteen or twenty other students to pay attention to. But at SAVE, it's only like nine people in your class and that even if everyone comes to school, they can pay attention to you. They can spend some time helping you, making sure you understand. Where the teachers at [mainstream] school, they could explain it maybe once or twice at the most, and then after that you're on your own.

(Donela 2008)

Jalil however, offered some troubling insights into how the smaller classes are achieved:

The kids, either they got sent out or they sleep. So it was easier for me to get my work done.

(Jalil 2008)

Jalil's observations conform to my experience visiting alternative schools and the stories that are told to me by my staff who work in these schools on a daily basis. Moreover, Jalil's remarks do not take into account the very high truancy rates that are characteristic of the alternative schools. So the small classes, an aspiration of many teachers and school districts, are achieved in alternative schools through a combination of truancy, suspension from class, or students sleeping in class.

The students also complained about the short school day. Rather than being glad that they had less time to spend in school, they realized they were being shortchanged, as Rosa's comments reveal: "And we get out early. So we got out like an hour before regular kids got out. . . . I don't think that was right because we barely learned anything and then we have to leave school early" (Rosa 2008).

Rosa was critical of the alternative school program where the school day is shortened by one hour. Some students lose even more academic time if they are sent to what is called the "three to five" program, which, as its name suggests, provides only two hours of school in the late afternoon. One of the school principals explained to me that students are sent to "three to five" for one of several reasons: to separate students who are believed to be in rival gangs, as a punishment for acting out in alternative school, or to alleviate an overflow at the alternative school. Donela ridiculed that program:

> I can't learn nothing in two hours that I could learn in six hours that I go to school for. I can't learn in two hours. They shoving a bunch of papers in your face and you supposed to do it in two hours because your time is up at five o'clock. When, instead, I could go to school at eight o'clock and I got until three o'clock—you know how much I could learn in them whole bunch of hours? What I can learn in two hours? I can't.
>
> (Donela 2008)

Jayda, who also spent time in three to five described it as "boring" and noted that there were never more than six students in attendance at any one time.

Rayquan summarizes the contradictions experienced in going to alternative school:

> In some ways it's good, better than other schools, because you get one-on-one. Then on other occasions, you know what I mean, it's not good because it's hurting your education. Even though you don't get one-on-one in regular schools, you get farther; you get like, more knowledge.
>
> (Rayquan 2008)

The sensibilities of these young people about the impoverished academic curriculum at their alternative schools belie the more commonly held notions that kids at the margins of education are cavalier about their education. To the contrary, many of the young people were both aware and concerned that their placement in alternative school would undermine their education. They were cognizant that the curriculum in alternative school is weaker than their regular school and that academics take a back seat to the fundamental warehousing purpose of these schools.

The youths' criticisms about the academic curriculum comports with research findings. A national telephone survey of directors of alternative education programs found that the directors most often described their schools in terms of discipline and behavioral change rather than educational curriculum, and success was measured by behavioral compliance rather than academic achievement (Lehr and Lange 2003). Foley and Pang (2006), in their survey of alternative school directors in Illinois, also questioned the quality of alternative school curricula in what they called "hand-me-down schools."

> General education curriculum was the predominant curriculum provided to students attending alternative education programs. However, lack of academic supports (e.g., science labs, computer labs, libraries) may suggest the integrity of state learner standards and academic expectations are being compromised for these youth.
>
> (Foley and Pang 2006, 18)

The pedagogical practices encountered and described by youths in alternative schools show that the kids are disconnected from content and/ or from the meaning of the subject matter. While none of the kids used expressions such as "more student-centered, culturally relevant pedagogy" (Ladson-Billings 1994), their comments indicate that they sought greater meaning in their classroom course work. The so-called lessons take place largely through the completion of handouts or worksheets. The measure of academic success is one's ability to complete and turn in these handouts. There is little description of the subject matter and the substantive information learned. The youths did not talk about why the work was assigned, its relationship to the course as a whole, or its significance. The image that came to mind was of students churning through meaningless tasks devoid of significance or relevance to one's thinking about the world. My discussion with Jalil is one example of the kids' detachment from the content of learning and the meaning of the subject matter:

> M: Tell me about your schoolwork. What do you think about the
>   work they give you in school?
> J: It was easy. Most of it is easy.
> M: Is it interesting? Do you find it interesting?

J: I just do it.

M: Is anything especially interesting to you?

J: It's not hard. There's nothing to do. It's just work.

(Jalil 2008)

Celia gave a description of the work in her English class, which brought to mind a tedious and unimaginative environment: "Now, like this week, we wasn't reading a book, we was just doing, like, little worksheets about capitalization, words, grammar, and stuff" (Celia 2008).

My conversation with Rayquan was especially depressing. When I asked him about his favorite subject, he told me:

> [I] [u]sed to [have a favorite subject], but now it's like, I don't really got no favorite classes. What do you need a favorite class for? I mean, you just go in there and do your work. Let it be that. Science used to be my favorite subject. This was, like, in elementary school, but now that I'm older, like, what you need a favorite subject for? I mean, just go to school and do what you can.
>
> (Rayquan 2008)

"I Go to School Because I Need My Education": Youth Appreciation of Education

School disciplinary practices and suspension in particular relegate kids to the margins of public education. Suspension classifies these kids as throwaways and permanent suspects who must be subjected to extensive searches to prevent what adults expect to be dangerous behavior. Over the years of working with kids in the alternative schools, I have heard administrators and teachers assert that these kids and their families do not value education. My interviews, however, suggest that we are missing opportunities to engage these young people. The young people sharply realize that they are being cheated out of an education when they are sent to schools that have a shorter schedule or give them "easy work." It matters to them as these many statements show:

[From Shayna:] To me, I like school because it's, like an education and that's something you gonna need.

[From Donela:] I know that when I get older I want to be something. . . . I want to be something. I want to make something of myself when I get older. And I feel that the only way that I'm going to be able to do that if my work is in and make sure that I got a passing grade. If I don't have that, what am I going to make for myself? Nothing. When I was in ninth grade last year, I did this program called LPP and we wrote to different colleges telling them how they should recommend us. And so many colleges are writing me back right now. I got so many papers at home and I'm going through the brochures and I'm looking at everything because I want to choose the right college that's really going to help me do what I got to do. I got a few colleges put up that I'm really going to write back and mail to because they brochures are really good. So many colleges want me to visit them this summer and I'm thinking about getting me in there to visit them.

[From Jalil:] I ain't going to quit school because I failed. I'm still moving on. I want to be a designer and to get there, I need to graduate from college and high school.

[From Jena:] I'm going to make sure that I graduate because I got goals and I got plans in life. I don't want to drop out and can't get a decent job. I want to be able to graduate. I am going to graduate even if I have to repeat the tenth grade three times; I'm gonna graduate and make it so I can have a high school diploma where I can go and get me a nice job. So if they gonna say, "you not going to make it," I'm gonna prove to them that I am going to make it. So, yes, I'm going to graduate from high school and I'm going to make sure I go to college and graduate from college.

[From Kendra:] I liked everything about Grant [her former school]. . . . Like, when I was also at Grant I got to do the extra classes. I had band and I was about to get into Spanish and I was going to get into AVID and I was going to have all these advanced classes. Then they were going to put me, like, in eighth grade classes. They were going to take away some of my seventh grade classes and put me in eighth grade classes.

[From Kwame:] Because I want to go to regular school. I know that at a regular school I have more chances of either getting scholarship so

I can go to college. I want to be a better student so I can go to college and stuff, so that I can get my family out of a bad place. I go to school because I need my education. I got to go places.

[From Rayquan:] I'm going to graduate so I can go to college. Even though I've been to SAVE and stuff, you know what I mean, I'm going to make it seem like it was nothing. People going to doubt me, but I'm going to try. And I know people that have dropped out. It's a shame.

[From Roland:] I love school. It's been plenty of times where ya know, I literally walk to school. There's been times where I rode my bike to school. People will, like some people, really be proud of me to actually see me walk to school or see me riding my bike. They say that if you walk to school or if you ride a bike to school or anything just to get to school, that actually shows that you really want to be there, that you really want to learn and want an education. I need an education. I don't want to be out in the streets and being dumb and don't have an education, don't know how to count, don't know how to do math and do certain things.

(Shayna 2008; Donela 2008; Jena 2008; Kendra 2008;
Jalil 2008; Kwame 2008; Rayquan 2008; and Roland 2008)

These statements are painful to read when juxtaposed to the physical, social, and educational exclusion that is imposed on these students in response to perceived and real misbehavior. Although they do not use the words of academicians, the kids' comments reveal that they well understand that without an education, they will become superfluous. Their appreciation and yearning for schooling and an education comes forward even as their works, grammar, and expressions demonstrate that they have already been shortchanged by the educational system. They tell me they "need" their education in order to become "something," in order to avoid being "out on the streets and dumb." Unfortunately, in the era of zero tolerance and mass incarceration, there is little public will to figure out how to translate the students' articulated commitment to education into reality.

The suspension segment of the school-to-prison pipeline begins with school authorities' responses to student behavior and misbehavior. It continues through the hearing and entry into the alternative school itself. There are common threads running through each piece of the suspension process—disrespect by peers or teachers, administrators, and school police that trigger or exacerbate student misbehavior; a zero tolerance philosophy and policy that makes it unimportant for school personnel to look for explanations for student behavior; responses other than school exclusion; and the stigma and labeling that attaches to each step along the process.

These students are identified as troublemakers early on in their school career, and the label becomes a self-fulfilling prophesy. The suspension process reinforces messages they believe they hear—that they are "bad" and of little value. The corrosive impact of suspension on the personae of youth is what I turn to next.

9

"We Have a Mike Tyson Here"

Labels, Rejection, and Stigma

[My suspension hearing was] horrible because of the things that they were saying. I thought in my mind that, you know, the things that they were saying, they was actually trying to make me look like, you know. I thought in my mind, that they were actually trying to make me look like I was a bad kid. They were actually trying to make me look like, you know, like I was a nobody. And so I was mad about the hearing, because, you know, I thought that they literally tried to make me look bad for real and it was horrible.

They were all talking about how I don't go to school, which I'm in school every day. They were talking about how I don't go to class, which I'm in class every day. I don't do my work, which I do. They was just trying to make me look like I was a bad kid, like I was literally a nobody, and that hurted me too.

—Roland

THE MOST DISTURBING COMMENTS I heard during my interviews with the kids were comments like those of Roland above, who perceived his suspension to be a rejection or dismissal of his essential humanity. The experience of public punishment sends powerful messages to youth about their value, about humiliation, and degradation, invading their sense of worth. The suspension process conveys a clear sense of how other authoritative entities see them.

The kids heard the authorities were suspending them because they are "tired" of them (a comment made by several youths—Kwame, Tyrel, and Jalil) or because he or she is "not a good kid," a conclusion reached by Jayda:

183

I went to the hearing with Ms. Richard[1] [a hearing officer] and . . . and she said she looked back on my records and she said, "Well, you came here a lot of times for fighting and stuff." I politely said, "Well, today this time, I don't know why should, I don't know why should I be here." We got onto the hearing and she put me into Steel for I think until January to January. The lady [Ms. Richard], she really didn't know me, but she seen my prior things coming from Brig and stuff, so basically it put out that I was a troubled child.

(Jayda 2008)

Jose, who was suspended for cursing out a teacher and throwing a pen[2] that hit a locker, reached a similar conclusion, telling me in a matter-of-fact manner:

And they didn't like me. The principal at Baines [his mainstream school] didn't like me. They was trying to do anything to evoke me to get in trouble. They wanted to hurry up and kick me out of their school. He [the principal] thought I was a bad kid.

(Jose 2008)

Children who are considered outside the social and behavioral norms of the school are stigmatized as troublemakers and dangerous (Casella 2003; Bowditch 1993). My interviews with youths show that they are well aware of how they are labeled. The messages they receive from the suspension process (as well as their prior school experience) impact their personal and cultural identities.

The kids perceive suspension to be a mechanism to get "rid of" them. Rayquan (2008) appears to accept this as part of the way that schools approach misbehavior, i.e., the deterrent ideology that is infused in zero tolerance policies:

1. Richard is a pseudonym.
2. This recalls Rayquan's (2008) previously quoted comment noting that anything can be a weapon, even a pen or pencil.

So now they [school authorities] say, "We have to get rid of you now because if we let you go back here, all the other students is going to look at us like yo, they just let him back in," and such and such. So it's not really a choice now. It's just, "you got to go."

Jena, too, thought that her "record" of poor attendance branded her and doomed her to out-of-school suspension:

When I went to the formal hearing, I think the reason why I got suspended, I think why they sent me to SAVE was because, like, they looked at my attendance, and, like, it was my first year and I skipped a lot, and so they looked and said, "Well, she's probably not a good kid."
(Jena 2008)

I then asked Jena how being thought of as "not a good kid" made her feel. She responded that it was

. . . pretty upsetting because I know that's not me. But, you know, there's nothing that I can do about what people think.
(Ibid.)

Kwame also took his suspension to alternative school as a classification of himself as a "bad" kid. When I asked why the school authorities suspended him, he said:

It was probably giving me a message saying, probably saying, Brig is a school for you and Brig is a school for bad kids. . . .
(Kwame 2008)

Rayquan summed up the message he got when he was suspended to Brig:

It makes people feel like they can't do nothing with their life. They just drop out. I went to an alternative school, ain't nobody gonna want to take me. If you write Brig on your thing, the schools you went to, they

look up your record . . . you might not even get into college. People hear
that you been to Brig, they gonna doubt you.

(Rayquan 2008)

Tyrel's experience with his math teacher, who suspended him, shows
how school discipline can sometimes be meted out because of guilt by
association. Tyrel is convinced that she (the teacher) did not like him
because of his family:

> She had my father and, like, one time we were sitting in class and she
> really got upset with me and she said I'm going to be like my father. And
> right now my father's not with me. Right now he's in jail and she said
> that I'm going to be like him. And after that—she was like one of my
> favorite teachers—but after that, every time I look at her, I'm like, she
> doesn't like me. She thinks negative about me. She thinks I'm going to
> be nothing.
>
> (Tyrel 2008)

Tyrel told me that this particular teacher repeatedly sent him to the principal's office. Both Tyrel and his mother appealed to the principal to transfer
him into a different math class, to no avail, even though the principal
seemed to be aware of the teacher's negative attitude:

> She [the math teacher] just kept kicking me out of her class and stuff
> because she doesn't like me, and the principal's been ripping up the
> referrals and stuff. And then he [the principal] just got tired of me, just
> keeping getting in trouble by her. I try to explain myself. . . . I was ask-
> ing, "Why can't you just switch me?" and he's like, "I can't do that, I
> can't do that." So I guess he kind of, he was trying to help me, but. . . .
> He was kind of . . . I don't know what he was doing . . . so yeah, I told my
> mom about it and then my mom called them and they had a meeting.
> And after that, she [the math teacher] really did not like me for nothing.
>
> (Tyrel 2008)

Eventually the teacher was successful in having Tyrel suspended after he
grabbed his MP3 player back from another student:

So then she wrote a lot of bad comments about me at the hearing and it made me look like I was a bad person, which I'm not.

(Tyrel 2008)

The teacher's attitude made Tyrel feel

. . . bad a little bit, but I wasn't going to let her put me down because I know for a fact that I'm not going to be put in jail. My life might be a little messed up right now but I'm going to get it together as soon as I get back in a regular school. I'm going to get it together. I'm not going to be like my dad. I mean, my dad's not a bad person. He just made a mistake. I feel really mad about that because, first of all, I'm not a bad student and she knows that I'm not a bad student. And she knows that my dad's not a bad person, he just made a mistake. So I was kind of upset but there's nothing I can do because she's a teacher and I'm a student.

(Tyrel 2008)

Tyrel's status as a child of an incarcerated parent leaves him more stigmatized, rather than supported. He is put in a position to have to distance himself from a parent he loves, yet stand up for that parent. He is given a lesson in powerlessness when his mother's advocacy causes his teacher to become even more disagreeable to him.

I asked Kwame what he felt about being in a school that was identified as the school for "bad kids." I am touched by Kwame's answer and his will to reject this label:

. . . Brig is a school for kids that don't know how to make the right choices, and kids who don't know what they going to do with their lives and just be bad in school for no apparent reason and get in trouble all the time and all that stuff. I don't think that I belong there . . . , because I want to go to regular school. I know that at a regular school I have more chances of either getting scholarship so I can go to college, or going to college instead of not going to college and not try to help my family to get out of a bad place. I want to be a better student so I can go to college and stuff so that I can get my family out of a bad place. The only thing I have in my life is my mom and my brothers and my sister. And if I lose my mom, then I lost everything and I'm not trying to lose it.

(Kwame 2008)

I felt encouraged to hear young people like Kwame resist being labeled as a throwaway or superfluous kid. Damian also offers moving insight about the damage created by adult insensitivity to how being kicked out of school is interpreted by kids:

I used to feel worthless . . . because teachers used to tell me that and junk. Like when you feel bad already and they tell you that you need to do this or you ain't going to be nothing. You going to be like a gang member. You going to be in jail or dead. That makes you feel worse. And I think that's what makes kids drop out of school faster and start gangs and stuff.

That's why a lot of young kids like my age don't care. They just want to make money and all this other dumb things. Just to prove a point that they aren't worthless. I think that's what they feel.

(Damian 2008)

Damian attributes his ability to counter feelings of worthlessness because of his bond with his family:

I used to feel like that, but I don't no more. I don't care [about being labeled worthless] after I promised my mom. I didn't care. Because I promised my brother [who did time in jail] that I'm going to stay in school. I promised my mom and my brother. . . . She said she wants— out of all her students, I mean out of all her children—she wants to see one of us with a diploma. I know I'm going to be the one. Like when I was younger, I used to be embarrassed to ask for help. Now I don't care. I don't care what nobody says about me. I'm trying to do, like graduate school. Get out of school. Trying to get a high school diploma.

(Damian 2008)

While listening to the kids try to wrest their self esteem from the assaults that bombard them with messages of their worthlessness, I was of course inspired by their efforts to repel these attacks. Upon reflection, however, I wonder how successful they will actually be. From my work with incarcerated and formerly incarcerated people, I know firsthand that these relentless messages, both verbal and material, take a toll that often leads to addiction and mental health problems, conditions that are often criminalized when manifested in poor people. Moreover, I was always struck by the extent to which the kids thought it was their sole responsibility to change how adults see them, and up to them to change the conditions of their behaviors. I often ended the interview, with the tape shut off, compelled to remind them that they were still children, in the best sense of the word. I could not help but commenting that as children they had the right to be treated with respect, cared for, and nurtured. At the end of the day, my words were unlikely to make a real difference, but I simply could not refrain from saying them.

"It Says on Your Record": Suspension, Stigma, and Reentry to Mainstream School

The young people knew that these negative labels followed them even after they served their time in the alternative school. Their stories again reminded me of the people who come into my office after being released from prison facing exclusion from employment, education, housing, and civic participation long after they have served their sentence. For example, when she returned to regular school, Donela had to again interact with the school police officer who was involved in her suspension. She knew he had a negative opinion of her and thought of her as a "bad girl." As described in chapter 8, Donela feels that she is placed under constant police surveillance in mainstream school because of her prior suspension history. But the negative labeling goes beyond the harassment that one feels under close scrutiny: it cuts to the core of a person's identity. Donela conveys profound despair when she complains that she is judged by her past record. She wants the officer (and other school staff) to know her as more than just a girl who was in a fight. She wants to be known as she describes herself to me: "I'm a good girl."

Jayda had a similar experience when she returned to her regular school after a year in the alternative school:

As a matter of fact, at Grayson, one of the administrators, he looked at my paper [and said], "Oh, so you came from Brig. What did you do to go to Brig?" I told him, fighting. "Oh, so you're a fighter," he said, and I said, "No I'm not a fighter." He said, "Well, it says on your record you're a fighter." And I said, "Well I'm not. That was just that one time." Then he would always see me in the hallway and he told another teacher, "Oh, we have a Mike Tyson here."

(Jayda 2008)

I continued to talk to Jayda about how she felt about being labeled "a Mike Tyson."

I don't like it. It made me dislike that teacher. I didn't know him and he didn't know me. He didn't take a chance to know me, where he could say, "Oh well, she fought, got in trouble, but she's a nice kid." We never got that chance. When I fought that boy in school, I know it probably made him think like I said, she's nothing but a fighter and that's not what I am. I'm respectful to adults, anyone—I'm very respectful. I'm a helping hand. If you ever needed a hand, I'm there if it could help you. So he just basically just threw it in the air, she's a fighter.

Jayda added that other people had stereotyped her because she had been sent to Brig: "Yeah, they saying that I'm a fighter. If they ask me and I tell them, I'm gonna tell them. I think they be like, oh, she's a fighter or she's a troubled child, and I'm not" (ibid.).

Many of the youths felt as if school authorities—teachers, administrators, and police—were just waiting for them to make a misstep once they returned from alternative school. The same officer that made Donela believe she was under surveillance also confronted Damian when he returned to the mainstream high school:

As soon as I went back, he tried to say as soon as I get in trouble I'm getting kicked right out. They say, anything I do, any wrong thing I do—I'm getting kicked out and sent right back to SAVE.

(Damian 2008)

Jena captured the reentry from alternative to mainstream school experience: "Sometimes, they just wait for you to do any little thing so they can kick you right back out" (Jena 2008).

The process of entry into and reentry from alternative school further alienates youth from the educational process. They return to schools where they are not wanted, and their status as "formerly suspended students" leaves them subject to ridicule, insult, and hyper-surveillance. Some students are directly told that they are expected to end up in jail. The school authorities' expectations that former alternative school students will recidivate becomes a self-fulfilling prophesy. According to a school administrator familiar with the district's suspension programs, the re-suspension rate for these students is at least 40 percent and their school drop-out rate is close to 80 percent.

The young people resent the way that school personnel jump to negative conclusions about their whole person without knowing who they really are. Jayda in particular articulates a sense of how she sees herself—as a helping hand and as a respectful young woman. I can attest to these characteristics after having spent ten days with her in Geneva, Switzerland. She was indeed a young woman who went out of her way to be helpful and certainly was respectful to me and the other chaperones on the trip, and interacted well with the other members of the US Human Rights Network delegation. Contrary to how school staff characterized her, many delegation members came up to me to comment on the way that Jayda and the other kids from our program comported themselves. These adults would shake their heads in disbelief when I reminded them that Jayda was there to testify on her experiences in the school-to-prison pipeline. They simply could not believe that such a young woman was tossed out by the school system.

When she returned to her mainstream school, Jayda quickly learned that school personnel, including the school police officer, were aware of her disciplinary record. The officer reminded her of this explicitly. Beyond the effect of a disciplinary record on a student's ability to reacclimatize to their mainstream school, this record now can impact a student's ability to enroll in higher education. The Common Application, used by more than 400 colleges across the country, explicitly asks the applicant to disclose his or her disciplinary history: "Have you ever been found responsible for a disciplinary violation at any educational institution you have attended from the ninth grade (or the international equivalent) forward, whether related to academic misconduct or behavioral misconduct, that resulted in a disciplinary action? These actions could include, but are not limited to: probation, suspension, removal, dismissal, or expulsion from the institution. Yes/No" (Common Application 2014).

The applicant is also required to provide a form to his or her guidance counselor, who is also asked to disclose the student's disciplinary record.

"You Get Kicked Out, You Go to Prison, and You Die": Kids' Reflections on the School-to-Prison Pipeline

Despite the rapidly growing exposure of the phenomenon of the school-to-prison pipeline by advocacy groups such as the National Association for the Advancement of Colored People (NAACP), the Children's Defense Fund, and the American Civil Liberties Union, few youths I interviewed were familiar with the term. They were, however, quite aware of the similarities between jail and school, and many believed that these similarities were intended to send them a message about their future prospects. As their comments reflect, suspension and alternative school was a sort of dress rehearsal for the criminal justice system.

Carlos made this point clearly when he told me how a visit to his uncle in jail brought to mind his school situation:

> I went to go visit him and it was like . . . , I didn't like the place. I was like, I never want to go to jail because sometimes jail is just like school. You get in trouble, you go to jail and that's regular life. In school, you get in trouble, you get kicked out, and you get sent to an alternative school like Steel or Brig. And in there you do your time and come back out and society don't look at you the same. Teachers don't look at you the same. Basically, that's what it is. . . . What I'm saying is they're trying to say that they'll kick you out, but they don't look back and say, "Oh, he's a good kid. Let's let him slide. He won't do it again, trust me." They'll be like, "Well, just send him to Steel or Brig and just leave him there and that will basically show him, like, straighten him out." Like jail. You get

straightened out, but sometimes people do the same thing over and over again. You gonna get in trouble some way or somehow and since you already got a record, the next time it's going to be worse.

(Carlos 2008)

Tyrel had a clear picture of the pathway to jail and prison that included how profiling and teacher attitudes reflect an expectation that students like him are prison bound. The son of an incarcerated father, Tyrel was one of the few young people who had some familiarity with the phrase "school-to-prison pipeline." When I asked him what it meant, he responded:

School-to-prison pipeline . . . : you get kicked out of school, you go to prison, and then you die.

(Tyrel 2008)

Tyrel returned to the example of his math teacher, who was the cause of his suspension, to point to how teachers push young people into the pipeline:

Like with the math teacher. Like, I could forget to raise my hand, to sharpen a pencil, and she will just send me out. Like she doesn't really care. She just wants me out because she thinks, why waste her time with me if I'm going to end up in jail anyways? She thinks I'm like my father.

(Ibid.)

Marla initially thought the phrase "school-to-prison pipeline" meant "somebody going to a bad school." When I explained to her what the phrase meant, that is, the relationship between suspension, dropping out, and the likelihood of incarceration, she saw the connection:

If they [young people] going to drop out, they going to go somewhere bad. They not going to get a good chance to get something good when they drop out. Yeah some teachers say it, like . . . , kids ain't going to be successful. Like, if they see somebody doing something wrong, they going to be, like, "Okay, you going to end up somewhere like prison."

(Marla 2008)

Of all the young people I interviewed, Rayquan seemed most aware of the problem of mass incarceration and the prison-industrial complex. He sadly thought that some school staff were even glad to think that kids would wind up in jail. He followed this up with an analysis that echoed the work of Loïc Wacquant and Bruce Western:

> Yeah, like they [school staff] looking forward to you going to jail or mess-ing up your life and not being nothing. . . . It's just the fact that it's not even those people [teachers] no more. It's like America itself, they just want to see people locked up, just for the fact of it.
>
> People can't maintain themselves; they put them in a cage. Because they just want to see us . . . , again, the whole thing about how they end up in jail or prison. When they come out, you may as well say they still inside because half of them now they on probation, they got somebody watching them. Or if they not on probation, they can't do too much. Like if they not on probation, like if you coming from prison, you can't vote. Then as soon as you get out of jail or prison you got to have a job in a certain amount of time or they taking you back or whatever. So once you come home, you really don't have too much rights. So you really may as well say you still there, a slave.
>
> (Rayquan 2008)

Ferguson (2000) observes that "bad boys" are made in part through school disciplinary and punishment processes that construct and shape how youth see themselves and how they are seen by others. Harsh school discipline procedures reinforce youth perceptions that their world is unfair and they are readily discardable. The stories told to me by these youths show that misbehavior, such as spitting, pulling off a fire alarm cover, or fighting with other students about amorphous issues of respect, are met with what Fallis and Opotow (2003, 114) term "moral exclusion":

> Moral exclusion helps us understand how schools—trusted social insti-tutions—can become locations of systemic violence in which a large proportion of students can be viewed as deserving invisibility, failure, and expulsion without eliciting a sense of injustice. Students are first seen as behaviorally, then as cognitively, and finally as morally deficient

and therefore outside the scope of justice, and ultimately, the cause of their own debilitation.

The words of the youths in the present volume show us that moral exclusion is apparent to youth. They know all too well that their teachers, their principals, and the school police—authoritative adults—see them as a "bad child," a "troubled child," "worthless," a "nothing." Systemic violence is surely illustrated when a school administrator calls out a fifteen-year-old girl as a "Mike Tyson."

Yet, despite the multiple levels of exclusion from the educational mainstream, the young people remain committed to education. In chapter 10, I turn to exploring what the young people say makes a difference in engaging them in learning—teachers who care and encouragement from the adults around them.

10

"At Least Somebody Wanted to See Me Do Good"

What Kids Think Makes a Difference

It was a social studies teacher, like, she was like the good kind of teacher. She give you, like, a chance. Instead of just kicking you out for something, she gave you a chance. She was the type, like, if you need help with something, she would help you. She would do what she got to do to make you pass and get good grades and make you understand stuff better.

—Shayna

THIS IS SHAYNA'S ANSWER to my question about what makes a good teacher. As I show in chapter 8, the kids in this study value education, at least for its instrumental use in positioning one for better employment opportunities. They also have some clear ideas about what might facilitate their learning. The young people uniformly endorse the idea that a good teacher is someone who "gives you chances" and help. They had ideas as well about what works in helping address behavioral problems in schools, solutions that emphasize social support, and counseling over punitive discipline. In essence the recommendations offered by the youths comport with a significant body of research about best practices in education. Yet educational policy in the United States has neither listened to students nor heeded research. Instead, it has been held hostage to social control policies that place order maintenance ahead of learning.

There is, of course, more to reforming education than social supports and smaller classes. Teaching and learning are complicated and span issues of curricula, cultural competence, and whole school culture,

196

among others. But the kids' suggestions about social supports, smaller classes, individual attention and help, and interactive learning opportunities are good places to start to dismantle the school-to-prison pipeline.

"He Will Push Us Up": Students' Definitions of a Good Teacher

I love social studies. He [the teacher] was honest. He kept track of us [to make sure] we aren't slacking on the work. He will help us with it. He will push us up to make us want to do work. He would explain to us what we are supposed to do instead of explaining one time. He made sure we are really getting it. He would ask, "Do you guys understand this?" If we say no or say yes, he'll help us more.

The English teacher, Ms. Putman [pseudonym], and that was one of my favorites. She also did the same thing. She taught us and she was English, so she read and read and read and taught us. She asked us the same thing, "Do you understand?"

Like I said, I like social studies and English. They always stayed on top of me. Mr. Owens [the social studies teacher, a pseudonym], me and him had a nice bond because he was like a nice teacher who you could relate to. He always used to stay on top of me, telling me, like, "Jayda, get to class, you got class with me."

I always stayed in the classroom. I felt like he wanted me there. He was one of the teachers who's gonna help you with stuff you need help with, instead of throwing it at you.

(Jayda 2008)

Jayda's description of a good teacher is virtually repeated by all of the young people interviewed. The core elements of being a good teacher involve time and patience. Teachers who take the time to explain the subject matter and who make sure that students understand the concepts and topic are much appreciated by the kids, as evident in Jena's summary of a good teacher:

They teach you something. They don't just give you something and tell you to do it. They go over it with you and if you need help, they help you. I think that's a good teacher.

(Jena 2008)

Kwame values teachers who seemingly go out of their way, or make an extra effort to help students:

> A good teacher to me is someone who is willing to take time, like after school or in the beginning of the day or even on breaks, something that they have, any time that they have to help a student get a question, or get . . . anything, if they need help on something.
>
> (Kwame 2008)

Norah also welcomes teachers who give her the time to process information.

> A good teacher is a teacher that gives you time to do all your work and don't rush, that will tell the things until you understand what they really mean. When they treat you well and treat you the same as they would treat the other students. Like that, and give you time to think whenever you need time to think.
>
> (Norah 2008)

Kendra, who rates herself as a good student and one who does not necessarily need additional help, nonetheless offered insights about what might help her peers who struggle in school:

> And the students that were struggling to get where they want to go or don't know where they want to go, they need the extra attention. They need the one-on-one connection. Not to say that they're stupid or anything. Like, that they just need more help than other people.
>
> (Kendra 2008)

Kendra has an inclusive view of education, one that sees potential in her fellow students even if they are struggling in class. She does not write them off or label them; she seems to instinctively recognize what the professionals call "different learning styles."

Carlos offered a similar insight about the need for teachers and other school staff to encourage kids who may be struggling in school:

> I think they don't give them much compliments. Like, they don't give compliments to people who try. They give compliments to the people

that already know the stuff. Like oh, you already know, "Good job." But for the people who are trying and struggling . . . , let's say like normally they get fifties, and they get a seventy on a test, they don't get a compliment. It's like, it's just boom for them. They don't get no glory or nothing. Kids would be more confident if teachers give them compliments. Tell them stuff like, "Oh, you did good today. You're really smart." [Without appreciation] they really start to slack. When they work, they be like, "Oh, I'm going to fail this test." They start believing what the teacher says: "Oh, I'm going to fail this test, I'm going to fail this test. I'm going to fail this class."

(Carlos 2008)

Carlos goes on to elaborate why encouragement is important:

Because to really want to do your work, teachers would be telling you, you did really good on this test, you tried, you tried your best, I seen you struggling. This would make you want to do more. When you do more, you get better grades. You study more often. You do your homework. And you're a better student. But when somebody doesn't show respect or anything, you don't really care about what you're doing anymore.

(Ibid.)

Carlos's words and the statements of the other young people show that teachers can have profound impact on students. Encouragement, patience, and demonstrating care that a student learns not only help kids to master subject matter, but encourages them to work harder.

In addition to teacher style, youths are also more likely to be engaged in learning if the curriculum is interactive. Carlos favorably recalls liking his mainstream classes because they allow him to work in groups. Several students shared their delight in biology classes where they dissected a frog.

It is obvious that adult approaches that reflect a belief in kids' capacities and their willingness to invest time and effort to help youths master new learning and develop new skills reap rewards. These are truisms in both academic fields of education and psychology and self-help arenas that deal with parenting. It is what most of us do in the day-to-day raising of our children. Yet, kids in the school-to-prison pipeline are denied these most basic of adult supports and are treated as throwaway children, unintelligent, and responsive to punishment but not encouragement.

There is such a contrast between what the kids do during their school day, such as it is, and what they do in programs that assume that they are capable, curious, and tender. When they come to my organization for an after-school program, they are met by staff who care about them, and who do their best to understand the burdens and pressures that affect their behavior. In such an environment, the kids eagerly take up tasks that schools think they are incapable of. They write poetry, like India's poem:

"The Music Within"

They say that they can't understand me
because I sing when there's no music
And I tell them it's the music within.
When I'm down and feel alone that's what
frees me the music within
That's what my ancestors were trying to
tell them it was the music within that set them free.
Even though they were beaten
Even though they couldn't read and write
Even though they were sold from their families
Even though they weren't physically free
in their heart, mind, and soul they were
freed by the music within.

(Calhoun 2001)

Or Donald's poem:

"INSIDE MY SOUL"

INSIDE MY SOUL
THERE IS AN OCEAN OF WATER
FLOODING WITH TEARS
THERE IS A PIRANHA OF DEATH
EATING AT MY SOUL

THE PIRANHA FEEDS OFF OF MY DEAD FRIENDS
LIKE DORE AND PRETTY RICKY
AND MY BOY CAV
THE LOSS I EXPERIENCE
IS THAT THEY TREATED ME
LIKE AN OLDER BROTHER
THAT I NEVER HAD
EVEN IF THEY WERE FROM DIFFERENT BLOCKS
IT FEELS LIKE SOMEONE
JUST WALKING UP TO YOU
AND RIPPING OUT MY HEART
INSIDE MY SOUL
THERE IS AN OCEAN
FLOODING WITH TEARS

(Pennyfeather 2001)

These kids, whose English classes often consist of worksheets on capitalization and punctuation, do not get to write poetry in school. Yet when offered this chance in an after-school program by a writer who knows that poetry can be an outlet for powerful emotion, they jump to the task. My staff entered many of the kids' poems in a countywide competition that included suburban schools, as well as mainstream city schools. Four of the sixteen poems selected for inclusion in a countywide publication were composed by the kids in our program.

Writing is not the only area that they become excited about. They learn biology in the context of HIV and AIDS, illnesses that have taken an enormous toll on their communities and families. They participate in research projects, identifying topics (e.g., "Why do members of Parent/Teacher Organizations (PTOs) focus on school fundraising rather than preventing school violence?"), conduct research (e.g., conducting focus groups with local PTOs), analyze data, and write reports. And, like Jayda and Jena, several of these students traveled to Switzerland to testify before the United Nations.

The experience of taking kids to a UN hearing showed me how easily schools track and channel kids based on preconceptions of what they are capable of. It also exposed the myopic view of what should be celebrated as success. When I learned that we would be able to take a delegation of kids to Geneva, I contacted school administrators to share the good news. They were delighted, and offered to help, particularly with the selection project. One administrator told me, "Don't worry, we have some great kids for you to consider from the superintendent's student cabinet." I thanked the individual and then went on to explain that we were taking four kids from our program—four kids who had attended alternative schools and had been in the juvenile justice system. My response was received by an awkward and lengthy silence followed by a more subdued offer to help.

When we returned from Geneva, another school administrator called me and said that the district wanted to honor the kids at a school board meeting. We were thrilled and told the kids and their parents, as well as other agency staff. About two weeks later, the administrator called me back and rescinded the invitation: the district had been monitoring the students' attendance and observed that they were still missing days of school or coming late to class. He thought that it would be embarrassing to recognize students who failed to meet these core measures of school success.

It was my turn to be dumbstruck. I took a deep breath, curtailed my anger, and tried to explain that a week in Geneva was not going to be the event that miraculously turned the kids from marginal students to members of the superintendent's student cabinet. I argued that what they did—their hard work in preparing their testimony, their effectiveness in presenting and speaking, and their capable representation of young people—were achievements worthy of recognition despite the fact that they were neither regular school attendees or grade-A students. The administrator simply did not get it; these kids lacked the behaviors, the "habitus" that are rewarded by schools. While a community agency might celebrate their success, the school district would not.

"I Should Not Have Ever Disrespected a Grown Lady": Kids' Reflections on Responsibility

Learning and behavior go hand in hand. Teachers who feel stymied in teaching because of disruptive students cannot impart the curriculum.

Teachers I have come to know, including my husband, often feel torn between their ability to give a disruptive student the attention he or she needs and keeping the rest of the class engaged. As this book focuses on school responses to perceived and real student misbehavior, it is important to consider what young people suggest might be helpful in reducing school behavioral problems.

It became clear to me as I spoke with the kids that they recognize their misbehavior and inappropriate actions. As described in earlier chapters, the youths take issue with how their misbehavior is responded to, but do not deny their roles and responsibilities. Zeke, Norah, Jayda, and Tyrel all provide examples of youths' sense of their own responsibility in getting suspended. Zeke reflected on his past behavior:

> Sometimes I was unrestrained and was being hyper, you know. I was just being a bad influence as a student. So I can see why a lot of times I did get kicked out. I wasn't humble enough going all those years through school. I wasn't humble enough about the situations I was going through and I know that now.
>
> (Zeke 2008)

Norah was also self-critical about yelling at a teacher who had been "screaming" at her:

> I think that I was wrong, that I was the one that was wrong. I think that I was wrong because that's a grown lady and I should not have ever disrespected a grown lady. My grandma's always telling me that.
>
> (Norah 2008)

Jayda, who staunchly thinks that she was wrongly accused and punished over the incident that placed her in Steel, nonetheless concedes that at other times:

> I knew sometimes, I knew I was in wrong . . . and I knew that I could have handled myself in a different way.
>
> (Jayda 2008)

Finally, Tyrel:

> I'm going to admit in front of you, sometimes I'm wrong. Sometimes I do stuff that I'm not supposed to do and I know that I'm not supposed to do it. But sometimes I be right and sometimes I be in the wrong place at the wrong time. And that's a problem I need to stop. I need to stop hanging out with some people that I used to hang out with. And I, when I'm wrong, I just shut up because they already know what I did. So I don't lie about it so I'm not going to get in more trouble.
>
> (Tyrel 2008)

Not only did these young people accept responsibility, they frequently identified anger as the antecedent to their behavior problems and explained how social supports, when available and offered, helped them to calm down and avoid responding in ways that got them in trouble. Tyrel told me,

> I got all this anger inside . . . because I never forget nothing. I got a lot of anger since I was little.
>
> (Ibid.)

He attributes this long-standing anger to having been a frequent target of neighborhood bullies. I also wondered whether having a father in prison contributed to his anger.

Kwame knows that underlying family issues trigger his anger. He is the child who has lost several relatives to street violence:

> Because I get mad. . . . I would be playing with somebody and stuff and then the next thing you know they just come out they just start saying. They just start making jokes about my family and it makes me mad. . . . They start bringing up the family and stuff and it makes me mad. . . . They talk about my aunts and uncles and stuff. And then, like, when they mention aunt, that makes me think of my aunt that died and it gets me mad.
>
> (Kwame 2008)

Celia's anger is also triggered by nasty comments about members of her family:

And she was talking about my mom and I got real mad. And I just punched her in her face. She started talking about my brother one day and I just asked her like, "What did you say about my brother?" and then she was like, "F—— you brother and your mom." And I was like, "My who?" She was like, "Your mother." And I got mad and I punched her and we started fighting.

(Celia 2008)

Raising Zeke's family issues also gets him angry, but in this case, he is set off by what he perceives to be insults when a vice principal compares Zeke to his father, who is a drug addict:

Well that day, I really felt really uncomfortable when he [the ISS teacher] called the vice principal down that day to the ISS room. He was just talking to me . . . , but then he said he knows my father. He said he recognizes me as my father's son. . . . He's like, "Go to the office, they'll handle you there." I'm like, "Why . . . ?" I'm like, I'm not even believing in this. But at the same time I'm getting—my conscience is getting—angry. And when you get angry you know you're not supposed to send it at all or that anger is just going to be exposed and you're going to feel like a fool afterwards. . . . It seems like he was just trying to pick an argument that day. They thought that I was getting ready to fight him. . . . I'm like, "You must want me acting like a tough guy because I'm about to. . . ." I'm sitting there getting stuck in the moment. I shouldn't have did it. I already know. But besides that, the dude knew my father. He came and picked me up and tried to walk me to the office like I'm a little baby or something.

(Zeke 2008)

Rosa gets angry because she cannot keep up with her schoolwork despite her efforts. She is frustrated and responds to teachers inappropriately:

[I was angry] about how the work was done and I was mad because I didn't get it. So I'll get mad and stuff. That gets me mad because I be really trying to do it so I can get it over with, so I can learn how to do it better.

(Rosa 2008)

Janella simply acknowledges an anger problem that she cannot understand:

> But I just . . . , I don't know. I just got an anger problem. I get angry real, real fast.
>
> (Janella 2007)

While the kids may not understand all of the roots of their anger, their life stories reflect how "socially toxic" conditions of family disruption, community violence, poverty, and other conditions that characterize marginalized communities contribute to behavior problems in school (Vorassi and Garbarino 2000; Watts and Erevelles 2004). The oppressive social conditions marginalize young people, especially young males of color, leaving them with feelings of anger and vulnerability. The kids seem to be simply at the end of their ropes. Zero tolerance school disciplinary policies ignore the structural, underlying conditions that define students' lives, and instead respond to symptoms of misbehavior by using social control processes that mimic the oppression these students experience in their home communities.

My conversations with the young people, however, show that being suspended simply contributes to their sense of anger. They are angry at what they perceive to be a lack of consideration of their side of the story, a perceived unfairness of the process, at the level of surveillance to which they are subjected, the denial of education, and the general stigma that attaches to their placement in the schools for "bad kids." Yet the interviews with the youths also reveal what the kids found helpful in gaining self-control, that is, support and encouragement from teachers and other school staff, and space to compose themselves.

Donela received a great deal of support from her guidance counselor:

> Yeah, me and Mr. Watson [pseudonym] is very close. Last year when I was with Mr. Watson, I went to his office probably every day. I would talk to him about, oh, "This teacher isn't really letting me catch up with my work. I have to stay after." Oh, "I need help," because he [Mr. Watson] does good with math and I'm bad in math so he'd always help me with my work and everything. So I would talk to him a lot. . . . He'd say

he'll come visit me and say, "How you doing in math? How you doing in this?" I'd tell him, "Good, but what's weighing me back is students. It's fighting time I guess." And he'd said, "It's never fighting time." He used to talk to me and tell me . . . , "Well what's the problem?"

(Donela 2008)

Malik also was helped by his guidance counselor:

Mr. Cybers [pseudonym], the guidance counselor—I looked at him as my father because me and him, we got along real well. Like anytime I had a problem situation or was mad, I could go talk to him. And he would talk to me and calm me down. He would let me know how to go about things and he would help me out.

(Malik 2008)

Kendra turns to a social worker in the school who is assigned there by my agency:

I talk to a social worker at my school, Ms. Iris [pseudonym]. She works at Brig and she works for [Center for Community] Alternatives. Like, she's taught me new ways to keep my anger down. Because at Brig it's really hard to keep my anger down and like I have a really bad temper. So, like, when somebody says something like really, really stupid. Like, I've gone through so much. Like, I've not gotten used to holding all my anger back. But she's taught me ways to keep my anger down—to just ignore the rumors and keep myself happy and just walk away. Teach me to like, keep your friends close and keep your enemies closer, kind of thing.

(Kendra 2008)

Kwame found a safe haven in his science teacher, Ms. Pleasant [pseudonym]:

Like when I get mad or stuff, she [Ms. Pleasant] would ask me if I needed to take a walk or something like that. Or she would try to help me fix problems or stuff. Any other teacher in there, they just won't give me no chance. They won't ask me if I need to take a walk or anything like that. They just write me up and send me to the office.

(Kwame 2008)

Some principals also step up to provide the support some kids need. Jose believes his principal is in his corner:

Ms. Warren [a pseudonym for the principal], I love her. She always cuts me a break too. She always wants to keep me in school. If I get in trouble one day, she'll help me out. She always tells me to come to her office and do my work. And I do it.

(Jose 2008)

Janela also gets support from her principal:

The principal, Ms. Lark [pseudonym], she mad nice. She was helping me out, like if I had a problem. I go to her and I would talk about the problem. She was just like, mad nice. She was just a nice person. Like if somebody was bothering me, I would talk to her about it. Like if I wanted to go to the dance and I didn't have no money, she would pay my way to the dance. She would make sure that I would do good so that I could go to the dance. She cared about me. It made me feel good. Like at least somebody wanted to see me do good.

(Janela 2007)

The elements that are common in these stories of support are adults who show an interest, who provide space for the kids to disclose their problems, who encourage solutions either through advice, or simply giving the kids time and space to pull themselves back together. These are examples of ways that adults can encourage self-control, rather than the imposition of external and punitive control.

The kids want to learn and they know that education is important for their future. In this way, they have absorbed the idea that education is a door to opportunity. They also can identify some of the difficulties that stand in the way of their learning. They know they need help in understanding the material, they know that they undermine their own success by misbehaving, and they know that their anger at slights and insults gets the better of them and takes them down a path that contributes to their exile from school.

They offer wise insights about what can help them and other kids get over these hurdles. Their advice is not "pie in the sky"; their solutions seem eminently practical. They want teachers who are invested in them, and demonstrate this investment by making sure that they are actually grasping the material being taught, giving extra time when needed, and giving them praise for their efforts and achievements. The kids want outlets for their anger; they need and respond to adults who give them space to vent, time to cool off, and advice for ways to handle the challenges in their lives.

So what makes these seemingly simple responses so hard to accomplish? I think that the answer lies not in a technocratic fix of schools, although certainly new policies, practices, and more resources for urban schools are needed. I think that the answer lies in confronting the role that schools play in perpetuating social stratification. The social reproduction process in urban schools in America now results in the production not of docile workers, but prisoners.

Schools, Social Reproduction, and the Making of Prisoners

Theory and Literature

THIS STUDY is located within an eclectic, but complementary group of theories that have relevance to what I learned from students. The main influence has been social reproduction theory and its derivative—resistance theory. In addition, the data collected from my interviews with young people who have been suspended from school are evocative of structural violence theory and reflective of critical race theory, as well as the literature on the evolution of the carceral state. Along with these conceptual approaches, I have also considered empirical research that examines the influence of family, neighborhood, and the structure of the school itself on the educational outcomes of youth.

In the previous chapters I discussed the phenomenon of mass incarceration, and the expansion of punitive school discipline practices that directly and indirectly connect to the criminal justice system. While the central question of the study is how young people make sense of school discipline and school suspension, their experiences can be located within a body of research and literature that shows how structural conditions create young people who are unable to fit into the dominant school culture, and how the school in turn prepares these outcasts to become subjects of the criminal justice system.

Outside the School: Research on Poverty and School Failure

Schools are located in communities and affected by the larger social, political, and economic environment of those communities. The students who attend schools come from families, interact with parents, siblings, peers, and adults before, during, and after school. Much has been written about how families and communities affect a range of youth outcomes, from delinquency to academic achievement and other school outcomes. Research on the role of poverty in school failure frames my interpretation of what I termed the "backstories," that is, the family and community lives of the kids included in this study.

Practitioner-focused studies in particular have typically focused on what Bronfenbrenner (1979) has defined as micro- and meso-level systems, that is, individual personal relationships involving families, peers, and immediate authority figures (microsystems), and the connections between individuals and immediate social institutions (mesosytems). This literature tends to focus on "dysfunctional" aspects, risk factors such as negative peers, family history of addiction, and mental health diagnoses.

Resiliencies or protective factors, a more recent addition to literature on youth development, are also concentrated on micro- and meso-level aspects: bonding with and social support from caring adults, temperament, and family stability (Hawkins and Catalano 1992; Howell 2003; Loeber and Farrington 2001). School disciplinary policies focus on these individual- and family-level risk and protective factors. While there are interventions that are intended to shore up resiliencies, school discipline has come to be dominated by the zero tolerance approach that assumes that risk factors must be addressed by punishment and isolation.

Through my professional work, I frequently interact with teachers and administrators in both mainstream and alternative schools. These experiences convince me that teachers and administrators lay the blame for out-of-control students on the doorstep of families, in general, and parental behavior, in particular. While school staff support attempts to help alternative school students, they are quick to dismiss the efforts as fruitless, believing that the kids' parents would undermine positive behavior. The poverty that envelops families is recognized but interpreted as an example of individual level failure. These judgments belie what the kids told me during our interviews. Their family stories reflect a more complex picture of the intermingling of risk and protective factors than is often conveyed by both practitioner-focused literature and the conclusions of school professionals. Families can appear both nurturing and chaotic, youth feel supported and besieged, and parents work hard for little material gain and go in and out of the workforce. Communities are sources of rich connections and frightening assaults.

The focus on individual- and family-level roles in the creation of risk is largely detached from consideration of the structural factors that manufacture risk, what Bronfenbrenner (1979) termed the meso- and exo-systems. As I have reported, poverty and race are the common characteristics among young people in the SCSD's alternative school: 100 percent of students qualify for free or reduced lunch and the overwhelming majority are children of color. Yet teachers and administrators rarely consider racism and structural poverty as factors that play a role in student misbehavior.

Students, of course, are not blank slates when they walk through the schoolhouse door. They carry not only their notebooks and texts, but also their daily experiences from their ecological contexts. For students who attend poor urban schools, these contexts have been beset by "savage inequalities" (Kozol 1991) that have been likened to the "toxic" conditions found in war-torn countries (Kostelny and Garbarino 2001). Unfortunately, zero tolerance disciplinary practices are focused on behaviors that are attributed to individual dysfunction and moreover assume that punishment and exclusion are ways to change or at least contain misbehavior.

Research shows that negative external factors, such as those depicted in what I termed the "backstories" of the kids' lives, contribute to poor school outcomes. Their lives can be dissected into pieces and parts of violence, negative peer relationships, parental incarceration, drug addiction, divorce, and separation (Patterson, Reid, and Dishion 1992; Rumberger 1995; Leventhal and Brooks-Gunn 2000). However, poverty is constant in the lives of the kids, whether they live with two parents or have a father in prison, whether parents work or are in rehab. The definition of poverty that most captures the condition of the kids in this study is offered by Holzer et al. (2007, 6, emphasis in original) and is not limited to money:

As a result [of still unresolved relationships between income and other family, school, community-level effects,] we interpret the causal effects of childhood poverty quite broadly. *They include not only the effects of low parental incomes, but also of the entire range of environmental factors associated with poverty in the U.S., and all of the personal characteristics imparted by parents, schools, and neighborhoods to children who grow up with or in them.* We define "poverty" broadly in this way in part because researchers have been unable to clearly separate low income from other factors that affect the life chances of the poor, and also because the set of potential policy levers that might reduce the disadvantages experienced by poor children go beyond just increasing family incomes. Of course, in defining poverty this way, we also assume that the entire range of negative influences associated with low family incomes would ultimately be eliminated if all poor children were instead raised in non-poor households.

This kind of poverty looms large in the lives of the kids and, as research shows, is the overarching factor in school failure. A US Department of Education study (Kennedy, Jung, and Orland 1986) determined that poverty is the single most important factor correlated with school failure, of greater importance than race, teen parenting, single-parent family, or geographical region. Additional research further confirms the relationship between family income and outcomes of children (McLanahan 1997; Duncan and Brooks-Gunn 1997; Duncan, Mendenhall, and DeLuca 2006; Rumberger 1987). While school-related factors, notably grade retention, are associated with dropping out of school, the impact of such grade retention is more pronounced among students from lower socioeconomic status (Rumberger 1995).

Poverty impacts every aspect of these children's lives. They and their families have poor health and less access to health care. They live in substandard housing, which subjects them to lead poisoning. The negative consequences of the conditions are documented in virtually every social domain. Poor children are almost twice as likely to report fair to poor health compared to non-poor children, and are three and one-half times more likely to have lead poisoning than nonpoor children (Duncan and

Brooks-Gunn 1997). Poor health links to school failure by increasing sick days, and, in the case of lead poisoning, affects cognitive capacity and behavior in ways that make it difficult for kids to learn, and contributes to impulsive and delinquent behavior (Lane et al. 2008). Poverty takes a toll on their parents, their material conditions, and psychological functioning. Poor kids lack access to stimulating, developmentally appropriate toys, materials, and experiences (Duncan and Brooks-Gunn 1997). Poverty affects family structure: the stressors of poverty contribute to divorce and absent fathers and in turn, single-parent [female-headed] families are more likely to be poor (McLanahan 1997). Poverty alone, however, has a greater impact on their educational outcomes than family structure. Dunbar and Brooks-Gunn (1997) show that poor children are twice as likely to repeat a grade and twice as likely to drop out of school compared to children who are not poor.

Poverty is not just a condition of the kids' families; it is neighborhood ecology also associated with negative educational outcomes. Garner and Raudenbush (1991) found significant negative associations between neighborhood deprivation and educational outcomes after controlling for individual- and family-level factors such as student ability and family background. Their study of 2,500 youths who left school in Glasgow, Scotland showed that neighborhood effects—which they defined in terms of an "area deprivation score"[1]—explained variations in educational attainment. They argued that as a result of their findings, the question becomes not, "Do neighborhood effects exist? But rather, How do they work?" (Garner and Raudenbush 1991, 261).

We know that neighborhood effects disadvantage poor youth in multiple ways that undermine their ability to learn and adapt to school. Environmental racism is increasingly recognized as a community-level factor that disadvantages poor youth and impairs their ability to learn and socially adapt to schools. The prevalence of environmentally induced

1. The area deprivation score was composed of twelve variables, the most salient of which were adult and youth unemployment, single parent family, low socioeconomic status, and chronic illness.

health problems, notably asthma and lead poisoning, results in missed school days as well as neurological damage, which appear as learning disabilities and behavioral problems in school (Kozol 1991; Books 2000; Lane 2008). High levels of community violence disrupt social networks and traumatize children (Upperman and Gauthier 1998).

Poverty creates a street culture, which ultimately gets brought into, but conflicts with, school values and expectations (Vigil 1999). Anderson (2000, 33) defines and describes street culture and its rules as a survival mechanism in ways that echo the stories told by the kids interviewed:

> At the heart of the code [of the street] is the issue of respect—loosely defined as being treated "right," or granted the deference one deserves. However, in the troublesome public environment of the inner city, as people increasingly feel buffeted by forces beyond their control, what one deserves in the way of respect becomes more and more problematic and uncertain. This in turn further opens the issue of respect to some-times intense interpersonal negotiation. In the street culture, especially among young people, respect is viewed as almost an external entity that is hard-won but easily lost, and so must constantly be guarded.

Scholars looking at the social disorganization of poor, marginalized communities resort to medical metaphors to convey the conditions that exist. Fagan, Wilkinson, and Davies (2007) refer to the "contagion of violence" that seems to require that kids be armed for self-protection, broadly defined. Vorassi and Garbarino (2000) describe how the confluence of "toxic" conditions results in an "accumulation of risk" wherein the cumulative nature of social pressures overwhelms children, causing behaviors antithetical to school norms, and resulting in their suspension or expulsion.

Yet, the evidence about how poverty affects student outcomes is set aside in the making and implementing of school disciplinary policies. None of the kids I interviewed were asked by school officials about whether and how these toxic conditions or the contagion of violence affected their behavior. And so Jena gets suspended without any adult wondering whether the premature death of her father to heart disease or the murder of her brother influences the "stupid" fight with another girl "who pushed her to the edge." The reliance on zero tolerance is not due to a lack of alternative ways to address kids' problem behaviors, but rather larger socio-economic issues and structural racism that marginalizes and excludes a large percentage of the US population. However, as argued under the frame of Critical Race Theory (CRT), racism and poverty are accepted as the norm, rather than identified as pathological structural conditions that influence every aspect of individual and family behavior and community conditions (Watts and Erevelles 2004). Instead of confronting structural racism, behaviors of kids of color are labeled under ostensibly race-neutral constructs of criminality and/or disability (Watts and Erevelles 2004; Crenshaw 1995; Ladson-Billings and Tate 1995).

Structural Violence, Alternative Schools, and the Shape of Youth Resistance

I argue that the pervasive and persistent harsh disciplinary policies of school are manifestations of what Galtung and others term "structural violence." First coined by Galtung (1969, 171), structural violence refers to the way that institutions limit or constrict access to opportunities and the ability to reach one's potential. Galtung explained structural violence as "indirect," not attributable to a personal actor, but causing harm nonetheless: "The violence is built into the structure and shows up as unequal power and consequently unequal life chances" (ibid.). Interpreting structural violence through the lens of critical race theory illuminates the way that institutional practices of harsh school discipline have resulted in ongoing, ossified racism in US society (Crenshaw 1995).

Structural violence takes the form of invisible punitive or harsh conditions that become normative. Less obvious than direct violence that inflicts personal injury, structural violence affects poor urban kids of color in insidious ways: public spending that prioritizes the military and prisons over schools, a lack of access to health and mental health services, and a high incidence of homelessness. Watts and Erevelles (2004, 281) explain: "Structural violence is embedded in the brutal poverty in which urban schools and their associated communities are situated and where even children have to struggle for their day-to-day survival in contexts that offer little in the way of hope and redemption."

Illuminating forms of structural violence is a necessary counterpoint to the hyperbole and politicized concern about school violence. While serious violence in school has decreased over the last decade, chaotic environments of urban schools coexist with more traditional student and student-teacher activities. Ethnographic studies, conducted in inner city school settings throughout the country, describe environments of disorder, disrespect, petty fights, and quieter tensions of apathy and truancy (Hemmings 2002; Vavrus and Cole 2002; Casella 2001; Devine 1996). These behaviors take place in environments of disrepair, overcrowding, and deprivation (Kozol 1991; Fine et al. 2004), not unlike the "bookless" library, unheated cavernous rooms, and classrooms without desks that I observed in my work in alternative schools and that the kids described in their conversations with me. Conditions that would be cause for outrage in suburban communities are accepted or condoned for poor kids. The violence of inequality is accepted as normal and obscured by the focus on interpersonal violence interpreted through the prism of individual- or community-level deficits (Barak 2006). The fighting and disruptive or inappropriate reactions that are associated with disrespect and humiliation are not examined for their structural origins.

Bombarded with messages about individual merit and how anyone can make it if they try, the kids do not assertively question the profound inequality that permeates every aspect of their lives. While dilapidated school conditions are sometimes subject to criticism, as in complaints about under-heated schools, these are not targets of their frustration. The interpersonal violence is directed at their peers, who are the most immediately visible sources of what they perceive to be disrespect. Nathan McCall, in his book *Makes Me Wanna Holler,* explains why violence occurs over petty and insignificant issues between peers, but does not directly challenge the more profound forms of oppression that constrain the lives of marginalized kids:

For as long as I can remember, black folks have had a serious thing about respect. I guess it's because white people disrespected them so blatantly for so long that blacks viciously protected what little morsels of self-respect they thought they had left. Some of the most brutal battles I saw in the streets stemmed from seemingly petty stuff. . . . But the underlying issue was always respect. You could ask a guy, "Damn, man, why did you bust that dude in the head with a pipe?" And he might say, "The motherfucka disrespected me."

That was explanation enough. It wasn't even necessary to explain how the guy had disrespected him. It was universally understood that if a dude got disrespected, he had to do what he had to do. It's still that way today. Young dudes nowadays call it "dissin'." They'll kill a nigger for dissin' them. Won't touch a white person, but they'll kill a brother in a heartbeat over a perceived slight. This irony was that white folks constantly disrespected us in ways seen and unseen, and we tolerated it. Most blacks understood that the repercussions were more severe for retaliating against whites than for doing each other in. It was as if black folks were saying, *I can't do much to keep whites from dissin' me, but I damn sure can keep black folks from doing it."*

(McCall 1995, 55, emphasis in original)

Structural violence is involved in urban schooling in complex and multifaceted ways. Urban school systems receive the human "victims" of structural violence, the children from communities whose populations are superfluous to American capitalism. Urban school districts in particular are also institutional victims of structural violence through the inequitable distribution of resources. Kozol describes this in *Savage Inequalities* (1991) when he compares the resource disparities between and among school districts. However, by their application of zero tolerance policies, urban school systems are complicit in the perpetration of structural violence, further victimizing the young people who attend these schools. As the kids' words demonstrate, schools replete with metal detectors, wands, random searches, lockdowns, and police presence are environments that marginalize, degrade, and disempower students.

School suspension and expulsion equates to "moral exclusion" characterized by "double standards," "concealing effects," and "disregarding, ignoring, distorting, or minimizing injurious outcomes" (Opotow, Gerson, and Woodside 2005, 307). Moral exclusion shows up when African

American boys are subject to more punitive discipline than experienced by Caucasian boys for similar behavior (double standards) (Skiba et al. 2000; Skiba, Peterson, and Williams 1997; Ferguson 2000; Gregory 1997; Gregory and Mosely 2004). It is demonstrated by the underestimation of school drop-out rates that characterized educational reporting until recently or the removal of reporting on alternative school outcomes on state report cards, which are illustrative of "the concealing effects of harmful outcomes" (Opotow, Gerson, and Woodside 2005, 307). Moral exclusion is glaringly apparent in the US State Department's official response to the UN Committee to End Racial Discrimination that "disregarded, ignored, distorted, or minimized injurious outcomes" (ibid, 307) that denied the federal role in school discipline and impact of school suspension on minority youth.

In its response to the UN Committee, the US Department of State (2008, 93) wrote:

> Regarding the Committee's concern about the "school-to-prison pipe-line," it may be helpful to explain how discipline issues in U.S. schools are typically addressed. In the United States, school boards elected by local citizens oversee local schools. A school principal working under the policies set by the local school board is responsible for the discipline and order in the school. Generally, schools may refer some, all, or none of their serious behavioral problems to law enforcement. Because school discipline and the environment of each school are individual to each school, a broad brush characterization such as the "school-to-prison" pipeline cannot be made, and no data documents such a phenomenon.

In this statement, the United States denied the primacy of the Safe and Gun-Free Schools Act, which, by making federal school aid contingent upon the local adoption of zero tolerance policies, usurped local school authority in disciplinary matters. The state department denied an accumulation of data, much of which is cited in this book, which clearly documents the relationship between school suspension, racial disparity, and juvenile and criminal justice system involvement.

Empirical work documents the impact of poverty and related aspects of marginalization on educational outcomes and structural violence theory provides a conceptual framework to understand how such unjust conditions are embedded within institutions and how system-level inequalities affect human life and human development, and physical and psychological well-being. Social reproduction theory, which I next discuss, helps us to understand how these system-level insults to youth development are kept hidden and, in fact, are perpetuated by the educational system.

Considering Social Reproduction in the Carceral State

Schools have long played a critical role in preparing individuals to assume social and economic roles in the workplace, family, community, and public life. One of the most fundamental and cherished of American values is equal opportunity, and education has been held up as the key to the door to opportunity. A good education is expected to level the playing field, allowing children to transcend the lives of their parents through better paid employment that translates into higher standards of living.

Social reproduction theory challenges this core American belief. It posits that schools play a critical role in transmitting privilege and status from generation to generation. Rather than a liberating function, schools are a means to preserve the status quo of class, race, and gender roles. The curriculum, structure, teacher expectations, rules, and resources of schools perpetuate social class, channeling young people into roles that perpetuate the extant social structure and inequality across generations (Anyon 1995; Bowles and Gintis 1976; MacLeod 1987; Warschauer 2003). Subsets of this literature—correspondence theory, cultural reproduction theory, and resistance theory—address the interaction between the school environment (culture, curricula, rules, policies) and the student and how the school experience readies youths for class-bounded social and economic roles.

Through the voices of young people, I describe how school suspension affects their educational experiences. Episodes of these narratives include an initial rush to judgment by school authorities in response to perceived misbehavior, confusing, alienating, and demoralizing processes that determine guilt, and exile to facilities that, while called schools, have metal detectors and a plethora of police but no libraries or librarians. I consider these experiences within the context of Katz's (2001, 710) broad and interesting definition of social reproduction as "the fleshy, messy, and indeterminate stuff of everyday life. It is also a set of structured practices that unfold in dialectical relation with production, with which it is mutually constitutive and in tension. Social reproduction encompasses daily and long term reproduction, both of the means of production and the labor power to make them work."

Bowles and Gintis in *Schooling in Capitalist America* (1976) elevated interest in social reproduction theory, arguing that schooling in the United States socializes students into assuming their roles in the workplace hierarchy and in this way, perpetuates existing social class divisions. They pointed to the similarities between the larger social structure of society and personal relationships: the division of labor between administrators and teachers, teachers and students, and students and other students corresponded to the hierarchical structure of the production workplace. Just as workers and managers have little control over the content of work or workplace conditions, students and even teachers, have little control over curriculum, the structure of the school day, or the organization of the school space.

Bowles and Gintis (1976) further contended that curriculum offerings for students differ by social class. Working class students are tracked toward a practical course of study preparatory to jobs in the service or manufacturing sectors. Teaching methods differed as well, with schools serving low-income students relying on rote memorization of basic facts, while schools that enroll students from professional and upper classes require a more rigorous, creative, and conceptual level of student participation (Anyon 1980). They challenged the idea that schools promote equal opportunity and social mobility. Rather, they assert that there is a "correspondence" between the social relations of education and the social relations of production. Schools are places "destined to legitimate inequality, limit personal development to forms compatible with submission to arbitrary authority, and aid in the process whereby youth are resigned to their fate" (Bowles and Gintis 1976, 266).

It is well accepted that schools have historically helped to cultivate a populace to fit the American political, social, and economic structure. The early promoters of public education argued that an educated citizenry was necessary to a democratic state and that sentiment has persisted through US history (Labaree 1997; National Commission on Excellence in Education 1983). Entwined with ideals of an educated citizenry and oftentimes eclipsing those concerns is the more practical goal of education as preparatory to a competent, competitive workforce. The organization of American schooling has been aligned and realigned to mesh with the changing economy of the country (Giroux 1982). From colonial time through the middle of the nineteenth century, schools were open but a few months in order to ensure that children were available to work the family farms. The current ten-month school calendar that runs from September to June is a remnant of that agrarian economy. By the late 1800s, in response to the industrialization of the economy, schools became more explicitly vocationally oriented, introducing curricula and training programs to prepare students to participate in manufacturing enterprises: "*Urban education in the nineteenth century did more to industrialize humanity than to humanize industry*" (Tyack 1974, 72, emphasis added).

The structure of schooling became more stratified to better prepare students for their eventual experiences in the workforce (Labaree 1997). As employers came to rely on schools as vocational training institutions, school attendance became more valuable, which resulted in children's more regular attendance. The percentage of youth completing high school rose from 6.3 percent in 1900 to a high of 79.1 percent in 1969 (Grubb and Lazerson 2005).

Race, gender, ethnicity, and culture, as well as the role of resistance and human agency, shape the interactions between school and students and make the social reproduction function of schools more complicated than described by Bowles and Gintis (Walker 2003; MacLeod 1995; Giroux 2003; Bourdieu and Passeron 1979; Willis 1977; Rikowski 1996, 1997). In a heterogeneous nation such as the United States, where people occupy multiple "social locations" (Cole and Omari 2003, 786) and where racial, class, ethnic, gender, and sexual orientation conflict and coexist, there are contradictory expectations of and reactions to the educational system. Cole and Omari (2003) and Ogbu (1986), for example, describe the push and pull of education in African American communities, where education is at once valued as the means of upward mobility and dismissed as destructive of culture and heritage, that is, "acting white" and selling out.

Schools privilege "habitus,"[2] a collection of behaviors, ideas, and values acquired through the social context in which one lives, as well as class (Bourdieu and Passeron 1979; Bourdieu 1984). Social and cultural capital are assets that are transmitted intergenerationally and give children from the privileged classes a head start in achieving academic and eventual economic and social success. Schools value the habitus of middle and upper class students that allow these children to enter school with behaviors, language, and expectations that resonate with the school structure, rules, and curriculum. Teachers and administrators interpret differential habitus and social capital in ways that reinforce the expectation that students will remain locked into their place in the social hierarchy. In MacLeod's (1995) words, this constitutes *"school mediated exclusion"* (16), where *"the process of social reproduction is accepted by the exploiter and exploited alike"* (15, emphasis added).

We see this in the stories of Zared, whose father is in drug rehab and Tyrel, whose father is in prison. They are both explicitly told by teachers that they are going to wind up like their fathers. Many of the other kids interviewed were not so directly and explicitly called out by their teachers or administrators; they were, however, often told that they were not going to amount to anything. While the kids rejected these negative connotations, I could see and hear that it affected them deeply. They went at great lengths to tell me that they are not and will not become "a nobody." These arguments to preserve self are the purview of the rejected and marginalized; they are not words or justifications that are made by [white] middle class kids. Those children enter school ready to "fit" into standards and are rewarded with grades and educational credentials that eventually translate into economic advantages (Bourdieu and Passeron 1979). The

2. Bourdieu (1977, 53) explains habitus as "systems of durable, transposable, dispositions, structured structures predisposed to function as structuring structures, that is, as principles which generate and organize practices and representations that can be objectively adapted to their outcomes without presupposing a conscious aiming at ends or an express mastery of the operations necessary in order to attain them."

kids I interviewed do not display such attributes and so they fail and are estranged from schools because they do not fit in.

However, the kids are also bombarded with what MacLeod (1995) refers to as the "achievement ideology," i.e., the notion that anything is possible through hard work, a seriousness of purpose, and discipline. I find it interesting that all of the kids in this study still believe that they can buckle down and attain the educational goals that they quite understand are needed for economic success. They cling to the achievement ideology even in the face of an educational experience that leaves them in schools with few books, short schedules, and work that seems meaningless. In fact, they worry about how getting kicked out of school will affect their education. Some of the kids, like Carlos, fear that the record of school suspension will harm their ability to get into college. This fear is not misplaced, since increasing numbers of college applications include questions about school disciplinary records as well as criminal records (Weissman et al. 2008).

If interpreted narrowly, social reproduction theory may seem to have little utility in explaining the school-to-prison pipeline. Bowles and Gintis focus on how schools help sort students into their future places in the workplace. In contrast, the pipeline metaphor does not foresee youth entry into the workforce. Rather, it maintains that youth in the pipeline will in fact be excluded from the workplace as they move from school suspension to dropping out of school, and ultimately entering the criminal justice system. Instead of meaningful work, these young people will enter the world of a permanent underclass, unable to work while incarcerated,[3] and, because of collateral consequences of a criminal record, unlikely to become employed after they are released.[4]

The empirical evidence on the association between a lack of adequate schooling and future imprisonment, particularly for African American men (Western 2006; Western and Pettit 2005), provides reason to consider

3. Prisoners are typically expected to "work" in prison, but earn on average between one and three dollars a day and work under conditions that do not reflect the free market economy (Blakely and Bumphus 2004).

4. Collateral consequences include formal prohibitions on a wide range of jobs, including home health aides, barbers, lawyers, and teachers (Mukamal 2001).

the role of the current educational system in reproducing prisoners. New forms of inequality emerge when "social reproduction gets unhinged from production" (Katz 2001, 709), as happens in the global economy when capital and production are highly mobile and move to where labor costs are lower. Labor, however, remains tied to place and boundaries, becoming "excessed groups of people who have no secure work future" (Katz 2001, 718). In the United States, these "excessed groups" are black and Latino young men who fill state prisons (Wacquant 2001, 2006).

The descriptions of school shared by the kids I interviewed give clear examples of the ways that alternative schools in particular have become acclimated to the carceral state and the preparation of prisoners. Education has become secondary to security and surveillance and learning; the dissemination of and acquiring of knowledge is superficial, at best. Recall kids' complaints about the short school days: "What can I learn in two hours?" is a rhetorical question posed to me by Donela. Other kids offer descriptions of school "work" as consisting of endless handouts and even crossword puzzles.

Much of the early scholarship on social reproduction and resistance focused on male, white, working class students, and was undertaken before major economic and social transformations in the United States. It seems reasonable to expect that social reproduction will look different in an economy that no longer supports working class jobs, but instead relegates so many young people to prisons. The increasingly punitive environment in public schools in urban America mirrors the expansion of social control in the larger society. The labeling of children as deviant or delinquent and the deprivation of learning through suspension are examples of structural violence inherent in school discipline.

These labels and exclusions shape the core identities of young people. My research shows that these negative labels are widely accepted by students, parents, teachers, administrators, and the public at large, which considers students in alternative schools as the "bad" kids (Syracuse City School District 2000). Even students who are suspended know that it means they are now lumped in with the "bad" kids and resist being so tagged. The images evoked in the Syracuse district are common to urban America, where inner city schools and the students who attend them have taken on a penal identity. School discipline, accepted as a necessary condition for imparting education, sorts out students as "good" and "bad," which become labels that persist beyond individual incidents and transgressions. Ferguson's (2000) study of in-school suspension in Chicago schools described "punishing rooms" in which even young elementary age students were "marked and categorized as they encounter state laws, school rules, tests and exams, psychological remedies, screening committees, penalties, and punishments, rewards and praise" (40–41).

Discipline is the method of imparting institutionally generated norms: those who conform to rules—Foucault's (1979) "docile bodies"—are rewarded, and those who do not are subject to punishment. While the essential elements of discipline—"hierarchical observation, normalizing judgments and examinations" (Foucault 1979, 170–192)—exist across institutional domains, they manifest themselves differently in different settings. In the age of the carceral state, penological methods of discipline have become ubiquitous in urban schools in the United States: armed police, security fences, surveillance cameras, and isolation rooms.

Resistance Theory and Student Reaction to Social Reproduction

It would be a mistake to consider that schools are monolithic in their ability to socially reproduce human beings in preordained slots, be those of workers or prisoners. The hegemony of schools is not unbreakable; rather, student resistance can be a force for individual and social transformation. The interaction between schools and children can be constraining or liberating (Giroux 1982).

Through ethnographic research, Willis (1977) and MacLeod (1995) explore the manifestations of resistance among working class youth and how actions of young people contribute to their becoming trapped in marginal social and economic positions. In *Learning to Labour* (1977), Willis studied disaffected white working class males in England in an effort to understand whether, how, and why these young people accept their restricted economic prospects. Willis found that the group of youths he called the "lads" resisted efforts to remold them into a middle or upper class lifestyle and culture. They rejected the efforts of the school, dismissing academic pursuits as unmanly and/or irrelevant. Their mode of resistance consisted of behaviors that got them into trouble in school. They were disruptive, boisterous, and openly hostile to school, recognizing the disconnect between the rhetoric about education as the gateway to upward mobility and the reality of the structural inequalities that impacted their working class lives. The resistance actions of Willis's lads destine these youths to underpaid factory jobs.

MacLeod (1995) studied two groups of young people living in a public housing project in Boston, Massachusetts, exploring the role of school in the formation of youth aspirations. One group, "the Hallway Hangers," are white working class youths who resemble Willis's lads, growing up in environments that eschew schooling and academics. The Hallway Hangers reject the achievement ideology: it "runs counter to the evidence in their lives" (MacLeod 1995, 139). The other group, "the Brothers," are African American, live in the projects and also come from essentially the same social class. Yet, the Brothers believe in the achievement ideology, influenced by their parents' faith that civil rights laws now open doors of opportunity for their children. They took school seriously and expected that getting an education would improve their life trajectory.

I found my students in Syracuse to be more like MacLeod's Brothers. They were surprisingly hopeful that if they worked hard, they could attain their aspirations, which were, contrary to popular rhetoric, not tied to NBA careers. They described goals ranging from professional careers in medicine and law to technical careers and entrepreneurship, and these would appear to be accessible had these students been born to white middle class families.

Despite their complaints about the process and impact of suspension, at the end of the day, the youths placed the responsibility to succeed in school solely on their own fragile shoulders. Similar to Macleod's Brothers, the youths I interviewed for this study are not in rebellion against the concept of education; rather, they largely embrace education as their ticket to success. Youths express their appreciation of the importance of an education and rue suspension policies that leave them without access to their education. They want to do well in school and yearn for the kinds of support that would help them achieve their educational goals.

The young people clearly value education and understand its importance even in the face of their exclusion from school. They accept their individual responsibility to work hard in school and are often self-critical of their lapses in this regard. They push back against the stigma of suspension, but their words also show that this experience has taken its toll on their psyches. The stories of student suspensions show that they are both displaced from school by their own actions, and also are pushed out through school responses to youth behaviors.

Their behaviors, however, can be understood as resistance to a curriculum they repeatedly describe as "work" that is accompanied by little discussion of its substantive meaning, and which is delivered by teachers whom they perceive do not care ("only in it for the paycheck" is the sense that kids take away from many classroom teachers). They are particularly resistant to a setting that subjects them to daily insults and nullification, and that they experience as uncaring and disrespectful of their cultural mores (Ogbu 2003; Valenzuela 1999). The kids in my study get in trouble for resisting disrespect from their peers, from their teachers, from school administrators, and from school police.

Behaviors that are considered counterproductive and delinquent may appear rational when viewed from the vantage point of youth. Student resistance that manifests itself as noncompliant behavior can be a reaction to a punitive school/classroom environment; uncaring, distant teachers; and authority that is perceived to be arbitrary and unfair. Many of the suspension incidents described by the young people I interviewed escalated when the child was confronted with disrespect by a teacher, school administrator, or police officer. Damian (2008) gets suspended after he tries to walk out of school after being confronted by a school police officer and a teacher who were "getting disrespectful to me." Kendra (2008) says that "she had a fit" and began flailing at school staff after a vice principal cut off her phone call to her father. These reactions and other forms of noncompliant behaviors are a means for students to exert some control over an environment that excludes their input: "In this light, student misconduct is viewed as resistance to a stultifying regime of frozen communication and work" (Stevick and Levinson 2003, 330). The double-edged sword of student resistance is well captured by Donna Gaines in her study *Teenage*

Wasteland (1998, 108): "Kids who refuse have always found something else to do. Sometimes it kills them. Sometimes it sets them free."

The kids in my study likened school to prison, and complained that the school is eager to throw them out for minor infractions or based upon their reputations. They react to this rejection with behaviors that make it easier for schools to suspend or expel them, including fighting and mouthing off. In this way, young people are not just pushed out of school—they also "jump" out to escape boredom, insult, and rejection.

Student disengagement from education was obvious to me in an incident that took place several years ago when I was invited to be a guest speaker at an alternative school class. There were seven students—three boys and four girls—present in the class whose official enrollment was eighteen. The room was rather small, with a long grey table surrounded by chairs, and without individual desks. There was not even a desk for the teacher.

The behaviors of the students were neither disruptive nor overtly hostile, but rather wholly at odds with what I, an older, white, middle class woman, expected in a classroom. The boys entered the class and did not interact with anyone. They simply sat down, put their heads on the table and promptly went to sleep. The girls gathered their chairs in a group toward the end of the table and sat down. The teacher entered the classroom and was greeted in a friendly manner by all the students (or at least those who were awake). He introduced me as the guest speaker and told them I was going to talk about prisons.

Almost as soon as I began my presentation, the girls repositioned themselves in a circle so as to be able to do a chain braiding of hair, i.e., each girl was getting her hair braided and braiding another girl's hair. They chatted quietly amongst themselves, occasionally breaking out into loud, friendly laughter. At one point a boy woke up and started to pace around the room. The teacher told him to sit down. He did and again laid his head on the table and dozed off.

I increased the level of my voice to try to command their attention. I was not harsh, nor did I criticize them for their obvious inattention. This raising of my voice did not change their demeanors; the girls continued with their business and the boys slept. Finally, I began saying "I'm sorry,

I'm sorry, I'm sorry." I increased the level of my voice until I was yelling. One boy woke and looked puzzled as if aroused from a dream and the girls all stopped what they were doing and looked up. They asked me what the matter was; they could tell I was distressed. I said that I was sorry that I was so boring, that I could not command their attention. I explained that I thought I prepared a topic that would be interesting to them, and again said that I was sorry that I was not. All the girls looked concerned. One girl got up from the table and came around and gave me a comforting pat on the back and said something to the effect of: "Don't worry, it's not you. This is what we always do in class." Other girls chimed in brief words to reassure me that their inattention had nothing to do with me. They seemed surprised that I would even care that they were not listening and were very concerned that my feelings were hurt.

There are multiple ways to interpret this event. The predominant labels that are typically applied to these behaviors connote deficits, including a lack of social skills, mental health problems, or learning disabilities such as Attention Deficit Disorder. Students who ignore classroom instruction are considered rude, lacking the habitus of appropriate deference for authority. In some school districts, braiding hair, a form of playing around, or sleeping is even considered infractions of the school disciplinary code and subject to sanctions.

However, through a lens of resistance theory, the braiding circle and the sleeping boys are ways that students reveal that school is irrelevant to them. Their bodies may be ensconced in class but their minds are not engaged in the lessons of the day. The braiding circle might reveal student responses to a classroom that had no student desks or chairs. Rather than accept the institutional metal table as appropriate for study, they reclaimed the physical structure for a more suitable activity. While these behaviors may not be tools for social change, they are also more than symptoms of deviance assumed by teachers and other school authorities. They are accessible means of confronting authoritarian elements of schooling; these behaviors are a form of "everyday resistance" directed both at adults in the school and other youths (Schultz 2005; Tobin 2005).

The strands of research and literature on poverty, structural violence, and social reproduction theory woven together help us to understand the school-to-prison pipeline. Poverty and marginalization are not taken into account in designing school responses to misbehavior. Structural violence theory suggests that the conditions in which kids live and the conditions that they are subjected to have become normalized. US policy does more than ignore the conditions, as shown in the US report to the United Nations; we deny their existence. Rhetoric about American education continues to perpetuate the myth of opportunity, rather than the ways that suspension leads to dropouts, and dropping out (particularly for African American males) leads to incarceration. The very process of suspension is quietly training marginalized kids for their place in the carceral state. They are learning how they will be charged, prosecuted, sentenced, and the kind of institution in which they will serve their time.

The convergence of schools and prisons has been remarked upon by Wacquant (2001), who includes schools in the "deadly symbiosis" between ghetto and prison; by Simon (2007), for whom schools are yet another institution that is "governed through crime"; and by Garland (2001b) and Noguera (2003), whose works suggest how schools are also invaded by a preoccupation with crime and security. The melding of schools and prisons are an aspect of how the "moral panic" of crime has come to dominate the governance of virtually all American institutions:

> At yet a third level we govern through crime when crime becomes a metaphor or analogy through which we apply the same technologies and mentalities established to govern crime onto very different issues, like child welfare and education, family integrity, worker security and satisfaction, and over consumption. This means that activists seeking to change conditions in any and all of these settings have real incentives to model their complaints as concerns about crime, construct themselves as victims of the willful wrongdoing of others, and invoke a prosecutorial-like response from government.
>
> (Simon 2002, 1417)

This is my view of how schools have come to produce prisoners, beginning the process of sending them down the pipeline.

12

Conclusion

"We All Activists Now"

HARDLY A DAY GOES BY without someone telling me about a wonderful achievement on the part of one or more of the youths who have been in our programs. One young man went on to become the president of his mainstream high school class; another young woman was accepted into an Ivy League college. But those stories are usually matched by a more dismal and depressing story of a former client arrested, a young man dropping out of school, a young woman pushed out of her mainstream school because she lacked sufficient credits and was haphazardly directed to a GED program. All these stories, the good and the not so good, compelled me to write this book. I wanted to learn directly about what these young people made of their school experience, and particularly their suspension experience.

Much of the research on the school-to-prison pipeline focuses on documenting the overt ways that the system moves young people from mainstream education to becoming dropouts and enmeshed in the criminal justice system. The research describes suspension practices (Skiba et al. 2000, 2003), the increase in the number of students suspended (Losen and Martinez 2013; US Department of Education 2006, 2012), the growing use of police in schools, and the attendant increase in the number of students arrested in schools (Advancement Project et al. 2013; Dahlberg 2012; Justice Policy Institute 2012; New York Civil Liberties Union 2007; Advancement Project 2005). While these studies document the problem and its policy implications, they do not explore how youth themselves describe their experiences of school exclusion.

This study looked at the extent to which students who have been suspended from school are cognizant of the role of school suspension in the
school-to-prison pipeline. The young people in this study are the very kids
most likely to wind up in prison by virtue of their status and characteristics: their poverty, their race, and their status as suspended students leave
them vulnerable to the carceral state. I wanted to illuminate what the kids
themselves make of their position. I found that while the pipeline is not
explicit to young people who are seemingly flowing through it, there are
other ways that the processes of school suspension and alternative school
placement signify their marginalization.

Social reproduction literature makes convincing arguments about how
schools reproduce class divisions, sort students according to their expected
place in the labor market, and reinforce these expectations (Bowles and
Gintis 1976; Oakes 2005; Oakes et al. 1992; Willis 1977). Yet in the inner
cities of the United States, viable work options have disappeared (Wilson 1996), moving first to the nonunionized South and Southwest, and
increasingly to developing economies in Asia and Latin America. Wacquant (2001, 2006) argues that prisons have become the new mode of
controlling the racially demarcated pool of surplus labor, and that prisons
and poor communities of color become merged in culture. In this study, I
looked at some of the ways that schools contribute to the reproduction of
prisoners from the pool of young people having little prospect of a place
in the labor force and who are likely to be relegated to prisons, instead.

As I described in chapter 9, students are not, for the most part, overtly
aware that the suspension process and their alternative school experiences
place them in the pipeline to prison. The students interviewed were not
familiar with the term "school-to-prison pipeline." Yet, as I listened to them
describe the behaviors that resulted in their suspension and the process of
suspension, the narratives eerily echoed those of my clients in the criminal justice system: what happens to them when they are arrested, what
they go through in court, and the prison environment. Like the criminal
justice system, schools' reliance on punitively oriented discipline excludes
young people without consideration of background factors or alternative
approaches. Also like defendants in the criminal justice system, the messages that kids receive are that they are "bad," the dangerous other unfit

to remain in their (school) community. They are put in a carceral environment replete with security, searches, and police, but bereft of books, computers, or even enough school hours sufficient for learning and study.

The young people were quite aware that they were vulnerable to suspension because of their own behaviors, because of school policies, and because they were already targeted as "bad kids." In some measure, the kids place themselves on the assembly line to prison: they fight amongst themselves and they challenge the authority of teachers, administrators, and school police, and in these ways they become complicit in their own marginalization. What sets kids off, whether it is against one another or in opposition to a teacher or police officer, is their perception of disrespect. It causes fights with other students when the rumor mill churns out stories about nasty comments about one's family or oneself. It causes kids to mouth off to school cops who challenge their right to be in a school corridor, or to teachers who liken them to their incarcerated parents.

The school-to-prison pipeline works in nuanced and subtle ways, preparing kids for an impersonal criminal justice system that does not look behind their behaviors, imposing punishments that do not change problematic behaviors, and setting kids on a path to permanent social exclusion, whether or not they go to prison.[1] There are, however, readily accessible mechanisms and approaches that would de-link schools from the carceral state. I conclude with policy and practice recommendations that flow from the comments and insights of the young people in this study.

Dismantling the School-to-Prison Pipeline

I was drawn to this topic as an activist and practitioner working with people caught in the criminal and juvenile justice system. I am not naïve with respect to what it will take to unravel the carceral state. Despite the activism, research, and examples of alternatives that emerged and flourished in

---

1. Student disciplinary records, for example, are now considered by colleges as part of the student application process, much in the same way that prior criminal records are considered (Weissman et al. 2008).

the years since the Attica prison rebellion (Weissman 2009a), New York State's incarceration level alone grew from 12,000 in 1971, peaking at about 71,000 in 2000. The state's prison population is now down to about 56,000, a number celebrated by state policy makers despite the fact that at roughly 300 people per 100,000, New York's incarceration rate is still significantly higher than incarceration rates in most of the world.

The dismantling of the school-to-prison pipeline will ultimately require transformation of the social system that at present renders these kids superfluous. While schools alone cannot completely change the trajectory for poor kids of color, they can do a better job at fulfilling the role of opportunity makers rather than prisoner producers. These changes are within our reach: there are models across the country that could be taken to scale, and my research indicates that the kids would welcome educational settings that give them opportunities to learn.

First, educators must reclaim their schools and eliminate or reduce mechanisms of social control that have become so pervasive in poor, urban schools, but which remain limited or nonexistent in wealthier, whiter school districts. Zero tolerance policies should and can be replaced with more sensible, student-centered approaches to school discipline that involve changing the whole school culture, teacher training, and involving students in the building and maintaining of safe and respectful school environments. The research on the ineffectiveness of zero tolerance is strong (Balfanz, Byrnes, and Fox 2013; Balfanz, Herzog, and Mac Iver 2007; Shollenberger 2013; Skiba et al. 2006), and there is a constituency that supports the elimination of zero tolerance policies that includes the American Bar Association, the American Psychological Association, and Mental Health America (formerly the National Mental Health Association), among others. There are state and local parent and student groups organizing against zero tolerance laws such as Community Asset Development Re-Defining Education (CADRE) in Los Angeles, Padres y Jóvenes Unidos in Denver, Make the Road by Walking in New York City, and Texas Zero Tolerance, which are having some success. In 2007, pushed by a parent-led group, CADRE, the Los Angeles Unified School District passed a new district-wide student discipline policy that is based on positive behavior support and developmentally appropriate discipline rather than zero tolerance (CADRE 2007). CADRE, in conjunction with other grassroots and advocacy groups, continued efforts to eliminate harsh school discipline and in 2013 achieved a groundbreaking victory that banned suspensions for "willful defiance," introduced restorative justice practices, expanded Positive Behavior Supports and Interventions, limited the role of police in schools, and created more transparent methods of accountability by making disciplinary and school arrest data available to students and parents.

Many state and local groups have joined in a national coalition, The Dignity in Schools Campaign (DSC), which supports national, state, and local efforts to end harsh school disciplinary policies. DSC has developed a model code for school districts to adapt to improve school discipline, reduce out-of-school suspensions, and minimize the role of police in schools. DSC-New York and other community groups successfully advocated for the passage of the Student Safety Act, which requires that New York City Police and the board of education report data on school-based arrests, summonses, and out-of-school suspensions. In the face of the now public data on suspensions in the Syracuse City School District, parents, youth, and community organizations in Syracuse are considering creating a DSC chapter.

States and localities are also revising school discipline-related laws and practices. In 2009, the Texas State Legislature passed a law that modifies zero tolerance policies requiring districts to take into account mitigating or extenuating circumstances when considering student misbehavior (Brown 2009). A court-led initiative in Clayton County, Georgia has resulted in a "school offense protocol" that significantly limits the types of behaviors that could result in a student's arrest. The new protocol has reduced school-based arrests and suspensions, increased school safety, and increased graduation rates. Suspensions have been reduced by more than half over a six-year period in Baltimore city schools through a combination of strong district leadership, revised discipline policy, and implementation of Positive Behavioral Supports and Interventions and other supportive interventions (Willoughby 2012). In Syracuse itself, the school board created a job description for police officers in school that limits their roles and responsibilities, is introducing advocates to help represent students and their families in disciplinary hearings, and is contracting to hire hearing officers who will be independent from the District.

Until the tragedy of the mass shooting in Newtown, Connecticut, there had been progress at the federal level, as well. President Obama's administration, through the secretary of education, indicated concern about the use of zero tolerance policies for minor misbehavior and the possible racially disparate impact of the policy (Aspen Institute 2009). Secretary of Education Arne Duncan's statement that *"education is the civil rights issue of our time,"* which he made before the Historical Black Colleges and Universities (HBCU) conference in Washington, DC on September 21, 2011, recast education as a fundamental element in US democracy (emphasis added). Nine months later, upon the release of the department's Office of Civil Rights (OCR) data on school discipline, Secretary Duncan added this powerful commentary: *"The undeniable truth is that the everyday educational experience for many students of color violates the principle of equity at the heart of the American promise. It is our collective duty to change that"* (emphasis added).

There has been movement on the federal level to expand positive school supports. First introduced by Barack Obama while a senator from Illinois, the "Positive Behavior for Effective Schools Act" expanded the use of positive behavioral supports and authorized federal funding for positive behavioral approaches. The act was reintroduced into the House of Representatives by Congressman Phil Hare in May 2009 (Positive Behavior for Safe and Effective Schools Act). In December 2012, Assistant Majority Leader Dick Durbin, Chairman of the Senate Judiciary Subcommittee on the Constitution, Civil Rights, and Human Rights, held the first congressional hearing on the school-to-prison pipeline. The hearing was held before an overflow crowd of almost 400 people from across the nation—so large that a room was set up to accommodate those who could not get into the hearing room itself. Testimony at the hearing called for an end to harsh school discipline, out-of-school suspensions, and the reduction, if not elimination of police in schools.

The elimination of zero tolerance policies does not, of course, eliminate the need for discipline and for ensuring safety in schools. The present study does not deny the presence of student behavior problems that disrupt the classroom and sometimes undermine the safety of other students and staff. The kids acknowledged they were at times out of control, fighting with each other, and being disruptive in class and in hallways. However, the "in your face" response by school police, the endless searches to which students are subjected, and their exclusion from regular school are not approaches that increase school safety or improve the school climate. Rather, these practices seem to escalate problems and kids' alienation from school (Noguera 1995, 2003). Unfortunately, the tragedy in Newtown, Connecticut, which took place two days after the historic Senate hearing, reinvigorated calls for armed police (and even armed teachers) in school.

Alternatives to school police and high-tech security exist on state, district, and school levels. The Center on Neighborhood Enterprise (CNE) Violence-Free Zone Initiative works in concert with local grassroots organizations to train young adults who then work in schools as youth advisors. The advisors intervene to reduce violence and conflict between students, and between students and teachers. Operating in twenty-seven schools in seven school districts, CNE reports—and a study of Violence-Free Zone schools in Milwaukee confirms—that sites with youth advisors show a reduction in disruptive behavior and reduced suspensions (Johnson and Wubbenhorst 2009).[2] A Justice Matters Institute report (Sandler 2003) profiles eight schools around the country that have created school environments that have reduced behavior problems and the use of suspension without relying on criminal justice approaches. Elements of positive school discipline include involving students in the creation and enforcement of school and classroom rules, consistency in enforcing these rules, high expectations of students on the part of principals and teachers, rewarding positive behavior, looking for causes of misbehavior, and addressing those causes and handling misbehavior in ways that nonetheless convey respect for the child.

Positive Behavioral Interventions and Supports (PBIS) is an approach that has been introduced in more than 9,000 schools around the country,

2. The Violence-Free Zone Youth Advisors did not replace Milwaukee police officers who are still assigned to Milwaukee public schools.

including a growing number of urban schools (McCurdy, Mannella, and Eldridge 2003). It addresses the whole school environment as well as individual student behavior issues. PBIS elements include building a positive school culture that all members of the school community buy into, and treating behavior as an issue for teaching and role modeling rather than punishment and exclusion. Data collection and analysis is embedded in the model, as its explicit goal is to reduce school disciplinary incidents and school suspensions. A body of research shows PBIS to be effective in reducing discipline problems in schools (Bradshaw et al. 2009; Bradshaw, Mitchell, and Leaf 2010; Horner et al. 2009), although reduction impacts may be less robust for youths of color, particularly African Americans (Vincent and Tobin 2010).

Restorative justice approaches aim to promote accountability, repair harm, and restore relationships by bringing together those who inflicted harm and those who were harmed. More widely used in New Zealand and Australia, evaluations have shown it to reduce the use of harsh school discipline and improved school climate (Cameron and Thorsborne 2001; Buckley and Maxwell 2007). There is emerging evidence of successful adaption of restorative justice approaches to discipline problems. Vanguard High School in Manhattan established a "Fairness Committee" comprised of teachers and students to sort out the "he said, she said" disputes of the type that were especially common among the girls whom I interviewed. Each party to the dispute gets a chance to tell his or her side of the story, with the facilitators asking clarifying questions and moving the discussion to solutions to the dispute. Cole High School in Oakland, California, where the majority of students were young people of color, also implemented a restorative justice program. Interviews with students and teachers indicated that they felt program elements improved school climate and reduced disciplinary infractions including fighting between students (Sumner, Silverman, and Frampton 2010). The study also showed a reduction in the school's suspension rate following the introduction of restorative justice. In the three years prior to program implementation, the average suspension rate was 50 suspensions per 100 students. In the two years after restorative justice was introduced, the suspension rate dropped to 6 suspensions per 100 students, reflecting an 87 percent decline.

Reducing or eliminating police in urban schools would not mean that schools are without police protection when such is needed. While the number of schools with assigned police officers has increased, 32 percent of schools in the United States have no permanently stationed police. Principals and administrators can simply call 911 as the rest of us do and the police respond when they are needed. In Syracuse, at least, this practice was estimated to save the school district $1.5 million, which it paid to the city police department for deploying police in schools. In the 2011–12 school year, the severity of cuts to the Syracuse City School District forced it to eliminate school police officers in the middle schools. In the first six months, at least, there were no reports of a spike in behavior problems in the schools, yet another indication that school police were not necessary from a school safety point of view. An economic crisis was not necessary in order to justify the removal of police from schools: one has only to visit the suburban schools that surround Syracuse to see how schools have successfully operated without armed law enforcement assigned to school buildings.

I propose the removal of police from schools rather than retraining; while retraining might improve police interaction with students, it will not change the fundamental role of the police in schools. As the Syracuse police chief explained at the parent and community meeting held after the fifteen-year-old girl was punched in the face by a school police officer, police roles and responsibilities remain the same whether the officer is assigned to a street, a highway, or a school. The officer might be "friendlier," but he or she is still responsible for discharging a police function. The Syracuse City Police Department, like most police agencies, defines its goals in terms of prevention and deterrence of crime and apprehension of criminals (Syracuse City Police Department 2009). Policing is officially authorized social control that is distinct from other means of control insofar as it permits use or threat of force (Manning 2000). A plethora of data show that increased police presence in schools, whether labeled as resource officers or school police, increases school-based arrests and may actually exacerbate behavioral problems in schools (Advancement Project et al. 2013).

Along with the removal of police from schools, surveillance technology should be either removed or sharply curtailed. Again, there are examples of urban schools in poor neighborhoods with high crime rates that do not use metal detectors yet have safe school environments. One such example is Urban Assembly School for Careers in Sports in the South Bronx with a student population, whose characteristics resemble those at New York City's Impact Schools, known for their high levels of school police and security. The Careers in Sports High School reports an 84 percent graduation rate compared to a 54 percent graduation rate at New York City schools with metal detectors (Ofer et al. 2009). School police play a limited role in the Careers in Sports High School, serving as "greeters" at the front doors at the beginning of the school day, and as back up for the rare occasions where police involvement is required. School police do not patrol school hallways. The school's suspension rate was 3.9 percent and the school had a 0 percent report of violent incidents.

The United States, particularly since 9/11, has become addicted to surveillance technology with little regard for its effectiveness and need. We are surrounded by messages of danger and violence that drive people to accept the façade of solutions represented by metal detectors, pat downs, and searches. My organization was not immune from this moral panic about dangerous kids. One summer, a few years back, the Syracuse papers were filled with stories of street violence. This in turn generated both casual discussion and discussions in community meetings about how violent the kids were and how they were ready to explode. While we knew that the kids we worked with were touched in various ways by the street violence, none of these behaviors were carried into our programs. Yet, the ubiquitous talk of impending violence instigated disquiet among my staff, who then came to me to request that we purchase a wand to search kids before they came into the office. We talked; I asked them whether a violent incident had taken place or whether they found knives or other weapons on the kids in the office. They said no, but wanted to take preventive measures given what they were hearing about the upcoming "hot summer." We talked more: I told them I wanted them to feel safe at work, but I was not convinced that the wands were either necessary or effective. I also reminded them that our organization was committed to removing stigma and so, if we were to institute a wand or similar security procedure, anyone coming in our door would be subject to the same security measures: public officials and program monitors who visited our programs, teachers, parents, other community professionals, and staff. This gave the staff pause; they thought of the hassles of security that they go through when they go into schools or airports and decided that they did not want this intruding into their work space as well. So we moved away from wands and talked about other ways to keep kids and ourselves safe. We involved the kids in discussion and rule setting that would give them the safe environment that they also wanted. They came up with ideas and ways that they could be directly involved. The kids made signs that we posted in our office that reminded everyone that our program was a safe space for all. Staff made sure that they escorted kids out of the building to their bikes or buses to avert fights that might take place outside on the streets. The hot summer was, instead, "chill."[3]

This was not an easy conversation for me to have with my staff. The staff was initially supported by their supervisors, less out of supervisors' sense of fear, but more to shore up staff morale and to show staff that we cared about their concerns. Buying a wand would be responsive to their request and a quick and easy thing to do. The net of social control is easy to fall into; a simple "yes" would have spared me several hours of conversation and would be relatively easy to implement. That said, the introduction of metal detectors in my organization would have made us yet another space that communicates to kids that we are afraid of them, that we think they are dangerous and unable to control themselves. I am glad we resisted.

Removing police and reducing, if not eliminating, high-tech and high-cost security technology would also free up money to be used for approaches and resources that would be more likely to engage students and help them address the very real problems in their lives. The kids'

---

3. As I write this, I need to add the words "knock on wood" as my way to acknowledge that the prospect of trouble has some basis in reality.

words provide guidance as to what helps them learn, and, for the most part, their ideas confirm research on best practices in education. These include small classes, better trained and culturally competent teachers, a relevant curriculum delivered in ways that get kids active and interactive in learning, and social supports including mental health services for traumatic events such as violence and family incarceration. We do not lack for models of programmatic approaches. Websites hosted by the US Department Education (What Works Clearinghouse), the US Department of Health and Human Services, Substance Abuse and Mental Health Agency (National Registry of Evidence-Based Programs and Practices), and the US Department of Justice Office of Juvenile Delinquency and Prevention (Model Programs Guide) have comprehensive lists and information about model programs and evidence-based practices. PBIS also posts information on its website and offers training and technical assistance to school districts and schools interested in implementing this approach.

I would conclude this list of eminently practical and accessible reforms with changes in school financing to reduce the disparities between inner city and suburban schools. School financial inequities, measured by spending per pupil, are largely due to differences in the property tax base per pupil; state aid formulas designed to make up some of the local differential have become so complicated, with so many exceptions, that they have not successfully equalized per-pupil spending. Reforms have varied from full state funding of education in the State of Hawaii, to 75 percent funding in several other states. In New York State, after years of litigation and the appointment of a special master's panel, poor urban school districts saw increases in state funding in the 2007–08 state budget, but this was followed by a roller-coaster ride of increases and decreases as well as a cap on property tax increases that likely will have long-term implications for school financing that relies on this source of revenue.

The changes above—elimination of zero tolerance policies, removal or at least reduction in law enforcement presence both human and technological, pedagogical improvements, and the expanding and deepening social supports—are not utopian. They exist right now in more prosperous school districts throughout the United States. The different paths traveled by urban school districts are tied to the very structural conditions that set in motion mass incarceration: the disappearance of decent paying jobs from the American landscape and the legacy of racism that makes it easy to make communities of color redundant.

Empirical evidence of the failure of zero tolerance policies and the availability of alternative practices alone will not lead to the abandonment of harsh discipline and out-of-school suspension. The barriers to ending zero tolerance are deeply embedded in America's social, political, economic, and ideological being and will require the mobilization of political will led by the young people, families, and community allies most harmed by the transformation of their schools into prison preparatories. There are local, state, and national efforts to mobilize constituencies to demand an end to policies that put kids on the track to prison. The Dignity in Schools Campaign brings together parent and student groups with community and legal advocates, teachers, and school administrators to reassert children's rights to education and to oppose policies and practices that push young people out of school. At its 2009 national conference in Chicago, Illinois, the campaign developed a National Resolution on Ending School Pushout. The campaign has developed a model code that emphasizes positive behavioral interventions and supports and removes police and law enforcement paraphernalia from schools.

It will likely be up to grassroots and community-based organizations to make sure that the voices of young people are at the forefront of efforts to sever the connection between carceral social control and schools. I don't underestimate what it will take to mobilize kids who have been socialized to expect that their voices will not be heard. Many of the kids I interviewed have come to believe that they are voiceless and powerless as captured by this statement from Jalil (2008): *"Teachers always believe other teachers over the child and they never want to listen to us,"* or that the system's rules are rigid and unyielding regardless of individual circumstances. As Roland (2008) said, *"they know I didn't do nothing wrong, but if my hand touches the knife then they have no choice but to send me to Brig and that's how I got to Brig."* It is immensely challenging to help kids to transform their resistance from self-defeating behaviors into politically astute and strategic criticism. Adult supporters like the people who work in my agency and who don't fall prey to the moral panic of kids as dangerous are focused on helping these young people negotiate day-to-day survival issues. We often do not have time to encourage their critical thinking skills and the kinds of actions that may accompany social critique.

Bringing youth forward to participate in systemic change is hard, but not impossible. To show this, I end the book with a concluding story about Jayda and her trip to the United Nations in Geneva. One of the most interesting experiences that Jayda and the other kids who traveled to Geneva had was attending a training session where the US Human Rights Network organizers were schooling the delegation on what to expect and how to "behave" when the official US response to the United Nation's committee hearing on the International Convention on the Elimination of All Forms of Racial Discrimination (ICERD) was presented. The organizers explained to the almost entirely adult audience how the reporting process would unfold and what the US representatives were likely to say. As they summarized the anticipated official US denials of racial discrimination in a range of domains—from housing, to criminal justice, to education—groans, moans, and call-outs expressed the delegations' profound disagreements with the US position. The trainers stopped their presentation and engaged us in a conversation about effective resistance and effective critique. They informed us that the UN's hearing on the ICERD was a formal event and the audience was expected to listen quietly without disruption. They pointed out that we (the Network Delegation) would have other opportunities to comment on the US presentation through a separate meeting with UN representatives, a written delegation response, and follow-up meetings held in the United States. The trainers urged us to conduct ourselves with dignity in the hearing. We nodded and agreed, and when the time came, followed the instructions.

After this training session, Jayda and I were walking back to the hotel, followed by the other kids. I asked her what she thought about the training session. She told me that she was surprised to hear grownups being told how to behave and was particularly interested in the advice we were given about effective ways of confronting perceived injustice. This prompted a discussion about community action and strategies for effecting change. As we turned the corner to the hotel, Jayda grabbed the kids and said: "*We all activists now!*"

While I can't be sure that Jayda will go on to become politically engaged, only activism on the part of students like Jayda, supported by her family and community allies, will deconstruct the pipeline to prison.

References • *Index*

References

Adams, A. Troy. 2000. "The Status of School Discipline and Violence." *Annals of the American Academy of Political and Social Science* 567:140–56.

Adimora, Adaora A., and Victor J. Schoenbach. 2005. "Social Context, Sexual Networks and Racial Disparities in Rates of Sexually Transmitted Infections." *Journal of Infectious Diseases* 191:S115–S122.

Advancement Project. 2005. *Education on Lockdown: The Schoolhouse to the Jailhouse Track.* Washington, DC: Advancement Project.

———. 2006. *Arresting Development: Addressing the School Discipline Crisis in Florida.* Washington, DC: Advancement Project.

Advancement Project, Alliance for Educational Justice, Dignity in Schools Campaign, NAACP, and Legal Defense Fund. 2013. *Police in Schools Are Not the Answer to the Newtown Shooting.* Washington, DC: Advancement Project.

Advancement Project and Civil Rights Project at Harvard University. 2000. *Opportunities Suspended: The Devastating Consequences of Zero Tolerance and School Discipline.* Washington, DC: Advancement Project.

Albonetti, Celesta A. 1997. "Sentencing under the Federal Sentencing Guidelines: Effects of Defendant Characteristics, Guilty Pleas, and Departures on Sentence Outcomes for Drug Offenses 1991–1992." *Law and Society Review* 31:789–813.

Althusser, Louis. 1971. *Lenin and Philosophy.* New York: Monthly Review Press.

American Academy of Pediatrics. 2003. "Policy Statement by the Committee on Child Health, Out-of-School Suspension, and Expulsion." *Pediatrics* 112 (5): 1206–9.

American Bar Association. 2001. *Committee Report on Zero Tolerance Policies.* Washington, DC: American Bar Association. http://www.abanet.org/crim just/juvjus/zerotolreport.html.

———. 2004. *Justice Kennedy Commission: 2004 Report to the House of Delegates.* Washington, DC: American Bar Association.

American Institute of Architects. 2006. *Sustainable Design Assessment Team: Communities Making Connections.* Syracuse, NY: American Institute of Architects. http://www.aia.org/about/initiatives/AIAS075426.

Anderson, Elijah. 2000. *Code of the Street: Decency, Violence, and the Moral Life of the Inner City.* New York: W. W. Norton.

Anyon, Jean. 1980. "Social Class and the Hidden Curriculum of Work." *Journal of Education* 162 (1): 67–92.

———. 1995. "Inner City School Reform: Toward Useful Theory." *Urban Education* 30 (1): 56–70.

Ares, Charles E., Anne Rankin, and Herbert Sturz. 1963. "The Manhattan Bail Project: An Interim Report on the Use of Pretrial Parole." *New York University Law Review* 38:67–92.

Aron, Laudan Y. 2003. *Towards a Typology of Alternative Education Programs: A Compilation of Elements from the Literature.* Washington, DC: Urban Institute.

Asner, Martha R., and James Broschart, eds. 1978. *Violent Schools—Safe Schools—The Safe School Study Report to the Congress.* Vol 1. Washington, DC: National Institute of Education.

Aspen Institute. 2009. "In Conversation with US Secretary of Education and Henry Crown Fellow Arne Duncan, Interviewed by Bob Schieffer of CBS News." Presentation at the Aspen Ideas Festival, Aspen, CO, July 1. http://www.aspeninstitute.org/leadership-programs/fellows-at-ideasfest.

Atkins, Marc S., Mary M. McKay, Stacy L. Frazier, Lara J. Jakobsons, Patrice Arvanitis, Tim Cunningham, Catherine Brown, and Linda Lambrecht. 2002. "Suspensions and Detentions in an Urban, Low-Income School: Punishment or Reward?" *Journal of Abnormal Child Psychology* 30 (4): 361–71.

Atlas, Randall. 2002. "Designing Safe Schools." *Campus Security and Safety Journal* (December): 16–42.

Austin, Roy L., and Mark D. Allen. 2000. "Racial Disparity in Arrest Rates as an Explanation of Racial Disparity in Commitment to Pennsylvania's Prisons." *Journal of Research in Crime and Delinquency* 37:200–220.

Baldus, David C., George Woodworth, David Zuckerman, Neil Alan Weiner, and Barbara Broffit. 1998. "Racial Discrimination in the Post-Furman Era: An Empirical and Legal Overview, with Recent Findings from Philadelphia." *Cornell Law Review* 83:1638–1770.

Balfanz, Robert, Vaughan Byrnes, and Joanna Fox. 2013. *Sent Home and Put Off-Track: The Antecedents, Disproportionalities, and Consequences of Being*

Suspended in the Ninth Grade Date. Prepared for the Center for Civil Rights Remedies and the Research-to-Practice Collaborative, National Conference on Race and Gender Disparities in Discipline, Los Angeles, CA, University of California at Los Angeles, January 10. Washington, DC: Civil Rights Project. http://civilrightsproject.ucla.edu/resources/projects/center-for-civil-rights -remedies/school-to-prison-folder/state-reports/sent-home-and-put-off-track -the-antecedents-disproportionalities-and-consequences-of-being-suspended -in-the-ninth-grade.

Balfanz, Robert, Liza Herzog, and Douglas J. Mac Iver. 2007. "Preventing Student Disengagement and Keeping Students on the Graduation Track in High-Poverty Middle-Grades Schools: Early Identification and Effective Interventions." *Educational Psychologist* 42 (4): 223–35.

Barak, Greg. 2006. "A Critical Perspective on Violence." In *Advancing Critical Criminology: Theory and Application*, edited by W. S. DeKeseredy and B. Perry, 133–54. Landham, MD: Lexington.

Beale, Calvin L. 1993. "Prisons, Population and Jobs in Nonmetro America." *Rural Development Perspective* 8 (3): 16–19.

———. 1997. "Rural Prisons: An Update." *Rural Development Perspectives* 11 (2): 25–27.

Beatty, Phillip, Amanda Petteruti, and Jason Ziedenberg. 2007. *The Vortex: The Concentrated Racial Impact of Drug Imprisonment and the Characteristics of Punitive Counties*. Washington, DC: Justice Policy Institute.

Beger, Randall R. 2002. "Expansion of Police Power in Public Schools and the Vanishing Rights of Students." *Social Justice* 29 (1–2): 119–30.

Berliner, David C., and Sharon L. Nichols. 2007. *Collateral Damage: How High-Stakes Testing Corrupts America's Schools*. Cambridge, MA: Harvard Educational Press.

Black History Preservation Project. n.d. "African Americans in Syracuse: From the First Great Migration to the 15th Ward." *Our Stories* (website). http:// ourstories.syr.edu/exhibit/.

Blakely, Curtis R., and Vic W. Bumphus. 2004. "Private and Public Sector Prisons: A Comparison of Select Characteristics." *Federal Probation* 68 (1): 27–31. http://www.uscourts.gov/fedprob/June_2004/prisons.html.

Blumstein, Alfred. 1982. "On the Racial Disproportionality of United States' Prison Populations." *Journal of Criminology* 73 (3): 1259–81.

Blumstein, Alfred. 1993. "Racial Disproportionality of U.S. Prison Populations Revisited." *University of Colorado Law Review* 64:743–60.

Blumstein, Alfred, Jacqueline Cohen, Susan E. Martin, and Morris H. Tonry, eds. 1983. *Research on Sentencing: The Search for Reform*. Vol. 1. Washington, DC: National Academy Press.

Bogdan, Robert C., and Sari K. Biklin. 2003. *Qualitative Research for Education: An Introduction to Theories and Methods*. Boston: Allyn and Bacon.

Books, Sue. 2000. "Poverty and Environmentally Induced Damage to Children." In *The Public Assault on America's Children: Poverty, Violence, and Juvenile Injustice*, edited by V. Polokow, 42–58. Teaching for Social Justice Series. New York: Teachers College Press.

Bourdieu, Pierre. 1977. *Outline of a Theory of Practice*. Cambridge: Cambridge University Press.

———. 1984. *Distinction: A Social Critique of the Judgment of Taste*. Translated by R. Nice. Cambridge, MA: Harvard University Press.

Bourdieu, Pierre, and Jean-Claude Passeron. 1979. *The Inheritors: French Students and Their Relation to Culture*. Chicago: University of Chicago Press.

Bowditch, Christine. 1993. "Getting Rid of Troublemakers: High School Disciplinary Procedures and the Production of Dropouts." *Social Problems* 40 (4): 493–509.

Bowles, Samuel, and Herbert Gintis. 1976. *Schooling in Capitalist America*. New York: Basic.

Bowling, Ben. 1999. "The Rise and Fall of New York Murder: Zero Tolerance or Crack's Decline." *British Journal of Criminology* 39 (4): 531–54.

Bradshaw, Catherine P., Christine W. Koth, Leslie A. Thornton, and Philip J. Leaf. 2009. "Altering School Climate through School-Wide Positive Behavioral Interventions and Supports: Findings from a Group-Randomized Effectiveness Trial." *Society for Prevention Research* 10:100–115.

Bradshaw, Catherine P., Mary M. Mitchell, and Philip J. Leaf. 2010. "Examining the Effects of School-Wide Positive Behavioral Interventions and Supports on Student Outcomes." *Journal of Positive Behavior Interventions* 12:133–48.

Brady, Kevin P., Sharon Balmer, and Deinya Phenix. 2007. "School–Police Partnership Effectiveness in Urban Schools: An Analysis of New York City's Impact Schools Initiative." *Education and Urban Society* 39 (4): 455–78.

Brantlinger, Ellen. 1991. "Low-Income Adolescents' Perceptions of Social Class: Related Peer Affiliations in School." *Interchange* 22:9–27.

Bronfenbrenner, Urie. 1979. *The Ecology of Human Development: Experiments by Nature and Design*. Cambridge, MA: Harvard University Press.

Brooks, Kim, Vincent Schiraldi, and Jason Ziedenberg. 1999. *School House Hype: Two Years Later.* San Francisco: Center of Criminal and Juvenile Justice.

Brown v. Board of Education, 347 U.S. 483 (1954).

Brown, Jessamy. 2009. "New Texas Law Seeks Common Sense Instead of 'Zero Tolerance' in Punishment of Students." *Star Telegram*, August 22. http://www.star-telegram.com/804/story/1552845.html.

Brown, Lionel H., and Kelvin S. Beckett. 2007. "Parent Involvement in an Alternative School for Students at Risk of Educational Failure." *Education and Urban Society* 39 (4): 498–523.

Buckley, Sean, and Gabrielle Maxwell. 2007. *Respectful Schools: Restorative Practices in Education: A Summary Report.* Wellington, New Zealand: Office of the Children's Commissioner and the Institute of Policy Studies, School of Government, Victoria University.

Burawoy, Michael C. 2003. "Revisits: An Outline of a Theory of Reflexive Ethnography." *American Sociological Review* 68:645–79.

Bureau of Justice Assistance. 1996. *National Assessment of Structured Sentencing.* Washington, DC: US Department of Justice, Bureau of Justice Assistance.

CADRE. 2007. *Parent-Led Victory in the Fight to End Pushout in Los Angeles Schools.* Los Angeles: CADRE. http://www.cadre-la.org/media/docs/3980_CADREarticle_060407FINAL_mc.pdf.

Calhoun, India. 2001. *The Music Within.* Syracuse, NY: Center for Community Alternatives.

Cameron, Lisa, and Margaret Thorsborne. 2001. "Restorative Justice and School Discipline: Mutually Exclusive?" In *Restorative Justice and Civil Society*, edited by Heather Strang and John Braithwaite, 180–94. Cambridge: Cambridge University Press.

Carlos [pseud.]. 2008. Interview by Director Marsha Weissman, Center for Community Alternatives, Syracuse, NY.

Carson, E. Anne, and William J. Sabol. 2012. *Prisoners in 2011.* Washington, DC: US Department of Justice, Bureau of Justice Statistics.

Casella, Ronnie. 2001. *Being Down: Challenging Violence in Urban Schools.* New York: Teachers College Press.

———. 2003. "Security, Schooling, and the Consumer's Right to Segregate." *Urban Review* 35 (2): 129–48.

Celia [pseud.]. 2008. Interview by Director Marsha Weissman, Center for Community Alternatives, Syracuse, NY, July 13.

Center on Juvenile and Criminal Justice. 2007. *Political Power of the CCPOA*. San Francisco: Center on Juvenile and Criminal Justice. http://www.cjcj.org /cpp/political_power.php.

Chaney, Reece, Don Linkenhoker, and Arthur Horne. 1977. "The Counselor and Children of Imprisoned Parents." *Elementary School Guidance and Counseling* 11 (3): 177–83.

Chang, Tracy F. H., and Douglas E. Thompkins. 2002. "Corporations Go to Prisons: The Expansion of Corporate Power in the Correctional Industry." *Labor Studies Journal* 27 (1): 45–69.

Chen, Greg. 2008. "Communities, Students, Schools, and School Crime: A Confirmatory Study of Crime in U.S. High Schools." *Urban Education* 43 (3): 301–18.

Civil Rights Cases, 109 U.S. 3 (1883) (Supreme Court opinion consolidating five cases: United States v. Stanley, United States v. Ryan, United States v. Nichols, United States v. Singleton, and Robinson v. Memphis & Charleston Railroad).

Clear, Todd, and James M. Byrne. 1992. "The Future of Intermediate Sanctions." In *Smart Sentencing: The Emergence of Intermediate Sanctions*, edited by J. M. Byrne, A. J. Lurigio, and J. Petersilia, 319–30. Newbury Park, CA: Sage.

Clinton, William J. 1996. "Remarks on Crime." Speech delivered at Webster Groves High School, Webster Groves, MO, May 17. http://www.presidency. ucsb.edu/ws/?pid=52829.

Clotfelter, Charles T. 2004. *After Brown: The Rise and Retreat of School Desegregation*. Princeton, NJ: Princeton University Press.

Cobb, Charles. (1963). "Prospectus for a Summer Freedom School Program in Mississippi." Reproduced at *Education and Democracy* (website), edited by Kathy Emery. http://www.educationanddemocracy.org/FSCfiles/B_05_Prosp ForFSchools.htm. Originally published in SNCC, *The Student Nonviolent Coordinating Committee Papers, 1959–1972*, 1982, (reel 39, file 165, page 75), Sanford, NC: Microfilming Corporation of America. The original papers are at the King Library and Archives, Martin Luther King Jr. Center for Nonviolent Social Change, Atlanta, GA.

Cohn, Jeffrey P. 2006. "Keeping an Eye on School Security: The Iris Recognition Project in New Jersey Schools." *National Institute of Justice Journal* 254:12–15. http://www.ncjrs.gov/pdffiles1/jr000254.pdf.

Cole, David. 1999. *No Equal Justice*. New York: New Press.

Cole, Elizabeth R., and Safiyah R. Omari. 2003. "Race, Class and the Dilemma of Upward Mobility for African Americans." *Journal of Social Issues* 59 (4): 785–802.

Coleman, James S. 1966. *Equality of Educational Opportunity.* Washington, DC: US Government Printing Office.

———. 1988. "Social Capital in the Creation of Human Capital." In *Organizations and Institutions: Sociological and Economic Approaches to the Analysis of Social Structure,* supplement, *American Journal of Sociology* 94:S95–S120.

Common Application. 2014. *The Common Application* (website). https://www.commonapp.org.

Confessore, Nicholas. 2007. "Spitzer Seeks Panel to Study Prison Closings." *New York Times,* February 5.

Correctional Association of New York. 2006a. *Basic Prison and Jail Fact Sheet.* New York: Correctional Association of New York. http://www.correctionalassociation.org/publications/factsheets.htm.

———. 2006b. *Offenders under Custody in NYS Prisons Calendar Years 1970–2005.* New York: Correctional Association of New York. http://www.correctionalassociation.org/publications/factsheets.htm.

Correctional Corporation of America. 2007. "About CCA" (website). http://www.correctionscorp.com/aboutcca.html.

———. 2010. "CCA Announces 2010 Fourth Quarter and Full-Year Financial Results." Press release available at http://ir.correctionscorp.com/phoenix.zhtml?c=117983&p=irol-newsArticle&ID=1527174&highlight=.

Costenbader, Virginia, and Samia Markson. 1994. "School Suspension: A Survey of Current Policies and Practices." *NASSP Bulletin* 78:103–8.

———. 1998. "School Suspension: A Study with Secondary School Students." *Journal of School Psychology* 36 (1): 59–82.

Crenshaw, Kimberley. 1995. "Race, Reform, and Retrenchment: Transformation and Legitimation and Anti-Discrimination Law." In *Critical Race Theory: The Key Writings that Formed the Movement,* edited by Kimberley Crenshaw, Neil Gotanda, Gary Peller, and Kendall Thomas, 103–22. New York: New Press.

Crutchfield, Robert D., George S. Bridges, and Susan R. Pitchford. 1994. "Analytical and Aggregation Biases in Analyses of Imprisonment: Reconciling Discrepancies in Studies of Racial Disparity." *Journal of Research in Crime and Delinquency* 31 (2): 166–82.

Dahlberg, Robin. 2012. *The Criminalization of School Discipline in Massachusetts' Three Largest School Districts.* New York: American Civil Liberties Union.

Damian [pseud.]. 2008. Interview by Director Marsha Weissman, Center for Community Alternatives, Syracuse, NY, January 30.

Darling-Hammond, Linda. 2007. "Race, Inequality, and Educational Accountability: The Irony of 'No Child Left Behind.'" *Race, Ethnicity and Education* 10:245–52.

Davis, Mike. 1995. "Hell Factories in the Field." *Nation,* February 20, 229–34.

Deering, Tara, Tom Alex, and Brianna Blake. 2003. "1 in 3 School Arrests Involved Blacks." *Des Moines Register,* June 17. http://www.uiowa.edu/~nrcfcp/dmcrc/pdf/DM%20Register%206-17-03.pdf.

Demuth, Stephen, and Darrell Steffensmeier. 2004. "The Impact of Gender and Race-Ethnicity on the Pretrial Release Process." *Social Problems* 51 (2): 234 and 237–38.

Devine, John. 1996. *Maximum Security: The Culture of Violence in Inner City Schools.* Chicago: University of Chicago Press.

DeVoe, Jill F., and Sarah Kaffenberger. 2005. *Student Reports of Bullying: Results from the 2001 School Crime Supplement to the National Crime Victimization Survey (NCES 2005–310).* Washington, DC: US Department of Education, National Center for Education Statistics.

Dinkes, Rachael, Emily Forrest Cataldi, and Wendy Lin-Kelly. 2007. *Indicators of School Crime and Safety: 2007 (NCES 2008-021/NCJ 219553).* Washington, DC: National Center for Education Statistics, Institute of Education Sciences, US Department of Education, and Bureau of Justice Statistics, Office of Justice Programs, US Department of Justice.

Donahue, Elizabeth, Vincent Schiraldi, and Jason Ziedenberg. 1998. *School House Hype: The School Shootings and the Real Risks Kids Face in America.* Washington, DC: Center for Juvenile and Criminal Justice.

Donela [pseud.]. 2008. Interview by Director Marsha Weissman, Center for Community Alternatives, Syracuse, NY, February 11.

Doster, Adam. 2007. "Correcting the Guards." *American Prospect,* July 2. http://prospect.org/cs/articles?article=correcting_the_guards.

Drakeford, William. 2004. *Racial Disproportionality in School Discipline: Practitioners' Brief.* Tempe, AZ: National Center for Culturally Responsive Educational Systems.

Ducre, K. Animashaun. 2012. *A Place We Call Home: Gender, Race and Justice in Syracuse.* Syracuse, NY: Syracuse University Press.

Dunbar, Christopher Jr. 2001. "From Alternative School to Incarceration." *Qualitative Inquiry* 7 (3): 158–70.

Duncan, Arne. 2011. "Remarks of U.S. Secretary of Education Arne Duncan to the National Historically Black Colleges and Universities Week Conference." Washington, DC, September 20. Available at http://www.ed.gov /news/speeches/engaging-world-anew-conference.

Duncan, Garrett Albert. 2000. "Urban Pedagogies and the Celling of Adolescents of Color." *Social Justice* 27 (3): 29–42.

Duncan, Greg J., and Jean Brooks-Gunn. 1997. *Consequences of Growing Up Poor.* New York: Russell Sage Foundation.

Duncan, Greg J., Ruby Mendenhall, and Stephanie DeLuca. 2006. "Neighborhood Resources, Racial Segregation, and Economic Mobility: Results from the Gautreaux Program." *Social Science Research* 35 (4): 892–923.

Duncombe, William W., Anna Lukemeyer, and John Yinger. 2006. *The No Child Left Behind Act: Have Federal Funds Been Left Behind?* Syracuse, NY: Syracuse University, Center for Policy Research, Education Finance and Accountability Program.

Eckenrode, John, Molly Laird, and John Doris. 1993. "School Performance and Disciplinary Problems among Abused and Neglected Children." *Developmental Psychology* 29:53–62.

Eisenhower, Dwight D. 1961. "Transcript of President Dwight D. Eisenhower's Farewell Address (1961)," January 17. *Our Documents* (website). http:// www.ourdocuments.gov/doc.php?doc=90&page=transcript. Original transcript provided courtesy of Dwight D. Eisenhower Presidential Library and Museum, Abilene, KS. http://www.eisenhowermemorial.org/speeches /19610117%20farewell%20addresshtm.

ERASE Initiative. 2002. *Profiled and Punished: How San Diego Schools Undermine Latino and African American Students.* Oakland, CA: Applied Research Center.

Fabelo, Tony, Michael D. Thompson, Martha Plotkin, Dottie Carmichael, Miner P. Marchbanks III, and Eric A. Booth. 2011. *Breaking Schools' Rules: A Statewide Study of How School Discipline Relates to Students' Success and Juvenile Justice Involvement.* New York: Council of State Governments Justice Center.

Fagan, Jeffrey, and Tom R. Tyler. 2005. "Legal Socialization of Children and Adults." *Social Justice Research* 18 (3): 217–41.

Fagan, Jeffrey, Deanna L. Wilkinson, and Garth Davies. 2007. "Social Contagion of Violence." In *The Cambridge Handbook of Violent Behavior*, edited by Daniel Flannery, Alexander Vazsonyi, and Irwin Waldman, 688–723. Cambridge: Cambridge University Press.

Fallis, R. Kirk, and Susan Opotow. 2003. "Are Students Failing School or Are Schools Failing Students? Class Cutting in High School." *Journal of Social Issues* 59 (1): 103–19.

Federal Bureau of Investigation. 2006. *Synopsis of Crime in Schools and Colleges: A Study of National Incident-Based Reporting System (NCIBRS) Data*. Rockville, MD: National Institute of Justice. http://www.fbi.gov/ucr/schoolviolence.pdf.

Ferguson, Ann A. 2000. *Bad Boys: Public Schools in the Making of Black Masculinity*. Ann Arbor: University of Michigan Press.

Figlio, David N. 2006. "Testing, Crime and Punishment." *Journal of Public Economics* 90 (4–5): 837–51.

Figlio, David N., and Lawrence S. Getzler. 2002. "Accountability, Ability and Disability: Gaming the System?" NBER Working Paper 9307. Cambridge, MA: National Bureau of Economic Research.

Fine, Michelle. 1991. *Framing Dropouts: Notes on the Politics of an Urban Public High School*. Albany: State University of New York Press.

———. 1994. "Dis-stance and Other Stances: Negotiations of Power inside Feminist Research." In *Power and Method: Political Activism and Educational Research*, edited by Andrew Gitlin, 13–35. Critical Social Thought Series. New York: Routledge.

Fine, Michelle, April Burns, Yassar Payne, and Maria E. Torre. 2004. "Civic Lessons: The Color and Class of Betrayal." In *Working Method: Research and Social Justice*, edited by Lois Weis and Michelle Fine, 53–75. New York: Routledge.

Fiscal Policy Institute. 2012. *Pulling Apart: The Continuing Impact of Polarization in New York State*. Albany, NY: Fiscal Policy Institute.

Florida Department of Juvenile Justice. 2011. *Delinquency in Florida's Schools: A Seven Year Study*. Tallahassee, FL: Florida Department of Juvenile Justice. http://www.djj.state.fl.us/docs/research2/2010-11-delinquency-in-schools-analysis.pdf?sfvrsn=0.

Foley, Regina M., and Lan-Sze Pang. 2006. "Alternative Education Programs: Program and Student Characteristics." *High School Journal* (February–March): 10–21.

Fordham, Signithia. 1996. *Blacked Out: Dilemmas of Race, Identity, and Success at Capital High*. Chicago: University of Chicago Press.

Fordham, Signithia, and John Ogbu. 1986. "Black Students' School Success: Coping with the Burden of 'Acting White.'" *Urban Review* 18:176–206.

Foucault, Michel. 1979. *Discipline and Punish: The Birth of the Prison*. New York: Vintage.

Franklin, John Hope. 1994. *Reconstruction after the Civil War*. Chicago: University of Chicago Press.

Free, Marvin D. 1997. "The Impact of Federal Sentencing Reforms on African Americans." *Journal of Black Studies* 28:268–86.

Freudenberg, Nick. 2008. "Health Research behind Bars: A Brief Guide to Research in Jails and Prisons." In *Public Health behind Bars: From Prisons to Communities*, edited by Robert Greifinger, 415–33. New York: Springer.

Frey, William H. 2010. *Census Data: Blacks and Hispanics Take Different Segregation Paths*. Washington DC: Brookings Institution. http://www.brookings.edu/research/opinions/2010/12/16-census-frey.

Frost, Natalie A., Judy Greene, and Kay Pranis. 2006. *HARD HIT: The Growth in the Imprisonment of Women, 1977–2004*. New York: Women's Prison Association.

Gaines, Donna. 1998. *Teenage Wasteland: Suburbia's Dead-End Kids*. Chicago: University of Chicago Press.

Gallagher, Kathleen, and Caroline Fusco. 2006. "I.D.ology and the Technologies of Public (School) Space: An Ethnographic Inquiry into the Neo-Liberal Tactics of Social (Re)production." *Ethnography and Education* 1 (3): 301–18.

Galtung, Johan. 1969. "Violence, Peace, and Peace Research." *Journal of Peace Research* 6 (3): 167–91.

Garland, David. 1990. *Punishment and Modern Society: A Study in Social Theory*. Oxford: Oxford University Press.

———. 2001a. "Introduction." In *Mass Imprisonment: Social Causes and Consequences*, edited by David Garland, 1–3. Thousand Oaks, CA: Sage.

———. 2001b. *The Culture of Control: Crime and Social Order in Contemporary Society*. Chicago: University of Chicago Press.

Garner, Catherine L., and Stephen W. Raudenbush. 1991. "Neighborhood Effects on Educational Attainment: A Multilevel Analysis." *Sociology of Education* 64 (October): 251–62.

Ghosh, Palash R. 2006. "Private Prisons Have a Lock on Growth." *Businessweek*, July 5. http://www.businessweek.com/print/investor/content/jul2006/pi2006 0706_849785.htm.

Gilmore, Ruth Wilson. 2007. *Golden Gulag: Prisons, Surplus, Crisis and Opposition in Globalizing California.* Berkeley: University of California Press.

Giroux, Henry A. 1982. "The Politics of Educational Theory." *Social Text* 5:87–102.

———. 2003. *The Abandoned Generation: Democracy Beyond the Culture of Fear.* New York: Palgrave Macmillan.

Glaser, Barney G., and Anselm L. Strauss. 1967. *The Discovery of Grounded Theory: Strategies for Qualitative Research.* New York: Aldine De Gruyter.

Glaze, Lauren E., and Laura M. Maruschak. 2008. *Parents in Prison and Their Minor Children.* Washington, DC: Bureau of Justice Statistics.

Glaze, Lauren E., and Erika Parks. 2012. *Correctional Populations in the United States, 2011.* Washington, DC: Bureau of Justice Statistics.

Goldkamp, John S. 1979. *Two Classes of Accused: A Study of Bail and Detention in American Justice.* Cambridge, MA: Ballinger.

Goldsmith, Susan. 2007a. "Unruly Schoolboys or Sex Offenders?" *Oregonian*, July 22, A1.

———. 2007b. "DA Pledges Review after Judge Tosses Swatting Case." *Oregonian*, August 21, A1.

Golub, Andrew, Bruce D. Johnson, and Eloise Dunlap. 2007. "The Race/Ethnicity Disparity in Misdemeanor Marijuana Arrests in New York City." *Criminology and Public Policy* 6 (1): 131–64.

Goodman, Paul. 1960. *Growing Up Absurd: Problems of Youth in the Organized Society.* New York: Random House.

Gordon-Reed, Annette. 2008. *The Hemingses of Monticello: An American Family.* New York: Norton.

Gregory, Anne, and Pharmacia Mosely. 2004. "The Discipline Gap: Teachers' Views on the Over-Representation of African American Students in the Discipline System." *Equity and Excellence in Education* 37:18–30.

Gregory, James F. 1995. "The Crime of Punishment: Racial and Gender Disparities in the Use of Corporal Punishment in U.S. Public Schools." *Journal of Negro Education* 64 (4): 454–62.

————. 1997. "Three Strikes and They're Out: African American Boys and American Schools' Responses to Misbehavior." *International Journal of Adolescence and Youth* 7:25–34.

Grubb, W. Norton, and Marvin Lazerson. 2005. "The Education Gospel and the Role of Vocationalism in American Education." *American Journal of Education* 111 (3): 297–318.

Hagan, John. 1974. "Extra-Legal Attributes and Criminal Sentencing: An Assessment of a Sociological Viewpoint." *Law and Society Review* 8:357–83.

————. 1993. "Structural and Cultural Disinvestment and the New Ethnographies of Poverty and Crime." Review of *Streetwise: Race, Class, and Change in an Urban Community*, by Elijah Anderson; *People and Folks: Gangs, Crime and the Underclass in a Rustbelt City*, by John M. Hagedorn; *Going Down to the Barrio: Homeboys and Homegirls in Change*, by Joan W. Moore; and *The Gang as an American Enterprise*, by Felix M. Padilla. *Contemporary Sociology* 22:27–32.

Harlow, Carolyn W. 2003. *Education and Correctional Populations*. Washington, DC: US Department of Justice, Bureau of Justice Statistics.

Harris, David A. 2000. "Driving while Black and Other African-American Crimes: The Continuing Relevance of Race to American Criminal Justice." In *The State of Black America 2000: Blacks in the New Millennium*, edited by Lee A. Daniels. New York: National Urban League.

Harrison, Paige M., and Alan J. Beck. 2006. *Prison and Jail Inmates at Midyear 2005*. Washington, DC: US Department of Justice, Bureau of Justice Statistics.

Hart, Timothy, and Brian A. Reaves. 1999. *Felony Defendants in Large Urban Counties, 1996*. Washington, DC: US Department of Justice, Bureau of Justice Statistics.

Harvey, Joel. 2007. *Young Men in Prison: Surviving and Adapting to Life Inside*. Uffculme, UK: William.

Hawkins, David, and Kenneth A. Hardy. 1989. "Black-White Imprisonment Rates: A State-by-State Analysis." *Social Justice* 16:75–95.

Hawkins, J. David, and Richard F. Catalano. 1992. *Communities That Care: Action for Drug Prevention*. San Francisco: Jossey-Bass.

Hazel, Neal, Ann Hagell, and Laura Brazier. 2002. *Young Offenders' Perceptions of Their Experiences in the Criminal Justices System*. London: Policy Research Bureau. http://tinyurl.com/cw39m.

Hemmings, Ann. 2002. "Youth Culture of Hostility: Discourses of Money, Respect and Difference." *Qualitative Studies in Education* 15 (3): 291–307.

Hemphill, Sheryl A., John W. Toumborou, Todd I. Herrenkohl, Barbara J. McMorris, and Richard F. Catalano. 2006. "The Effect of School Suspensions and Arrests on Subsequent Adolescent Antisocial Behavior in Australia and the United States." *Journal of Adolescent Health* 39 (5): 736–44.

Henry, Stuart. 2000. "What Is School Violence?: An Integrated Definition." *Annals of the American Academy of Political and Social Science* 567:16–29.

Hermann, Robert, E. Single, and J. Boston. 1977. *Counsel for the Poor.* Lexington, MA: Lexington.

Holt, John. 1964. *How Children Fail.* New York: Pitman.

Holzer, Harry, Diane W. Schanzenbach, Greg J. Duncan, and Jen Ludwig. 2007. *The Economic Costs of Growing Up Poor in the United States.* Washington, DC: Center for American Progress.

Horner, Robert H., George Sugai, Keith Smolkowski, Lucille Eber, Jean Nakasato, Ann W. Todd, and Jody Esperanza. 2009. "A Randomized, Wait-List Controlled Effectiveness Trial Assessing School-Wide Positive Behavior Support in Elementary Schools." *Journal of Positive Behavior* 11 (3), 133–44.

Hosp, John L., and Michelle K. Hosp. 2001. "Behavior Differences between African-American and Caucasian Students: Issues for Assessment and Intervention." *Education and Treatment of Children* 24:336–50.

Howard, Tyrone C. 2003. "A Tug of War for Our Minds: African American High School Students' Perceptions of Their Academic Identities and College Aspirations." *High School Journal* (October–November): 4–14.

Howell, James C. 2003. *Preventing and Reducing Juvenile Delinquency: A Comprehensive Framework.* Thousand Oaks, CA: Sage.

Human Rights Watch. 2000. *Punishment and Prejudice: Racial Disparities in the War on Drugs.* New York: Human Rights Watch. http://www.hrw.org/reports/2000/usa/.

Hyman, Irwin A., and Donna C. Perone. 1998. "The Other Side of School Violence: Educator Policies and Practices That May Contribute to Student Misbehavior." *Journal of School Psychology* 36 (1): 7–27.

Illich, Ivan. 1972. *Deschooling Society.* New York: Harper and Row.

Institute on Money in State Politics. 2006. *Policy Lockdown: Prison Interests Court Political Players.* Helena, MT: Institute on Money in State Politics. http://www.followthemoney.org/press/Reports/200605021.pdf.

Irons, Peter. 2002. *Jim Crow's Children: The Broken Promise of the Brown Decision.* New York: Viking.

Jacob, Brian A. 2005. "Accountability, Incentives and Behavior: The Impact of High Stakes Testing in the Chicago Public Schools." *Journal of Public Economics* 89 (5–6): 761–96.

Jacobs, Ann L. 1995. "Protecting Children and Preserving Families: A Cooperative Strategy for Nurturing Children of Incarcerated Parents." Speech presented to the Annie E. Casey Foundation Family-to-Family Initiative Conference, Baltimore, MD, October.

Jacobs, David, and Robert M. O'Brien. 1998. "The Determinants of Deadly Force: A Structural Analysis of Police Violence." *American Journal of Sociology* 103 (4): 837–62.

Jalil [pseud.]. 2008. Interview by Director Marsha Weissman, Center for Community Alternatives, Syracuse, NY, March 25.

Janella [pseud.]. 2007. Interview by Director Marsha Weissman, Center for Community Alternatives, Syracuse, NY, December 27.

Jayda [pseud.]. 2008. Interview by Director Marsha Weissman, Center for Community Alternatives, Syracuse, NY, June 19.

Jena [pseud.]. 2008. Interview by Director Marsha Weissman, Center for Community Alternatives, Syracuse, NY, January 6.

Johnson, Byron R., and William Wubbenhorst. 2009. *The Center for Neighborhood Enterprise Violence-Free Zone Initiative: A Milwaukee Case Study.* Waco, TX: Baylor Institute for Studies in Religion.

Johnson, Elizabeth, and Jane Waldfogel. 2002. "Parental Incarceration: Recent Trends and Implications for Child Welfare." *Social Service Review* (September): 460–79.

Jose [pseud.]. 2008. Interview by Director Marsha Weissman, Center for Community Alternatives, Syracuse, NY, April 16.

Justice Policy Institute. 2012. *Education under Arrest: The Case against Police in Schools.* Washington, DC: Justice Policy Institute.

Kaeser, Susan C. 1979. "Suspensions in School Discipline." *Education and Urban Society* 11:465–84.

Karla [pseud.]. 2008. Interview by Director Marsha Weissman, Center for Community Alternatives, Syracuse, NY, February 23.

Katz, Cindi. 2001. "Vagabond Capitalism and the Necessity of Social Reproduction." *Antipode* 33 (4): 708–28.

Kaufman, Philip, Xianglei Chen, Susan P. Choy, Sally A. Ruddy, Amanda K. Miller, Jill K. Fleury, Kathryn A. Chandler, Michael R. Rand, Patsy Klaus, and

Michael G. Planty. 2000. *Indicators of School Crime and Safety, 2000.* Washington, DC: US Department of Education and US Department of Justice.

Kendra [pseud.]. 2008. Interview by Director Marsha Weissman, Center for Community Alternatives, Syracuse, NY, April 29.

Kennedy, Mary M., Richard K. Jung, and Martin E. Orland. 1986. *Poverty, Achievement and the Distribution of Compensatory Education Services.* Washington, DC: US Department of Education.

Kerbow, David. 1996. "Patterns of Urban Student Mobility and Local School Reform." *Journal of Education for Students Placed at Risk* 1 (2): 147–69.

Kerka, Sandra. 2003. *Alternatives for At-Risk and Out-of-School Youth.* Columbus: Ohio State University. http://eric.ed.gov/?q=sandra+kerka&ff1=dtySince_1995&id=ED482327.

King, Ryan S., and Marc Mauer. 2002. *Distorted Priorities: Drug Offenders in State Prison.* Washington, DC: Sentencing Project.

King, Ryan S., Marc Mauer, and Malcolm Young. 2005. *Incarceration and Crime: A Complex Relationship.* Washington, DC: Sentencing Project.

Klehr, Deborah G. 2009. "Addressing the Unintended Consequences of No Child Left Behind and Zero Tolerance: Better Strategies for Safe Schools and Successful Students." *Georgetown Journal on Poverty Law and Policy* 16:585–610.

Kleiner, Brian, Rebecca Porch, and Elizabeth Farris. 2002. *Public Alternative Schools and Programs for Students at Risk of Educational Failure: 2000–01.* Washington, DC: US Department of Education, National Center for Educational Statistics.

Kneebone, Elizabeth, Carey Nadeau, and Alan Berube. 2011. *The Re-Emergence of Concentrated Poverty: Metropolitan Trends in the 2000s.* Washington, DC: Brookings Institution.

Kollali, Sapna. 2008. "Groups Question Police in School." *Syracuse Post Standard*, November 22.

Kora [pseud.]. 2008. Interview by Director Marsha Weissman, Center for Community Alternatives, Syracuse, NY, June 19.

Kostelny, Kathleen, and James Garbarino. 2001. "The War Close to Home: Children and Violence in the United States." In *Peace, Conflict, and Violence: Peace Psychology for the 21st Century*, edited by Daniel J. Christie, Richard V. Wagner, and Deborah A. Winter, 110–99. Englewood Cliffs, CA: Prentice-Hall.

Kozol, Jonathan. 1967. *Death at an Early Age*. New York: Penguin.

————. 1972. *Free Schools*. Boston: Houghton Mifflin.

————. 1991. *Savage Inequalities*. New York: Crown.

Krezmien, Michael, Peter E. Leone, and Georgianna M. Achilles. 2006. "Suspension, Race, and Disability: Analysis of Statewide Practices and Reporting." *Journal of Emotional and Behavioral Disorders* 14 (4): 217–26.

Kvale, Steinar. 1996. *InterViews: An Introduction to Qualitative Research Interviewing*. Thousand Oaks, CA: Sage.

Kwame [pseud.]. 2008. Interview by Director Marsha Weissman, Center for Community Alternatives, Syracuse, NY, April 8.

Labaree, David A. 1997. "Public Good, Private Goods: The American Struggle over Educational Goals." *American Educational Research Journal* 34 (1): 39–81.

Ladson-Billings, Gloria. 1994. *The Dreamkeepers: Successful Teachers of African American Children*. San Francisco: Jossey-Bass.

————. 1998. "Just What Is Critical Race Theory and What's It Doing in a Nice Field Like Education?" *International Journal of Qualitative Studies in Education* 11:1 and 7–24.

————. 2001. *Crossing Over to Canaan: The Journey of New Teachers in Diverse Classrooms*. San Francisco: Jossey-Bass.

Ladson-Billings, Gloria, and William F. Tate IV. 1995. "Toward a Critical Race Theory of Education." *Teachers College Record* 97 (1): 47–68.

Lane, Sandra D. 2008. *Why Are Our Babies Dying? Pregnancy, Birth and Death in America*. Boulder, CO: Paradigm.

Lane, Sandra D., Robert A. Rubinstein, Rob Keefe, Noah Webster, Alan Rosenthal, Donald Cibula, and Jesse Dowdell. 2004. "Structural Violence and Racial Disparity in Heterosexual HIV Infection." *Journal of Health Care for the Poor and Underserved* 15 (Aug): 319–35.

Lane, Sandra D., Noah Webster, Brooke A. Levandowski, Robert A. Rubinstein, Rob Keefe, Martha A. Wojtowycz, Donald A. Cibula, Johanna E. F. Kingson, and Richard H. Aubry. 2008. "Environmental Injustice: Childhood Lead Poisoning, Teen Pregnancy, and Tobacco." *Journal of Adolescent Health* 42:43–49.

Langan, Patrick A. 1985. "Racism on Trial: New Evidence to Explain the Racial Composition of Prisons in the United States." *Journal of Criminal Law and Criminology* 76 (3): 667–83.

Lange, Cheryl M., and Sandra J. Sletten. 2002. *Alternative Education: A Brief History and Research Synthesis*. Alexandria, VA: National Association of State Directors of Special Education.

Learning Point Associates. 2006. *Final Report: Syracuse City School District*. Naperville, IL: Learning Point Associates.

Lehr, Camilla A., and Cheryl M. Lange. 2003. *Alternative Schools and the Students They Serve: Perceptions of State Directors of Special Education*. Alternative Schools Research Project, Policy Research Brief 14 (1). Minneapolis: University of Minnesota, Institute on Community Integration.

Leschied, Alan W., Anne L. Cummings, Marvin van Brunschot, Allison Cunningham, and Angela Saunders. 2000. *Female Adolescent Aggression: A Review of the Literature and the Correlates of Aggression*. Ottawa, ON: Solicitor General of Canada. http://ww2.ps-sp.gc.ca/publications/corrections/200004_Leschied_report_e.pdf.

Leventhal, Tama, and Jeanne Brooks-Gunn. 2000. "The Neighborhoods They Live In: The Effects of Neighborhood Residence on Child and Adolescent Outcomes." *Psychological Bulletin* 126 (2): 309–37.

Levitt, Steven D. 2004. "Understanding Why Crime Fell in the 1990s: Four Factors That Explain the Decline and Six That Do Not." *Journal of Economic Perspectives* 18 (1): 163–90.

Lietz, Jeremy J., and Mary K. Gregory. 1978. "Pupil Race and Sex Determinants of Office and Exceptional Education Referrals." *Educational Research Quarterly* 3 (2): 61–66.

Lipsey, Mark W. 1992. "Juvenile Delinquency Treatment: A Meta-Analysis Inquiry into the Variability of Effects." In *Meta-Analysis for Explanation: A Casebook*, edited by T. D. Cook, H. Cooper, D. S. Cordray, H. Hartmann, L. V. Hedges, R. J. Light, T. A. Louis, and F. Mosteller, 83–127. New York: Russell Sage Foundation.

Livingston, Andrea. 2006. *The Condition of Education 2006 in Brief*. Washington, DC: US Department of Education, National Center for Education Statistics.

Loeber, Rolf, and Davis P. Farrington, eds. 2001. *Child Delinquents: Development, Intervention, and Service Needs*. Thousand Oaks, CA: Sage.

Losen, Daniel, and Tia E. Martinez. 2013. *Out of School and Off Track: The Overuse of Suspensions in American Middle and High Schools*. Los Angeles, CA: Center for Civil Rights Remedies at the Civil Rights Project at the University of California, Los Angeles. http://www.civilrightsproject.ucla.edu.

MacArthur Foundation Research Network on Adolescent Development and Juvenile Justice. n.d. *Adolescent Legal Competence in Court.* Issue Brief #1. Philadelphia, PA: MacArthur Foundation Research Network on Adolescent Development and Juvenile Justice. http://www.adjj.org/content/page.php?cat _id=2andcontent_id=28.

MacDonald, Robert, and Jane Marsh. 2004. "Missing School: Educational Engagement, Youth Transitions and Social Exclusion." *Youth and Society* 36 (2): 143–62.

MacLeod, Jay. 1995. *Ain't No Makin' It: Aspirations and Attainment in a Low-Income Neighborhood.* Boulder, CO: Westview.

Maeroff, Gene I. 2012. *Rebuilding Communities: Education's Central Role in Mobilizing Community Reform.* New York: Say Yes to Education. http://www .sayyestoeducation.org/pressrelease/say-yes-announces-new-paper-creating -city-wide-change.

Mahoney, Barry, Bruce D. Beaudin, John A. Carver III, Daniel B. Ryan, and Richard B. Hoffman. 2001. *Pretrial Services Programs: Responsibilities and Potential.* Washington DC: National Institute of Justice.

Malik [pseud.]. 2008. Interview by Director Marsha Weissman, Center for Community Alternatives, Syracuse, NY, March 25.

Manning, Peter K. 2000. "Policing New Social Spaces." In *Issues in Transnational Policing,* edited by James W. E. Sheptycki, 177–200. New York: Routledge.

Marla [pseud.]. 2008. Interview by Director Marsha Weissman, Center for Community Alternatives, Syracuse, NY, March 21.

Martin, Nancy, and Samuel Halperin. 2006. *Whatever It Takes: How Twelve Communities Are Reconnecting with Out-of-School Youth.* Washington, DC: Youth Policy Forum.

Massachusetts Advocacy Center. 1986. *The Way Out: Student Exclusion Practices in Boston Middle Schools.* Boston, MA: Massachusetts Advocacy Center.

Matza, David. 1990. *Delinquency and Drift.* New Brunswick, NJ: Transaction.

Mauer, Marc. 1994. *Americans Behind Bars: The International Use of Incarceration.* Washington, DC: Sentencing Project.

———. 2001. "The Causes and Consequences of Prison Growth in the United States." In *The Culture of Control: Crime and Social Order in Contemporary Society,* edited by David Garland. Chicago: University of Chicago Press.

———. 2006. *The Race to Incarcerate.* New York: New Press.

Mayer, Matthew J., and Peter E. Leone. 1999. "A Structural Analysis of School Violence and Disruption: Implications for Creating Safer Schools." *Education and Treatment of Children* 22:336–56.

McCall, Nathan. 1995. *Makes Me Wanna Holler: A Young Black Man in America.* New York: Vintage.

McCarthy, John D., and Dean R. Hoge. 1987. "The Social Construction of School Punishment: Racial Disadvantage Out of Universalistic Process." *Social Forces* 65:1101–20.

McCracken, Grant. 1998. *The Long Interview.* Newbury Park, CA: Sage.

McCurdy, Barry L., Mark C. Mannella, and Norris Eldridge. 2003. "Positive Behavior Support in Urban Schools: Can we Prevent the Escalation of Antisocial Behavior?" *Journal of Positive Behavior Interventions* 5 (3): 158–70.

McFadden, Anna C., George E. Marsh, Barrie J. Price, and Yunhan Hwang. 1992. "A Study of Race and Gender Bias in the Punishment of Children." *Education and Treatment of Children* 15 (2): 140–46.

McLanahan, Sara S. 1997. "Parent Absence or Poverty: Which Matters More?" In *Consequences of Growing Up Poor,* edited by Greg J. Duncan and Jeanne Brooks-Gunn, 35–48. New York: Russell Sage Foundation.

Merriam, Sharan B. 1998. *Qualitative Research and Case Study Applications in Education.* San Francisco: Jossey-Bass.

Miles, Matthew B., and Michael A. Huberman. 1994. *Qualitative Data Analysis.* Thousand Oaks, CA: Sage.

Miller, Jerome G. 1996. *Search and Destroy.* New York: Cambridge University Press.

Miller, Ron. 2002. *Free Schools, Free People: Education and Democracy after the 1960s.* Albany: State University of New York Press.

Mukamal, Deborah. 2001. *From Hard Time to Full Time: Strategies to Help Move Ex-offenders from Welfare to Work.* Washington, DC: US Department of Labor.

Mukuria, Gathogo. 2002. "Disciplinary Challenges: How Do Principals Address This Dilemma?" *Urban Education* 37:432–53.

Mustard, David B. 2001. "Racial, Ethnic, and Gender Disparities in Sentencing: Evidence from the U.S. Federal Courts." *Journal of Law and Economics* 44 (1): 285–314.

Nadeau, Debra Fuchs. 2003. *The Impact of Legislation on School Safety: A Policy Examination of Selected New York State Districts.* Research Brief 2.

New Paltz, NY: New York State Center for School Safety. http://nyscenter-forschoolsafety.org/brief2.pdf.

Nagel, Mechthild. 2002. "Prisons, Big Business, and Profit: Whither Social Justice?" In *Diversity, Multiculturalism, and Social Justice*, edited by Seth Asumah and Ibipo Johnston-Anumonwo, 361–85. Binghamton, NY: Global.

National Association of School Resource Officers. 2012. *To Protect and Educate: The School Resource Officer and the Prevention of Violence in Schools.* Hoover, AL: National Association of School Resource Officers. http://nasro.mobi/cms/index.php?option=com_contentandview=articleandid=157andItemid=334.

National Center on Crime and Delinquency. 1998. *1996 National Survey of State Sentencing Structures.* Washington, DC: US Department of Justice, Bureau of Justice Statistics.

National Coalition to Abolish Corporal Punishment in Schools. 2007. "Facts about Corporal Punishment." Columbus, OH: Center for Effective Discipline. http://www.stophitting.com/disatschool/facts.php#Punishment%20in%20U.S.%20Public.

National Commission on Excellence in Education. 1983. *A Nation at Risk.* Washington, DC: National Commission on Excellence in Education, US Government Printing Office. http://www.ed.gov/pubs/NatAtRisk/risk.html.

National Organization of Blacks in Law Enforcement. 2001. *A NOBLE Perspective: Racial Profiling—A Symptom of Bias-Based Policing.* Alexandria, VA: National Organization of Blacks in Law Enforcement.

Nelson, James F. 1995. *Disparities in Processing Felony Arrests in New York State, 1990–1992.* Albany: New York State Division of Criminal Justice Services, Bureau of Research and Evaluation.

New Jersey Office of the Attorney General. 1999. *Final Report of the State Police Review Team.* Trenton: New Jersey Office of the Attorney General. http://www.state.nj.us/lps/Rpt_ii.pdf.

New York Civil Liberties Union. 2007. *Criminalizing the Classroom: The Over-Policing of New York City Schools.* New York: New York Civil Liberties Union.

———. 2009. *The Rockefeller Drug Laws: Unjust, Irrational, Ineffective.* New York: New York Civil Liberties Union.

———. 2012. "Stop and Frisk Data" (website). New York: New York Civil Liberties Union. http://www.nyclu.org/issues/racial-justice/stop-and-frisk-practices.

New York State Community Action Association. 2009. *Poverty Report*. Guilderland, NY: New York State Community Action Association. http://www
.nyscaaonline.org/.

New York State Department of Correctional Services. 2010. *Under Custody
Report: Profile of the Inmate Population under Custody on January 1, 2010*.
Albany: New York State Department of Correctional Services.

New York State Department of Corrections and Community Supervision. 2011.
*Under Custody Report: Profile of the Inmate Population under Custody on
January 1, 2011*. Albany: New York State Department of Corrections and
Community Supervision.

———. 2012. *Under Custody Report: Profile of Incarcerated Offender Population
under Custody on January 1, 2012*. Albany: New York State Department of
Corrections and Community Supervision.

New York State Department of Education. 2005. *Five Schools Named as Persistently Dangerous under NCLB*. Albany: New York State Department of
Education.

———. 2008a. "Glossary of Terms Used in Reporting Violent and Disruptive
Incidents." New York State Department of Education (website). http://www
.emsc.nysed.gov/irts/violence-data/.

———. 2008b. *The New York State Public Schools Report Card*. Albany: New
York State Department of Education. https://www.nystart.gov/publicweb
-external/2007statewideAOR.pdf.

———. 2008c. "VADIR—Violent and Disruptive Incident Reporting." New
York State Department of Education (website). http://www.emsc.nysed.gov
/irts/violence-data/.

———. 2010. "New York Wins Nearly $700 Million in Race to the Top Competition." New York State Department of Education (website). http://www.oms
.nysed.gov/press/NewYorkWinsNearly700MinRacetotheTopCompetition
.html.

———. 2011. "The New York State District Report Card: Syracuse City School
District Accountability and Overview Report 2010–2011." New York State
Department of Education (website). https://reportcards.nysed.gov/schools
.php?district=800000040902& year=2011.

———. 2012. "The New York State District Report Card." New York State
Department of Education (website). https://reportcards.nysed.gov/counties
.php?year=2012.

New York State Department of Health. 2000. *Community Needs Index for the Central New York Region.* 2000 ed. Menands: New York State Department of Health AIDS Institute.

———. 2006. "Child and Adolescent Health Indicators, Onondaga County." *Department of Health Information for a Healthy New York* (website). Albany: New York State Department of Health. http://www.health.state.ny.us/nysdoh /chac/chai/docs/cah_onondaga.htm.

Noguera, Pedro A. 1995. "Preventing and Producing Violence: A Critical Analysis of Responses to School Violence." *Harvard Educational Review* 65 (2): 189–212.

———. 2003. "Schools, Prisons, and Social Implications of Punishment: Rethinking Disciplinary Practices." *Theory Into Practice* 42:341–50.

Norah [pseud.]. 2008. Interview by Director Marsha Weissman, Center for Community Alternatives, Syracuse, NY, April 17.

Oakes, Jeannie. 2005. *Keeping Track: How Schools Structure Inequality.* 2nd ed. New Haven, CT: Yale University Press.

Oakes, Jeannie, Molly Selvin, Lynn Karoly, and Gretchen Guiton. 1992. *Educational Matchmaking: Academic and Vocational Tracking in Comprehensive High Schools.* Berkeley, CA: National Center for Research in Vocational Education, University of California at Berkeley. http://www.eric.ed.gov/ERIC Docs/data/ericdocs2sql/content_storage_01/0000019b/80/29/a3/1a.pdf.

Ofer, Udi, Angela Jones, Johanna Miller, Deinya Phenix, Tara Bahl, Cristina Mokhtar, and Chase Madar. 2009. *Safety with Dignity: Alternatives to the Over-Policing of Schools.* New York: New York Civil Liberties Union, Annenberg Institute for School Reform at Brown University, and Make the Road.

Ogbu, John U. 1986. "Class Stratification and Racial Stratification and Schooling." In *Race, Class and Schooling,* edited by Lois Weis, 163–82. Buffalo: State University of New York at Buffalo, Comparative Education Center.

———. 2003. "Black American Students in an Affluent Suburb: A Study of Academic Disengagement." Mahwah, NJ: Lawrence Erlbaum.

Opotow, Susan, Janet Gerson, and Sarah Woodside. 2005. "From Moral Exclusion to Moral Inclusion: Theory for Teaching Peace." *Theory Into Practice* 44 (4): 303–18.

Orfield, Gary, and Daniel Losen. 2012. "Response to the Release of the 2009– 10 Civil Rights Data." *Civil Rights Project* (website). March 8. http://civil rightsproject.ucla.edu/research/k-12-education/civil-rights-data-collection -1/03.08.12-response-to-the-release-of-the-2009-10-civil-rights-data.

Orfield, Gary, Daniel Losen, Joanna Wald, and Christopher B. Swanson. 2004. *Losing Our Future: How Minority Youth Are Being Left Behind by the Graduation Rate Crisis.* Cambridge, MA: Civil Rights Project at Harvard University. http://www.urban.org/UploadedPDF/410936_LosingOurFuture.pdf.

Osypuk, Theresa L., Sandro Galea, Nancy McArdle, and Dolores Acevedo-Garcia. 2009. "Quantifying Separate and Unequal: Racial-Ethnic Distributions of Neighborhood Poverty in Metropolitan America." *Urban Affairs Review* 45 (1): 25–65.

Owen, Stephen S. 2005. "The Relationship between Social Capital and Corporal Punishments in Schools: A Theoretical Inquiry." *Youth and Society* 37 (1): 85–112.

Parents Involved in Community Schools v. Seattle School District No. 1; and Meredith, Custodial Parent, and Next Friend of McDonald v. Jefferson County Bd. of Ed., 551 U.S. 701 (2007) (combined Supreme Court cases).

Pastore, Ann L., and Kathleen Maguire. 2007. *Sourcebook of Criminal Justice Statistics.* 31st ed. http://www.albany.edu/sourcebook/.

Patterson, Gerald R., John B. Reid, and Thomas J. Dishion. 1992. *Antisocial Boys.* Eugene, OR: Castaila.

Payne, Charles M. 1997. "Education for Activism: Mississippi's Freedom Schools in the 1960s." Paper presented at the Annual Meeting of the American Educational Research Association, Chicago, IL, March 24–28. http://www.eric.ed.gov/ERICDocs/data/ericdocs2sql/content_storage_01/0000019b/80/14/ed/13.pdf.

Pennyfeather, Donald. 2001. *My Soul.* Syracuse, NY: Center for Community Alternatives.

Perez, Luis. 2003. "More Lead Poisoning Targeted." *Syracuse Post Standard*, February 7.

Perlstein, Daniel. 1990. "Teaching Freedom: SNCC and the Creation of the Mississippi Freedom Schools." *History of Education Quarterly* 30 (3): 297–324.

Perry, Steve W. 2008. *Justice Expenditure and Employment Extracts, 2006.* NCJ 224394. Washington, DC: US Department of Commerce, Bureau of the Census.

Petteruti, Amanda. 2011. *Education under Arrest: The Case against Police in Schools.* Washington, DC: Justice Policy Institute.

Pew Center on the States. *One in 100: Behind Bars in America 2008.* Washington, DC: The Pew Charitable Trusts.

Phillips, Mary T. 2007. "Bail, Detention and Non-Felony Case Outcomes." In *CJA Research Brief No. 14.* New York: New York Criminal Justice Agency.

Poe-Yamagata, Eileen, and Michael A. Jones. 2000. *And Justice for Some.* Washington, DC: National Center on Crime and Delinquency.

Pope, Carl, and William Feyerherm. 1990. "Minority Status and Juvenile Justice Processing." *Criminal Justice Abstracts* 22:327–36.

Potts, Randolph G. 2003. "Emancipatory Education versus School-Based Prevention in African American Communities." *American Journal of Community Psychology* 31 (1–2): 173–83.

Raffaele Mendez, Linda M., and Howard M. Knoff. 2003. "Who Gets Suspended from School and Why: A Demographic Analysis of Schools and Disciplinary Infractions in a Large School District." *Education and Treatment of Children* 26 (1): 30–51.

Raffaele Mendez, Linda M., Howard M. Knoff, and J. M. Ferron. 2002. "School Demographic Variables and Out-of-School Suspension Rates: A Quantitative and Qualitative Analysis of a Large, Ethnically Diverse School District." *Psychology in the Schools* 39 (3): 259–77.

Ramirez, Debra, Jack McDevitt, and Amy Farrel. 2000. *A Resource Guide on Racial Profiling Data Collection Systems: Promising Practices and Lessons Learned.* Washington, DC: US Department of Justice.

Rausch, M. Karenga, and Russell Skiba. 2004. *Disproportionality in School Discipline among Minority Students in Indiana: Description and Analysis.* Children Left Behind Policy Briefs. Supplementary Analysis 2-A. Bloomington: Center for Evaluation and Education Policy, Indiana University. http://ceep .indiana.edu/ChildrenLeftBehind/pdf/2a.pdf.

Rayquan [pseud.]. 2008. Interview by Director Marsha Weissman, Center for Community Alternatives, Syracuse, NY, January 4.

Raywid, Mary Anne. 1994. "Alternative Schools: The State of the Art." *Educational Leadership* 52 (1): 26–31.

Reyes, Augustina H. 2006. "The Criminalization of Student Discipline Programs and Adolescent Behavior." *St. John's Journal of Legal Commentary* 21 (1): 73–110.

Rikowski, Glenn. 1996. "Left Alone: End Time for Marxist Educational Theory." *British Journal of Sociology of Education* 17:415–52.

———. 1997. "Scorched Earth: Prelude to Rebuilding Marxist Educational Theory." *British Journal of Sociology of Education* 18:551–74.

Robbins, Christopher G. 2008. *Expelling Hope: The Assault on Youth and the Militarization of Schooling*. Albany: State University of New York Press.

Robers, Simone, Jijun Zhang, Jennifer Truman, and Thomas D. Snyder. 2012. *Indicators of School Crime and Safety: 2011*. Washington, DC: National Center for Educational Statistics, US Department of Education and the Bureau of Justice Statistics, Office of Justice Programs, US Department of Justice.

Roland [pseud.]. 2008. Interview by Director Marsha Weissman, Center for Community Alternatives, Syracuse, NY, January 7.

Rosa [pseud.]. 2008. Interview by Director Marsha Weissman, Center for Community Alternatives, Syracuse, NY, April 2.

Rose, Dina R., and Todd R. Clear. 1998. "Incarceration, Social Capital and Crime: Examining the Unintended Consequences of Incarceration." *Criminology* 36 (3): 441–80.

———. 2004. "Who Doesn't Know Someone in Jail? The Impact of Exposure to Prison on Attitudes toward Formal and Informal Controls." *The Prison Journal* 84 (2): 228–47.

Ross, Catherine E., and Chia-Ling Wu. 1996. "Education, Age and the Cumulative Advantage in Health." *Journal of Health and Social Behavior* 37:104–21.

Rothman, David. 1971. *The Discovery of the Asylum*. Boston: Little Brown.

Rouse, Cecilia E., and Lisa Barrow. 2006. "U.S. Elementary and Secondary Schools: Equalizing Opportunity or Replicating the Status Quo?" *Future of Children* 16 (2): 99–124. http://www.futureofchildren.org/usr_doc/Volume _16_Number_2_Fall_2006.pdf.

Rubel, Robert J. 1978. "Trends in Student Violence and Crime in Secondary Schools from 1950 to 1975: A Historical View." In *Theoretical Perspectives on School Crime*. Vol. 1. Hackensack, NJ: NewGate Resource Center and National Council on Crime and Delinquency.

———. 1986. "Student Disciplinary Strategies: School Systems and Police Response to High Risk and Disruptive Youth." Paper presented at the Working Meeting on Student Disciplinary Strategies Analysis of the Office of Research, Office of Educational Research and Improvement, US Department of Education, Washington, DC, November 6–7.

Rumberger, Russell W. 1987. "High School Dropouts: A Review of Issues and Evidence." *Review of Educational Research* 57 (2): 101–21.

———. 1995. "Dropping Out of Middle School: A Multilevel Analysis of Students and Schools." *American Educational Research Journal* 32 (Fall): 583–625.

S.B. 1070, 49th Leg., 2nd Reg. Sess. (Ariz. 2010), "Support Our Law Enforcement and Safe Neighborhoods Act," codified at Ariz. Rev. Stat. Ann. §§ 11-1051, 13-1509, 13-3883 (2010).

Sabol, William J. 1999. *Crime Control and Common Sense Assumptions Underlying the Expansion of the Prison Population.* Washington, DC: Urban Institute.

Sabol, William J., Todd D. Minton, and Paige M. Harrison. 2007. *Prison and Jail Inmates at Midyear 2006.* Washington, DC: US Department of Justice, Bureau of Justice Statistics.

Sabol, William J., Katherine Rosich, Kamala M. Kane, David P. Kirk, and Glenn Dubin. 2002. *The Influences of Truth-in-Sentencing Reforms on Changes in States' Sentencing Practices and Prison Populations.* Washington, DC: Urban Institute.

Sack, William H. 1977. "Children of Imprisoned Fathers." *Psychiatry* 40:163–74.

Sack, William H., Jack Seidler, and Susan Thomas. 1976. "Children of Imprisoned Parents: A Psychosocial Exploration." *American Journal of Orthopsychiatry* 46 (4): 618–28.

Sampson, Robert J., and Janet L. Lauritsen. 1997. "Racial and Ethnic Disparities in Crime and Criminal Justice in the United States." *Crime and Justice* 21:311–74.

Sandler, Susan. 2003. "Turning to Each Other, Not on Each Other." *Justice Matters* (website). San Francisco: Justice Matters. http://www.justicematters.org/jmi_sec/jmi_dwnlds/turning.pdf.

Santos, Fernanda. 2008. "Plan to Close Prisons Stirs Anxiety in Rural Towns." *New York Times,* January 27.

Schlosser, Eric. 1998. "The Prison-Industrial Complex." *Atlantic Monthly,* December 1, 51–77.

Schmitt, Christopher. 1991. "Plea Bargaining Favors Whites, as Blacks, Hispanics Pay Price." *San Jose Mercury News,* December 8.

Schultz, Sarah. 2005. "Finding Meaning in the Resistance of Preschool Children: Critical Theory Takes an Interpretative Look." In *Rethinking Resistance in Schools: Power, Politics, and Illicit Pleasures,* edited by Jonathan G. Silin, 6–15. Occasional Paper Series 14. New York: Bank Street College of Education.

Schwartz, Robert, and Len Rieser. 2001. "Zero Tolerance as Mandatory Sentencing." In *Zero Tolerance: Resisting the Drive for Punishment in Our Schools,* edited by William Ayers, Bernadine Dohrn, and Rick Ayers, 126–35. New York: New Press.

Sentencing Project. 2011. *Trends in U.S. Corrections*. Washington, DC: Sentencing Project.

Seward, Zack. 2012. "A City Faces Its 'Berlin Wall': An Interstate Highway" (radio broadcast). National Public Radio series, *NPR Cities: Urban Life in the 21st Century*, July 24. http://www.npr.org/2012/07/24/155917247/a-city -faces-its-berlin-wall-an-interstate-highway.

Sexton, George. 1995. *Work in American Prisons: Joint Ventures with the Private Sector*. Washington, DC: US Department of Justice.

Shabazz Sanders, G. Rashad. 2008. "'They Imprison the Whole Population': U.S. and South African Prison Literature and the Emergence of Symbiotic Carcerality, 1900–Present." PhD diss., University of California, Santa Cruz. ProQuest (UMI No. 3317409).

Shader, Michael. 2004. Risk Factors for Delinquency: An Overview. Washington, DC: Office of Juvenile Justice and Delinquency Prevention.

Shaw, Steven R., and Jeffrey P. Braden. 1990. "Race and Gender Bias in the Administration of Corporal Punishment." *School Psychology Review* 19:378–83.

Shayna [pseud.]. 2007. Interview by Director Marsha Weissman, Center for Community Alternatives, Syracuse, NY, December 15.

Shollenberger, Tracey L. 2013. "Racial Disparities in School Suspension and Subsequent Outcomes: Evidence from the National Longitudinal Survey of Youth 1997." Prepared for the Center for Civil Rights Remedies and the Research-to-Practice Collaborative, National Conference on Race and Gender Disparities in Discipline, Washington, DC, January 10. http://civilrights project.ucla.edu/resources/projects/center-for-civil-rights-remedies/school -to-prison-folder/state-reports/racial-disparities-in-school-suspension-and -subsequent-outcomes-evidence-from-the-national-longitudinal-survey-of -youth-1997.

Sieh, Maureen. 2003. "Half of Latino Children Here in Poverty." *Syracuse Post Standard*, May 25.

Simkins, Sandra, Amy Hirsh, Erin Horvat, and Majorie Moss. 2004. "The School to Prison Pipeline for Girls: The Role of Physical and Sexual Abuse." *Children's Legal Rights Journal* 24 (4): 56–72.

Simon, Jonathan. 2001. "Fear and Loathing in Late Modernity: Reflections on the Cultural Sources of Mass Imprisonment in the United States." In *The Culture of Control: Crime and Social Order in Contemporary Society*, edited by David Garland, 15–27. Chicago: University of Chicago Press.

————. 2002. "Introduction: Crime, Community, and Criminal Justice." *California Law Review* 90 (5): 1415–22.

————. 2007. *Governing through Crime: How the War on Crime Transformed American Democracy and Created a Culture of Fear.* New York: Oxford University Press.

Skiba, Russell J., and Kimberly Knesting. 2002. "Zero Tolerance, Zero Evidence: An Analysis of School Disciplinary Practice." *New Directions for Youth Development: Theory, Practice and Research* 92:17–43.

Skiba, Russell J., Robert S. Michael, Abra Carroll Nardo, and Reece L. Peterson. 2000. "The Color of Discipline: Sources of Racial and Gender Disproportionality in School Punishment." *Policy Research Report #SRS1.* Bloomington: Indiana Education Policy Center.

Skiba, Russell J., and Reece Peterson. 1999. "The Dark Side of Zero Tolerance: Can Punishment Lead to Safe Schools?" *Phi Delta Kappa* 80:372–76.

Skiba, Russell J., Reece L. Peterson, and Tara Williams. 1997. "Office Referrals and Suspension: Disciplinary Intervention in Middle Schools." *Education and Treatment of Children* 20:295–315.

Skiba, Russell J., Cecil R. Reynolds, Sandra Graham, Peter Sheras, Jane C. Conoley, and Enedina Garcia-Vazquez. 2006. "Are Zero Tolerance Policies Effective in the Schools? An Evidentiary Review and Recommendations." Washington, DC: American Psychological Association, Zero Tolerance Task Force.

Skiba, Russell J., Lauren Shure, and Natasha Williams. 2012. "Racial and Ethnic Disproportionality in Suspension and Expulsion. In *Disproportionality in Education and Special Education,* edited by Amity L. Noltemeyer and Caven S. Mcloughlin, 89–118. Springfield, IL: Charles C. Thomas.

Skiba, Russell J., Ada Simmons, Lori Staudinger, Marcus Rausch, Gayle Dow, and Renae Feggins. 2003. "Consistent Removal: Contributions of School Discipline to the School-Prison Pipeline." Paper presented at the Harvard Civil Rights Conference on the School-to-Prison Pipeline, Cambridge, MA, May 16–17.

Small, Margaret, and Kelley Dressler Tetrick. 2001. "School Violence: An Overview." *Juvenile Justice Journal* 8 (1): 3–12.

Smith, Brian J. 2000. "Marginalized Youth, Delinquency and Education: The Need for Critical Interpretive Research." *Urban Review* 32:293–312.

Smith, Jean Louise M., Hank Fien, and Stan C. Paine. 2008. "When Mobility Disrupts Learning." *Educational Leadership* 65 (7): 59–63.

Solomon, R. Patrick, and Howard Palmer. 2004. "Schooling in Babylon: When Racist Profiling and Zero Tolerance Converge." *Canadian Journal of Educational Administration and Policy* 33:1–16.

Solzhenitsyn, Alexander I. 1973. *The Gulag Archipelago, 1918–1956: An Experiment in Literary Investigation.* Vol. 1. New York: Harper and Row.

Spelman, William. 2000. "The Limited Importance of Prison Expansion." In *The Crime Drop in America,* edited by Alfred Blumstein and Joel Wallman, 97–129. Cambridge: Cambridge University Press.

Spohn, Cassia. 2000. "Thirty Years of Sentencing Reform: The Quest for a Racially Neutral Sentencing Process." In *Criminal Justice 2000,* edited by Julie Horney, 427–50. Rockville, MD: National Institute of Justice.

Staples, William G. 2003. "Surveillance and Social Control in Postmodern Society." In *Punishment and Social Control: Essays in Honor of Sheldon L. Messinger,* edited by Thomas G. Blomberg and Stanley Cohen, 191–210. New York: Aldine Transaction.

Stemen Don, Andres Rengifo, and James Wilson. 2006. *Of Fragmentation and Ferment: The Impact of State Sentencing Policies on Incarceration Rates, 1975–2002.* New York: Vera Institute of Justice.

Stevick, E. Doyle, and Bradley A. U. Levinson. 2003. "From Noncompliance to Columbine: Capturing Student Perspectives to Understand Noncompliance and Violence in Public Schools." *Urban Review* 35 (4): 323–49.

Stoops, Nicole. 2004. *Educational Attainment in the United States: 2003.* Washington, DC: US Census Bureau.

Sullivan, Laura. 2010. "Prison Economics Help Drive Arizona Immigration Law" (radio news story). National Public Radio, October 28. Washington, DC: National Public Radio. http://www.npr.org/2010/10/28/130833741/prison-economics-help-drive-ariz-immigration-law.

Sumner, Michael D., Carol J. Silverman, and Mary Louise Frampton. 2010. *School-Based Restorative Justice as an Alternative to Zero-Tolerance Policies: Lessons from West Oakland.* Berkeley: University of California, Berkeley School of Law, Thelton E. Henderson Center for Social Justice.

Syracuse City Police Department. 2000. *1998–2000 Statistical Report.* Syracuse, NY: Syracuse City Police Department.

———. 2009. *2008 Annual Report.* Syracuse, NY: Syracuse City Police Department.

Syracuse City School District. 2000. *Report of the District-Wide Sub-Committee Brig, SAVE, and Homebound Programs.* Syracuse, NY: Syracuse City School District.

————. 2006. *Syracuse City School District School Calendar and District Handbook, 2006–2007.* Syracuse, NY: Syracuse City School District. http://www.syracusecityschools.com/webcalendar.pdf.

————. 2007. *District-Wide Reconstruction Project: Master Plan.* Syracuse, NY: Syracuse City School District. http://docs.google.com/gview?a=vandq=cache:lw4UPJxk5ZkJ:www.Syracusecityschools.com/board%2520of%2520ed/SpecialMtgMin06-26-07.pdf+condition+of+Syracuse+city+schoolsandhl=enandgl=us.

————. 2013. *Disciplinary Data Analysis, 2010–2011 and 2011–2012.* Syracuse, NY: Syracuse City School District.

Syracuse Community Geography. 2013. "Maps, Data & Profiles." *Syracuse Community Geography* (website). http://communitygeography.org/maps-data-profiles/.

Tanza [pseud.]. 2007. Interview by Director Marsha Weissman, Center for Community Alternatives, Syracuse, NY, December 11.

Taylor, Jean, Thomas Stanley, Barbara DeFlorio, and Lynn Seekamp. 1972. "An Analysis of Defense Counsel in the Processing of Felony Defendants in San Diego, California." *Denver Law Journal* 49:233–75.

Taxman, Faye S., James Byrne, and April Pattavina. 2005. "Racial Disparity and the Legitimacy of the Criminal Justice System: Exploring Consequences for Deterrence." *Journal of Health Care for the Poor and Underserved* 16 (4): 57–77.

Texas Appleseed. 2007. "Texas School-to-Prison Pipeline: Dropout to Incarceration." *Texas Appleseed* (website). http://www.texasappleseed.net/index.php?option=com_content&view=article&id=115:publications&catid=27:texas-school-to-prison-pipeline&Itemid=298.

Thompson, Jacquelyn, Meghan Neary, Scott Joftus, and Monica Rosen. 2011. *Executive Summary—Syracuse City School District: Special Education System Review.* Report published by Cross and Joftus (no publishing location provided). http://edstrategies.net/.

Tobin, Joseph. 2005. "Everyday Tactics and the Carnivalesque: New Lenses for Viewing Resistance in the Preschool." In *Rethinking Resistance in Schools: Power, Politics, and Illicit Pleasures,* edited by J. G. Silin, 32–38. Occasional Paper Series 14. New York: Bank Street College of Education.

Tolan, Patrick H., and Deborah Gorman-Smith. 1997. "Families and Development of Urban Children." In *Urban Children and Youth: Interdisciplinary Perspectives on Policies and Programs,* edited by H. J. Walberg, O. Reyes, and R. P. Weissberg, 67–91. Thousand Oaks, CA: Sage.

Tonry, Michael H. 1995. *Malign Neglect: Race, Crime and Punishment in America*. New York: Oxford University Press.

Townsend, Brenda L. 2000. "Disproportionate Discipline of African American Children and Youth: Culturally-Responsive Strategies for Reducing School Suspensions and Expulsions." *Exceptional Children* 66:381–91.

Travis, Jeremy, and Sarah Lawrence. 2002. *Beyond the Prison Gates: The State of Parole in America*. Washington, DC: Urban Institute.

Tyack, David. 1974. *One Best System: A History of American Urban Education*. Cambridge, MA: Harvard University Press.

Tyack, David, and Robert Lowe. 1986. "The Constitutional Moment: Reconstruction and Black Education in the South." *American Journal of Education* 94 (2): 236–56.

Tyler, Tom R. 1990. *Why People Obey the Law*. New Haven, CT: Yale University Press.

———. 2008. "Procedural Justice and the Courts." *Court Review* 44 (1–2): 26–31.

Tyrel [pseud.]. 2008. Interview by Director Marsha Weissman, Center for Community Alternatives, Syracuse, NY, March 16.

Uggen, Christopher, Jeff Manza, and Melissa Thompson. 2006. "Citizenship, Democracy and the Civic Restoration of Criminal Offenders." *Annals of the American Academy* 605:281–310.

United Nations Committee on the Elimination of Racial Discrimination in All Forms. 2008. "Consideration of Reports Submitted by States Parties under Article 9 of the Convention. Concluding Observations of the Committee on the Elimination of Racial Discrimination, United States of America." New York: United Nations. http://www1.umn.edu/humanrts/CERDConcluding Comments2008.pdf.

US Census Bureau. 2000. "Census 2000 EEO Data Tool." US Census Bureau (website). http://www.census.gov/cgi-bin/broker.

———. 2010. "Employed Civilians by Occupation, Sex, Race and Hispanic Origin: 2010." *Labor Force, Employment, and Earnings* (website). http://www .census.gov/compendia/statab/cats/labor_force_employment_earnings.html.

———. 2013. "State and County Quickfacts." US Census Bureau (website). http://quickfacts.census.gov/qfd/states/36/3673000.html.

US Department of Education. 2000. *Office for Civil Rights Elementary and Secondary School Survey: 2000 National and State Projections*. Washington,

DC: US Department of Education, Office for Civil Rights. http://vistademo .beyond2020.com/ocr2000rv30/Table 1 -.

———. 2006. *Civil Rights Data Collection.* Washington, DC: US Department of Education, Office for Civil Rights, Civil Rights Data Collection. http:// ocrdata.ed.gov/Projections_2006.aspx.

———. 2006. *Elementary and Secondary School Survey: 2006.* Washington, DC: US Department of Education. http://ocrdata.ed.gov/ocr2006rv30/VistaView /dispview.aspx.

———. 2012. *The Transformed. Civil Rights Data Collection (CRDC): Revealing New Truths about Our Nation's Schools.* Washington, DC: US Department of Education. http://www2.ed.gov/about/offices/list/ocr/ . . . /crdc-2012-data -summary.pdf.

———. n.d. *What Works Clearinghouse.* US Department of Education, Institute for Education Sciences (website). http://ies.ed.gov/ncee/wwc/.

US Department of Health and Human Services. 2001. *Youth Violence: A Report of the Surgeon General.* Rockville, MD: US Department of Health and Human Services, Office of the Surgeon General. http://www.surgeongeneral .gov/library/youthviolence.

———. 2007. "Results from the 2007 National Survey on Drug Use and Health: National Findings 25." US Department of Health and Human Services, Substance Abuse and Mental Health Services Administration (website). http://www.oas.samhsa.gov/nsduh/2k7nsduh/2k7Results.pdf.

———. n.d. *National Registry of Evidence-Based Programs and Practices.* US Department of Health and Human Services, Substance Abuse and Mental Health Agency (website). http://nrepp.samhsa.gov/.

US Department of Justice. 2002. "Trends in Justice Expenditure and Employment, Table 1." Washington, DC: US Department of Justice, Bureau of Justice Statistics. http://www.ojp.usdoj.gov/bjs/data/eetrnd01.wk1.

———. 2007. "Local Police Departments for 1997, 2000, 2003, and 2007." Washington, DC: US Department of Justice, Bureau of Justice Statistics. http:// bjs.ojp.usdoj.gov/index.cfm?ty=tp&tid=71.

———. 2009. *Report to Governor David A. Patterson, Re: Investigation of the Lansing Residential Center, Louis Gossett, Jr. Residential Center, Tryon Residential Center, and Tryon Girls Center.* Washington, DC: US Department of Justice, Civil Rights Division. http://www.usdoj.gov/crt/split/findsettle.php #Juveniles%20Findings%20Letters.

———. n.d. "Model Programs Guide." US Department of Justice, Office of Juvenile Delinquency and Prevention (website). http://www.ojjdp.gov/mpg/.

US Department of State. 2008. *Questions Put by the Rapporteur in Connection with the Consideration of the Combined Fourth, Fifth and Sixth Periodic Reports of the United States of America* (February 18–March 7). Geneva, Switzerland: Committee on the Elimination of Racial Discrimination. http://ourhumanrights.files.wordpress.com/2008/02/us-report-back-to-cerd-committee.pdf.

US Human Rights Network Working Group on Juvenile Justice. 2008. *Children in Conflict with the Law: Juvenile Justice and the U.S. Failure to Comply with Obligations under the Convention for the Elimination of Racial Discrimination.* Atlanta, GA: US Human Rights Network. http://www.ushrnetwork.org/files/ushrn/images/linkfiles/CERD/8_Juvenile%20Justice.pdf.

US Sentencing Commission. 1995. *Special Report to the Congress: Cocaine and Federal Sentencing Policy, 1995.* Washington, DC: US Sentencing Commission.

Upperman, Kate, and Anne Hélène Gauthier. 1998. "What Makes a Difference for Children? Social Capital and Neighbourhood." *Options Politiques* (September): 24–27.

Valenzuela, Angela. 1999. *Subtractive Schooling: U.S.-Mexican Youth and the Politics of Caring.* Albany: State University of New York Press.

Vanguard High School. 2010. *Need a Fairness Hearing* (website). http://www.vanguardnyc.net/need-a-fairness-hearing.

Vavrus, Francis, and KimMarie Cole. 2002. "'I Didn't Do Nothin': The Discursive Construction of School Suspension." *Urban Review* 34 (2): 87–111.

Verdugo, Richard R. 2002. "Race-Ethnicity, Social Class, and Zero Tolerance." *Education and Urban Society* 35 (1): 50–75.

Vey, Jennifer S. 2007. *Restoring Prosperity: The State Role in Revitalizing America's Older Industrial Cities.* Washington, DC: Brookings Institute.

Vigil, James Diego. 1999. "Streets and Schools: How Educators Can Help Chicano Marginalized Gang Youth." *Harvard Educational Review* 69 (3): 270–88.

Viljoen, Jodi L., Jessica Klaver, and Ronald Roesch. 2005. "Legal Decisions of Preadolescent and Adolescent Defendants: Predictors of Confessions, Pleas, Communication with Attorneys, and Appeals." *Law and Human Behavior:* 29 (3): 253–77.

Vincent, Claudia G., and Tary J. Tobin. 2010. "The Relationship between Implementation of School-Wide Positive Behavior Support (SWPBS) and

Disciplinary Exclusion of Students from Various Ethnic Backgrounds with and without Disabilities." *Journal of Emotional and Behavioral Disorders* 10 (5): 1–16.

Violent Crime Control and Law Enforcement Act of 1994, H.R. 3355, Pub.L. 103–322 (1994).

Vorassi, Joseph A., and James Garbarino. 2000. "Poverty and Youth Violence: Not All Risk Factors Are Created Equal." In *The Public Assault on America's Children: Poverty, Violence and Juvenile Injustice*, edited by V. Polakow, 59–77. New York: Teachers College Press.

Wacquant, Loïc. 2001. "Deadly Symbiosis: When Prison and Ghetto Meet and Mesh." *Punishment and Society* 3 (1): 95–134.

———. 2006. *Punishing the Poor: The New Government of Social Insecurity.* Durham, NC: Duke University Press.

Wagner, Peter. 2003. "Rural Areas Have 20% of Population but 60% of New Prisons." *Prison Policy Initiative, Prison Gerrymandering Project* (website). July 28. http://www.prisonersofthecensus.org/news/fact-28-7-2003.html.

Wald, Joanna, and Daniel F. Losen. 2003. *Defining and Redirecting a School-to Prison Pipeline.* San Francisco: Jossey-Bass.

Walker, Elaine M. 2003. "Race, Class and Cultural Reproduction: Critical Theories in Urban Education" [Raza, clase y reproducción cultural: Teorías críticas en educación urbana]. Published in English in Spanish-language journal. *Revista Electrónica de Investiagación Educativa* 5 (2): 1–28. http://redie.uabc.mx/index.php/redie/article/view/79.

Warschauer, Mark J. 2003. "Social Capital and Access." *Universal Access in the Information Society* 2 (4): 315–30.

Wasik, Barbara H. 2004. *Handbook of Family Literacy.* Mahwah, NJ: Lawrence Erlbaum.

Watts, Ivan Eugene, and Nirmala Erevelles. 2004. "These Deadly Times: Reconceptualizing Youth Violence by Using Critical Race Theory and Disability Studies." *American Educational Research Journal* 41 (2): 271–99.

Weissman, Marsha. 2008. "The School to Prison Pipeline and Criminalizing Youth: Costs, Consequences and Alternatives." *Link* 6 (4): 6–9 and 15–17.

———. 2009a. "Aspiring to the Impracticable: Alternatives to Incarceration in the Era of Mass Incarceration." *New York University School of Law Review of Law and Social Change* 33 (2): 235–69.

———. 2009b. "Look What Those 'Bad Kids' Can Accomplish." *Syracuse Post Standard*, April 2.

Weissman, Marsha, Alan Rosenthal, Patricia Warth, Roberta Meyers-Peeples, and April Frazier. 2008. *Closing the Doors to Higher Education: Another Collateral Consequence of a Criminal Conviction.* Syracuse, NY: Center for Community Alternatives. http://www.communityalternatives.org.

West, Heather C., and William J. Sabol. 2009. *Prison Inmates at Midyear 2008—Statistical Tables.* Washington, DC: US Department of Justice, Office of Justice Programs, Bureau of Justice Statistics.

———. 2010. *Prisoners in 2009.* Washington, DC: US Department of Justice, Office of Justice Programs, Bureau of Justice Statistics.

Western, Bruce. 2006. *Punishment and Inequality in America.* New York: Russell Sage Foundation.

Western, Bruce, and Katherine Beckett. 1999. "How Unregulated Is the U.S. Labor Market? The Penal System as a Labor Market Institution." *American Journal of Sociology* 104 (4): 1030–60.

Western, Bruce, and Becky Pettit. 2005. "Black-White Wage Inequality, Employment Rates, and Incarceration." *American Journal of Sociology* 111 (2): 553–78.

Western, Bruce, Becky Pettit, and Joshua Guetzkow. 2002. "Black Economic Progress in the Era of Mass Imprisonment." In *Invisible Punishment: The Collateral Consequences of Mass Incarceration,* edited by M. Chesney-Lind and Marc Mauer, 165–90. New York: New Press.

Wicker, Tom. 1975. *Time to Die: The Attica Prison Revolt.* New York: Quadrangle/New York Times Book Company.

Wilkinson, Richard G., Ichiro Kawachi, and Bruce P. Kennedy. 1998. "Mortality, the Social Environment, Crime and Violence." *Sociology of Health and Illness* 20 (5): 578–97.

Williams, Heather A. 2005. *Self-Taught: American Education in Slavery and Freedom.* Chapel Hill: University of North Carolina Press.

Williams, Marian R. 2003. "The Effect of Pretrial Detention on Imprisonment Decisions." *Criminal Justice Review* 28 (2): 299–316.

Willis, Paul. 1977. *Learning to Labour.* Farnborough, UK: Saxon House.

Willoughby, Brian. 2012. "Suspending Hope." *Teaching Tolerance* 41:47–49. http://www.tolerance.org/print/magazine/number-41-spring-2012/feature/suspending-hope.

Wilson, William J. 1996. *When Work Disappears: The World of the New Urban Poor.* New York: Knopf.

Wolf, Elaine, and Marsha Weissman. 1996. "Revising Federal Sentencing Policy: Some Consequences of Expanding Eligibility for Alternative Sanctions." *Crime and Delinquency* 42 (2): 192–205.

Woolard, Jennifer L., Samantha Harvell, and Sandra Graham. 2008. "Anticipatory Injustice among Adolescents: Age and Racial/Ethnic Differences in Perceived Unfairness of the Justice System." *Behavioral Sciences and the Law* 26:207–26.

Wu, Shi Chang, William T. Pink, Robert L. Crain, and Oliver Moles. 1982. "Student Suspension: A Critical Reappraisal." *Urban Review* 14:245–303.

Zahn, Margaret A., Susan Brumbaugh, Darrell Steffensmeier, Barry C. Feld, Merry Morash, Meda Chesney-Lind, Jody Miller, Allison Ann Payne, Denise C. Gottfredson, and Candace Kruttschnitt. 2008. *Violence by Teenage Girls: Trends and Context*. Washington, DC: US Department of Justice, Office of Juvenile Justice and Delinquency Prevention.

Zeke [pseud.]. 2008. Interview by Director Marsha Weissman, Center for Community Alternatives, Syracuse, NY, January 11.

Index

abuse, physical, 93

academic achievement, 5, 177–78

accountability, 62, 72–73, 76–77, 79, 168, 236, 239

"accumulation of risk," 215–16

achievement ideology, 7–8, 224, 227

activism, 11n3, 49–51, 64–67, 231, 244–46

administrators. *See* school administrators

Advancement Project, 36

advocates/advocacy: defender-based, 62–63; groups, 63, 192, 235–36, 244; parents as, 64, 141–42, 146, 147, 187; student, 81, 168, 235–36, 244; suspension process and, 13, 67, 141–42, 146–47, 154, 187, 236–37. *See also specific group or organization*

African Americans: arrests of, 4, 26–28; drug laws and, 23; incarceration rates, 4, 19, 21–22, 27–28, 53, 224–25, 226; inflated earnings of, 32n9; mass imprisonment as tool of employment for, 31–32; in Syracuse, 3–4, 70–72

African American students: achievement ideology and, 227; "acting white," 9, 223; arrests of, 35–36, 39; dropout rates, 5–6, 38–40; history of education, 49–51, 54–56; link between schooling and imprisonment, 224–25; moral exclusion and, 218–19;

suspension and expulsion of, 39–40, 53, 56–59, 114–17, 123, 153–54, 218–19; Syracuse City School District, 2, 3, 53, 74, 115–17, 153–54

agency, 7, 8–9, 222

Albonetti, Celesta A., 27

alienation, 33, 127, 238

Alliance for Educational Justice, 36

alternative schools, 157–82, 199–202, 225, 243, curriculum, 174–79; behavior vs. learning, 175, 177–78; characteristics of students in, 212; classroom size, 174, 175–76, 177, 243; conditions of, 217–18; contradictory expectations for, 52–53; enrollment statistics, 57; first impressions on attending, 157–60; goals and mission of, 49–53, 177–78; location of, 52, 64, 79–80; overflow issues, 177; pathways to, 53–54; prison comparisons, 13–14, 103–4, 166, 225; progressive origins of, 49–51; school hours, 176–77; three-to-five programs, 135n1, 176–77; transfer limitation policies and, 159; types of, 52; as warehouses, 51–53. *See also specific school*

Althusser, Louis, 6–7

American Academy of Pediatrics, 57

American Bar Association, 26, 235

287

172–73; school surveillance and, 12; zero tolerance and, 155

Rahsheem (student), 137

Raudenbush, Stephen W., 214

Rayquan (student): on alternative school learning, 177, 179, 181; on attending alternative school, 165; family relationships, 90; on school-based police, 171–72; on school-to-prison pipeline, 194; on stigmatization, 184–85, 185–86; suspension hearings, 142; suspension incidents, 129–30

Reagan, Ronald, 20

recidivism, 60

Reconstruction, education during, 54–55

reentry to mainstream school, 62–63, 82, 91, 135, 174, 189–92

rehabilitation, 25, 62

reintegration, 62

rejection, 145, 183–95

Renewal Academy (Syracuse), 79, 147n3

Report on Programs for Students at Risk of Education Failure (US Dept. of Education), 51–52

Republican power, 20

resiliencies, 211

resistance theory, 6–8, 127, 210, 220, 225, 226–31

respect, importance of, 215, 217–18, 228–29, 234

responsibility, 202–9, 227–28

restorative justice, 155, 239

restraining, 11–12, 36, 76, 136, 141

rioting, 18–19, 44, 49, 235

risk factors, 7–8, 210–16

Rockefeller Drug Laws, 22–23

Roland (student): on alternative school learning, 181; on attending alternative school, 161; family relationships, 95; on powerlessness, 244; on

school-based police, 170; suspension hearings, 148–49, 183; suspension incidents, 127, 130, 136–37

Rosa (student): on alternative school learning, 175; on attending alternative school, 159, 164, 176; family relationships, 92, 97; living with community violence, 105–6; on responsibility, 205; suspension incidents, 118–19, 122–23

Rose, Dina R., 82–84

Rubel, Robert J., 44

rules, fairness and, 148–56

rural communities, prison economy in, 20, 30

Safe and Crime Free Schools Act, 44

Safe and Drug-Free Schools and Communities Act, 43

Safe and Gun-Free Schools Act, 7, 43, 219

Sanders, Shabazz, 33, 34

San Diego, CA, 57

Sandy Hook Elementary School (CT), 45–46, 237, 238

Savage Inequalities (Kozol), 218

SAVE Alternative School (Syracuse), 78–79, 147n3

Say Yes to Education Foundation, 74–75

school administrators: complaints about by students, 139–40, 148–56; eroding power of, 140; interpretation of student behavior, 53–54, 57–59, 148, 215–16, 220; policing as undermining of, 36–37; school policies and, 135, 136–38, 146, 148–56, 159; studies and survey of, 48; views of student's families, 8, 112, 146, 179

school-based crime and violence, 42–46;
changes in terminology, 46–47;
Columbine High School shooting,
43, 45–46, 167–68; girls and fighting, 117–23, 138–39, 153–54; media
depictions of, 36, 43, 44; Sandy Hook
Elementary School shooting, 45–46,
237, 238; suburbs and, 44. *See also*
attitudes and behaviors; zero tolerance policies
school-based police: alternatives to,
238; costs of, 240; growth of, 34–35,
140; laws regarding, 11–12, 236;
manuals for, 49; media depictions,
36; in New York City, 27, 35, 36,
167, 236; perceptions of by parents,
172–73; perceptions of by students,
166–74; reducing or eliminating,
236–37, 240, 244; relations with
administration, 36–37; role of, 136;
school resource officers (SROs)
vs., 34–35, 167, 240; in Syracuse,
10–12, 36–37, 127, 166–74, 236–37,
240. *See also* arrests, school-based;
surveillance
Schooling Capitalist America (Bowles &
Gintis), 221
school resource officers (SROs), 34–35,
167, 240
school rioting, 44, 49
schools, role of, 2–7, 140, 209–16,
220–26, 221–22
school shootings, 43, 45–46, 167–68,
237, 238
"school-to-prison pipeline": defined,
6–7, 34; dismantling of, 234–46; first
congressional hearing on, 237, 238;
first national conference addressing,
34, 60, 63–64; research on, 232–33;

student perceptions of, 192–95;
suspension segment, 181–82; US
Department of State on, 219
Seattle, WA, 56n3
secrecy, incarceration and, 102n4,
104–5
security. *See* surveillance
Security Management (journal), 37
segregation and desegregation of
schools, 3, 6, 44, 55–56
segregation and suspension, 42, 49, 52
Selton, Officer, 11–12
sentencing: alternative options, 62–63;
for cocaine, 24n4; laws and legislation, 20, 21, 22–25, 155; mandatory,
21, 22–25, 155; prison-industrial
complex and, 28–30; reductions for
whites, 27–28; stage-based discrimination and, 25–28
sexual assault, 46–47
Shamiya (student), 98–99
Shane High School (Syracuse), 168–69
Shayna (student): on alternative school
learning, 180; on attending alternative school, 159, 160–61; family
health, 94; family relationships, 99,
100; on school-based police, 169–70;
on what makes good teacher, 196
Simon, Jonathan, 17, 47, 231
Skiba, Russell J., 58, 60, 123
slavery, education and, 21, 32, 54–55
social control, 19–21, 28–33, 194, 235
social reproduction theory, 6, 210,
220–31, 233
social stratification, 209
sociocultural aspects, 7–9, 66–72,
220–26
socioeconomic conditions, 2–4, 66–72,
74, 210–16, 220–26, 233. *See also*

Vavrus, Francis, 59
Verdugo, Richard R., 58, 123
Vestermark, Seymour, 49
victims' rights groups, growth of, 29–30
violence. *See* crime and violence
Violence-Free Zones, 238
Violent Crime Control and Law
    Enforcement Act of 1994, 24–25
Vorassi, Joseph A., 215

Wackenhut Corporation, 29
Wacquant, Loïc: on carceral state, 17;
    on deadly symbiosis, 4, 231; on mass
    incarceration as social control of Afri-
    can Americans, 21, 32, 194; on prison
    as mechanism for unemployment,
    31–32, 233; on prisons as "hyper-
    ghetto," 32–33
War on Drugs, 4, 22–25
Watts, Ivan Eugene, 216–17
weapons possession, 10, 38, 45–46,
    48, 128–31, 160–66, 241–42. *See
    also* gun violence; metal detectors;
    surveillance
Western, Bruce, 31–32, 38, 194
white counterculture movement, 50
white flight, 3, 56, 65, 68, 74
whites, 3, 4, 21–22, 23, 27–28, 31, 54–56,
    226–27
white students: "acting white," 9, 223;
    discipline and, 219; dropout to prison
    rates, 38–39; economic advantages,
    223–24; Free School Movement and,

49–51; incarcerated parents, 102; in
SCSD, 74; sentencing reductions
and, 27–28; suspension and expul-
sion of, 39–40, 53, 57–58, 114–16,
123
Wilkinson, Deanna L., 215
Williams, Natasha, 58, 123
Willis, Paul, 7–8, 226–27
Wilson, Pete, 20
Woolard, Jennifer L., 154–55

Zared (student), 127, 222, 223
Zeke (student): family health, 94; family
    relationships, 99–100; on responsibil-
    ity, 203, 205; suspension hearings,
    143
zero tolerance policies, 6, 37–61, 77,
    212, 216; as contributor to structural
    violence, 218; criminalizing student
    behavior, 46–48; in Denver, CO,
    168; dismantling and modification
    of, 235–36, 237–38, 244; effects on
    personal power of school administra-
    tors, 140; expulsion and, 38; growth
    of carceral state and, 17–18, 34;
    negative effects of, 13, 14–15, 61,
    123, 148–49, 154–56, 181–82, 206; in
    New York State, 38; origins of, 7, 38;
    racial profiling aspects, 155; school
    financing and, 38, 43, 78; stereo-
    types and, 126; support for, 41–42;
    suspensions and, 7, 9, 34, 37–40, 122,
    181–82, 184–85; in Texas, 235–36